DOMINANCE AND RESISTANCE IN COLONIAL INDIA

DOMINANCE AND RESISTANCE IN COLONIAL INDIA

Editor

K. Venugopal Reddy

KALPAZ

Dominance and Resistance in Colonial India

ISBN: 978-81-7835-888-8

Published in 2012 in India by
Kalpaz Publications
C-30, Satyawati Nagar,
Delhi-110052
E-mail: kalpaz@hotmail.com
Phone : 9212729499

Lasser Type Setting by: Rudra Computer Graphics, Delhi
Printed at : Chawla Offset Printers, Delhi

Contents

Preface

Understanding the theme of dominance and resistance is critical to understand the dynamics of social process and social transformation in colonial India. The book makes a modest attempt in this direction. It emerges out of articles presented at a National Seminar organized on the theme of Dominance and Resistance in colonial and post-colonial India in March 2009 at the Department of History, Pondicherry University. My special thanks are particularly due to the Indian Council of Historical Research, New Delhi, and Pondicherry University, Puducherry for their financial and other kinds of necessary support in organizing the event. I am indebted to Prof. J.A.K. Tareen, Vice-Chancellor, Pondicherry University, whose inspiration has gone a long way to make this work possible. I am equally indebted to Prof. A.M. Pathan, Vice-Chancellor, Central University of Karnataka for his encouragement and support in completing the work early. I am indeed beholden to Professor Bipan Chandra, who always remains a fountain of intellectual inspiration and guidance for all of intellectual endeavours. Also I thank Professor Sabyasachi Bhattacharya, Professor Aditya Mukherjee and Professor Mridula Mukherjee for their encouragement and help in bringing out the book.

I am very much beholden to my colleagues at the Department of History, Pondicherry University for their unstinted cooperation and help in all of my intellectual forays. Particularly Professor Venkata Raghotham, Head, Department of History, Professor, K. Rajan, Professor G. Chandhrika, who always have responded to my call for any help. Perhaps it may not be exaggeration to mention that without their support and encouragement, this book would not have been published. Also I thank my other faculty colleagues at School of Social and International Studies, Pondicherry University for their support and encouragement. Particularly, my thanks are due to Professor D. Sambandhan, Dean, School of Social and International Studies, Professor B.B. Mohanty, Head, Department of Sociology, Professor. B. Mohanan Pillai, Head, Department of International Studies, Professor Murthy, Co-ordinator, Centre for Gandhian Studies, Dr. B. Krishna Murthy, Department of International Studies.

Specially, I am grateful to the contributors for having immediately responded to my call to revise their papers and sent them to me in time. My repeated requests for clarifications met with very eager and patient response. I am thankful to the students and other supporting staff of the Department of History, Pondicherry University for all the help extended in making this publication a possibility.

I am particularly grateful to Kalpaz Publications for having readily accepted my proposal to bring out the book in time.

List of Contributors

1. **Prof. Shri Krishan**, Dept. of History Post-Graduate Regional Centre (M.D. University), Rewari, Haryana India
2. **Prof. Devireddy Subramanyam Reddy (Retd.)** Dept. of History S.V. University Tirupati Andhra Pradesh India
3. **Dr. B. Rama Chandra Reddy** Dept. of History K.M.C.P.G. Studies (Autonomous) Puducherry India
4. **Dr. B. Krishnamurthy** Dept. of Politics and International Studies Pondicherry University Puducherry India
5. **Dr. M. Lakshmanan** Dept. of History Presidency College (Autonomous) Chennai Tamil Nadu India
6. **S. Mahaboob Basha** Dept. of History Babasaheb Bhimrao Ambedkar Central University Lucknow Uttar Pradesh India
7. **Dr. G. Samba Siva Reddy** Dept. of History Yogi Vemana University Kadapa Andhra Pradesh India

Introduction

K. Venugopal Reddy

India was known for its extensive trade in cotton textiles which were in high demand in the entire world particularly the Africa, Europe, and west Asia. It is noted that '...India had a massive balance of trade surplus with Europe and some with west Asia, based mostly on its more efficient low cost cotton textile production and also of course on pepper for export. These went westwards to Africa, west Asia, Europe, and from there on across the Atlantic to the Caribbean and the Americas.'[1] India had thus witnessed a robust and "...continued economic expansion... through the 17th century."[2] However, the conquest of India and the establishment of British colonial rule in the second half of 18th century and the consolidation of colonial rule by mid 19th century had irretrievably altered the basic contours of its political, economic and social landscape.[3] India thus became a prey to British colonizer's relentless economic quest,[4] leaving it at last extremely emaciated in 1947.

The British dominance thus established around the mid 18th century got entrenched in all spheres of India[5] and it was amply demonstrated in the representation of Indian people and their history.[6] The alien dominance also got deeply embedded in the "distorted representation" of India denying it the "voice, autonomy, and agency".[7] Further its materialization was marked in "...objectification and re-ordering through the application of European scholarly methods on Indian thought and culture..."[8] Colonial power was demonstrated not just through the spread of its 'English ideas here and there, but upon the systematic redefinition and transformation of the terrain on which the life of the colonized was lived.'[9] The perception of India and its history, attitudes, morals, culture and customs were thus coloured by the prejudices of the colonizers.[10] Significantly, they presented their perception of history of India.[11] It should be read in that mode only. To argue that they presented an objective account of the history is only to think the colonizers way.[12]

Thus, the colonial dominance was firmly buttressed through 'baring the differences, real or assumed and stamping its supremacy.'[13] It subsisted on continued perpetuation of violence and brutality, which were used as essential means for maintaining its control over colonized. The colonial regime was always conscious of maintaining its image of power as something "unshakable in its expansive dominance". In India as elsewhere, "deference and distance" were considered necessary to maintaining white dominance.[14] The colonial regimes universally are known for "marginalization of resistance".[15] Therefore an attempt is made to present the trajectory of this colonial dominance and the resistance that it engendered in colonial India.

Contemporary social theory is awash with hermeneutics of key concepts of 'Dominance' and 'Resistance'.[16] Theoretical interventions by historians namely the Subalterns have not adequately addressed the two concepts and it is forcibly argued that "Certainly, there is no concerted attempt to construct a theory of domination as *hegemony*, as the invocation of Gramsci might have led us to expect...The concepts of power which have actually been developed in the series are fragmentary and somewhat disconnected."[17] Similarly, on the aspect of the subalterns resistance to the domination of the colonial State or the 'elites' sections, these historians have failed to offer a convincing "theory of popular consciousness and resistance."[18]

The two key concepts refer to 'complex of interconnections and relations' that constitute the society. In this sense, dominance and resistance are the two key concepts, with which the nature of social relations is to be grasped. They do signify the multiple layers of internal as well as external social reality. The book initiates a serious exercise in critical discourse of the two key concepts and how they are implicated in holding out reference to (in pointing to) the social process. The collective contributions of the scholars seek to explore the essentiality of the two key concepts to comprehend the social, political and economic milieu during the colonial era.

'The geographies of dominance and resistance are treated in a dynamic and networked way'.[19] It is argued that the 'spatialities of domination' and 'geographies of resistance' are both constitutive of the domain of the relations of power and they are not separated by the spatiotemporal activity. It is explained that resistance is incessantly intertwined with the relations of power and domination since "resistance turns up in domination' and 'domination turns up in resistance'.[20] On the manifestation of colonial power and its diverse forms of domination, Rosalind O' Hanlon explains thus "...it imposes a total milieu, institutions as well as intellectual and informational, to whose hegemonic sway its subjects must inevitably succumb. Colonial power thus derives its strength from two sources: from the material ability to coerce which it brings with it in its armies, and from the Orientalist discourses of its second, shadow army of textual scholars, linguists, historians, anthropologists and so on.[21]

Dominance operates systematically to reinforce and reproduce dominant social relations for instance the male domination of woman and the upper caste domination of the lower caste and this process of perpetuation of dominant social relations are resisted by diverse social groups in the society. In Indian context, the different forms of dominance, be they male domination or caste dominance, were intricately interconnected and implicated with the foundation and consolidation of colonial rule.[22] This position of interconnectedness of colonial interests would point to the "...the contradictory approach of the British government to women's position in India.[23] Therefore the British claims of "liberalizing" the Indian society were shallow[24] as the British rulers pursued their espoused policy of "non-interference in Indian culture and religion".[25]

Just as there are myriad forms of dominance, there are also numerous modes of resistance against the structures of dominance. What constitutes resistance and who names it are challenging questions, which perhaps provoke equally challenging responses from those who dominate and those who offer resistance on "everyday" basis. Their perceptions can be diametrically apart. The scholars who 'developed this concept of resistance argued that opposition to domination takes myriad forms'.[26] Similarly the responses to such 'opposition to domination' can also take myriads forms. Many scholars have focused on the term *resistance* explaining "a wide variety of actions and behaviors at all levels of human social life (individual, collective, and institutional) and in a number of different settings, including political systems, entertainment and literature and workplace. Indeed, everything from revolutions to hairstyles has been described as resistance. The term is defined variously as, for example, "acting autonomously, in [one's] own interests"; "active efforts to oppose, fight, and refuse to cooperate with or submit to ... abusive behaviour and control"; "engaging in behaviors despite oppositron"; or simply "questioning and objecting".[27]

The scholars explained that the word 'Resistance' implies 'two elements' which 'were common to nearly explanations of the term'. The first is 'a sense of *action*' and the second involves 'a sense of *opposition*.' Hence the core elements which

'Resistance' embodies are 'action and opposition.'[28] The resistance can be expressed through open and massive protest movements or revolutions. It can also be articulated through "everyday" forms, which are 'prosaic and constant struggle.' These everyday forms of resistance constitute 'the ordinary weapons of relatively powerless groups: foot dragging, dissimulation, false compliance, pilfering, feigned ignorance, slander, arson, sabotage, and so forth.'[29] These acts of 'everyday' forms of resistance may not make "headlines" but surely and quietly they leave their footprints on the oppressive system.[30] *Ibid*, p. xvii.

Resistance or protest movements are not "...mechanically determined by social structure." And it may be stated that the "defiance" could also be "contingent on historical circumstance."[31] The subaltern historians explain the resistance of the subalterns located in "...a long tradition of exploitation, or a shorter-term economic dislocation, which provokes resistance and rebellion: challenges to landlords or the agents of the state, the appropriation or destruction of the signs and instruments of their authority. This action, which independently generated and pursued, draws on the insurgents' own original culture for its values, symbols and its means of organizing."[32]

How is resistance suppressed? In a colonial situation, the colonial state had the power of defining of what constituted opposition to its authority. Therefore, in a colonial situation, the dominance of colonial state was overwhelmingly experienced by the colonized particularly the subaltern classes and it constituted the core aspect of contested political process. The dominance of the elites be they the landlords, zamindars, capitalists and money lenders vis-à-vis the tenants, landless peasants, workers and the hapless bonded or indebted peasants and labourers were yet other sites of political and social contest or spaces of domination strengthened and abetted strongly by the colonial state. The dominance of the upper castes vis-à-vis the lower castes and the male dominance vis-à-vis female are also most important sites of contested social terrain. It is these multiple forces of dominance, which engender the myriad forms of resistance among the subalterns in colonial India. Therefore, the domination and resistance at the individual or group level constitute a core and re-defining aspect of contested social process. Therefore, dominance and resistance have "a cyclical relationship: domination leads to resistance, which leads to the further exercise of power, provoking further resistance, and so on."[33]

In India what the colonial State symbolized was the "*political domination of a foreign State*."[34] The colonial State which gained political dominance through coercion had subsequently encountered a series of resolute resistance from the colonized in India. The colonial State was thus formed in the crucible of resistance. The resistance of the oppressed against the multiple forms of exploitation by colonial, landlord and capitalist masters has thus a long tradition. So, throughout the period of British colonial rule in India, the process of interrogating and confronting the existing and also emerging social, religious, political, economic, and cultural systems, had become manifest in the varied forms, i.e., in the form of the social and religious reform movements, the popular revolt of 1857 by Indian sepoys and many tribal, peasant and working class struggles throughout the late eighteenth century, through nineteenth century to the second half of the twentieth century. The tradition of resistance and protest was thus not sporadic in the history of colonial India.[35]

This process of resistance signified blistering protest against the prevailing regimes of dominance and the emerging value systems. The struggles articulated the growing or failed aspirations of diverse social groups representing varied identities like caste, class or gender. These resistance movements by their critical interrogation and intervention in colonial India threw very serious and at times determined challenge to hegemony of colonial State and also other hegemonic socio-cultural practices. The chief thrust of the book is therefore to present the nature of transformation triggered by the colonial State in varied fields and the beginning of resistance against the different forms of entrenched dominance buttressed by colonial penetration in India. It focuses on the multiple zones of conflict and collective actions of the diverse social groups in colonial India.

Therefore the impact of the colonial policies, transformations in social, economic, political and cultural realms, the peasant resistance against the dominance of the landowning classes and the colonial State, the Tribal revolts against the multiple forms of exploitation and the intrusion of the colonial State through its interventionist forest policies abridging their traditional and customary rights, the anti-caste movements interrogating the established forms of dominance and seeking social justice and equality are the chief themes of critical interrogation.

The work endeavors to focus on the interrogation of the anatomy and the internal dynamics of the resistance movements in colonial India. While focusing on the multiple sites and the sources of resistance of the oppressed, it also aims to explore and debate the plurality or myriad forms of resistance and the nature of their manifestation. It attempts to articulate on the need to look for new sources i.e., non-archival sources to construct or reconstruct the genealogy of the resistance movements in colonial India. It re-examines the 'politics of the people', the common people or the masses and the paradigms of resistance movements. It also focuses on the process of spontaneous and organized expressions of discontent against oppression, domination and marginalization and how the protests turn into institutionalized movements. It also addresses the issue of how new identities were forged among the oppressed and how they came out with new strategies for survival and resistance. It aims to address the emergence of alternative perspectives on history and historiography of the oppressed and the marginalized in colonial India. The book debates the Indian experience on the formation of identities and resistance against the multiple forms of oppression. It seeks to focus on the issues that are of enduring relevance to the perception of the resistance movements in colonial India.

The contributors have investigated the theme of dominance and resistance deeply exploring and decoding the structures of dominance and representing the multiple and diverse forms of resistance. Indeed the most notable aspect present in all the papers of the contributors in general is the "...task of recovering lost or suppressed experience".[36]

Shri Krishan, through his contribution on 'Drug-use in History, Colonial Dominance, and Resisting Drugs: Some Implications for Contemporary Social policy' locates the significance of Drugs in the enterprise of empire building by the western powers, the evolution of a modern drug policy in India, and the resistance to the policy of colonial government by the Indians with focus on revisiting post-colonial context and continuities.

The perceptions of resistance vary depending on the context in which resistance was organized. Hence the resistance against the British colonial order by different classes of India in 1857 did constitute an act of resistance against the colonial order in the wider meaning be it was by the old feudal elements of India supported by the subaltern forces. If the resistance against the British colonial authority in 1857 had acquired any historical import, it has to be necessarily interpreted as the single most remarkable anti-colonial event, which threatened almost uprooting of colonial control from India's political horizon. Devireddy Subramanyam Reddy in his paper on 'Andhra Pradesh in 1857' discusses the revolt of 1857 in colonial Andhra and Nizam Andhra tracing its critical significance to the establishment of British rule in India. He explores the nature of indigenous resistance involving diverse social groups to the expansion of British dominance particularly in colonial Andhra in 1857.

They are very few studies dealing with tribal movements in colonial south India particularly with reference to Andhra province.[37] Though there has been some serious research work on tribal uprisings in colonial Andhra[38], many of the tribal movements 'remained unexplored.'[39] B. Rama Chandra Reddy makes an attempt to fill the lacunae. His paper on 'A Messianic Movement among the Tribals of Andhra in 1900' traces the emergence and course of a messianic movement among the Tribals in the Vizagapatam District of Madras Presidency (presently Andhra Pradesh) in 1900. He analyses the movement in the light of Stephen Fuchs ideas on messianic movements in India. He explains that the political subordination, economic exploitation and social degradation of the tribals during the British colonial regime paved the way for the revitalization movement. Subsequently, the movement had metamorphosed from the religious into a movement with political overtones. The leaders vainly tried to enlist support of a deposed and a reigning Raja of the locality. However, the British promptly suppressed the movement. Curiously, it had occurred only months after a similar well recorded Birsa Munda movement took place in Chotanagpur area.

The phenomenon of colonialism and the experience undergone by the colonized during the process of colonization was not dissimilar globally. However resistance against the multiple forms of oppression by the colonizers was articulated through diverse ways. B. Krishnamurthy in his paper on 'Colonial Dominance and Constitutional Resistance in French India' aims to explore the uniqueness of the case of French India, where the colonized people resisted the colonial as well as elite dominance through constitutional means and tries to draw some lessons to present day impasse.

M. Lakshmanan in his paper on 'Contractual Work and Fragmented Social Security' discusses the various methods that the employers had used to recruit workmen. He articulates on the methods of work organized in various firms and the sort of authority that the employers had possessed over their workmen in legal terms. Contextually, he focuses on the attitude of the employers to social security measures in colonial Madras. He argues that social security measures cut across caste/

community differences among the workers and were administrated within the framework of the low level of industrial development.

There are concerns raised on the marginalization of the voices of protest by women in the course of the study of resistance movements. It is forcefully stated that 'Studies of resistance often overlook the significance of gender.'[40] Some efforts have been made since then to bridge the gap and the book attempts modestly to address this lacuna. The study of S. Mahaboob Basha takes up the study of the issue of how women began to raise their voice to break the shackles of tradition and reconstruct the conventional predominant image of women as passive by courageously moving "into a sphere in which men have long been dominant."[41] In his paper on "Ending up Making a Monkey While Intending to Portray a Gentleman" Controversy in a Women's Organisation in Colonial Andhra– Story of the *Shri Vidyarthini Samajamu*, 1902-1947', he makes a study of women's organizations in different parts of colonial Andhra. He narrates the story of the *Shri Vidyarthini Samajamu*, also known as the *Kakinada Vidyarthini Samajamu*, which emerged at the very beginning of the twentieth century.[42] He also presents in detail the eruption of controversy surrounding the *Samajamu* and the nature and limitations of the Womens' organization in colonial Andhra. The study squarely addresses the issue of women's subordination in the contemporary colonial Andhra and the relentless efforts made by the *Shri Vidyarthini Samajamu* to counter the dominant patriarchal forces "constructing their demands around women's domestic... oppression."[43] The paper demonstrates the most significant aspects of women's movement articulating on its strengths and weaknesses and the singular contribution made by the organization to highlight the progress of the women's movements.

The first quarter of the twentieth century witnessed the emergence of backward castes movement against the Brahminical superiority, resistance to social hierarchy and the assertion of the demands for social equality. The non-Brahmin castes of south India 'resented the dominance of the Brahmins. They raised the issue of exploitation and oppression, both economic and cultural, by the Brahmins.'[44] G. Samba Siva Reddy in his paper on 'Non-Brahmin Movement in Colonial Rayalaseema, 1916-1937' traces the emergence of non-Brahmin movement in colonial Rayalaseema between 1916 and 1937. He probes the failures and successes of the movement in countering the hegemony of the Brahmins in different realms. He argues that the non-Brahmin movement fizzled out primarily due to the failure of elite non-Brahmin upper castes to develop a coherent policy of inclusion of other lower castes in the society.

Thus all the contributions presented here will surely further our perceptions in their own way of the complexly knotted and multi-layered underpinnings on the theme of 'Dominance and Resistance in colonial India'.

References

1. Andre Gunder Frank, 'India in the World Economy, 1400-1750', *Economic and Political Weekly*, Vol. 31, No. 30 (Jul. 27, 1996), p. 50.
2. *Ibid.*, p. 54.
3. Bharat Patankar and Gail Omvedt, 'The Bourgeois State in Post-Colonial Social Formation', *Economic and Political Weekly*, Vol. 12, No. 53 (Dec. 31, 1977), p. 2172.
4. Eugene F. Irschick, 'Order and Disorder in Colonial South India', *Modern Asian Studies*, Vol. 23, No. 3 (1989), p. 459; Note: Colonialism ... "was a system of exploitation of people of a geographically defined area with definite ethic and cultural characteristics by an alien group which was ethnically and culturally distinct and which did not regard India as a home." See Amiya Kumar Bagchi, Colonialism and the Nature of 'Capitalist' Enterprise in India', *Economic and Political Weekly,* Vol. 23, No. 31 (July. 3, 1988), PE-45.
5. Bharat Patankar and Gail Omvedt, *op.cit,* p. 2171.

6. Note: 'India came to be described as a vast pathological reservoir, "overlaid perennially by a thick layer of maladies". The new 'code words' were sudden, severe, decline, decadence, deterioration, degeneration and the worst, putrefaction'; See Deepak Kumar, 'Medical Encounter in British India, 1820-1920', *Economic and Political Weekly*, Vol. 32, No. 4 (Jan. 25-31, 1997), p. 166; Also see Ronald Inden's 'Orientalist Constructions of India', *Modern Asian Studies*, Vol. 20, No. 3 (1986), pp. 401-446.
7. David Scott, 'Colonial Governmentality', *Social Text*, No. 43 (Autumn), 1995, p. 192.
8. Rosalind O'Hanlon, Recovering the Subject Subaltern Studies and Histories of Resistance in Colonial South Asia', *Modern Asian Studies*, Vol. 22, No. 1 (1988), p. 217.
9. David Scott, *op.cit*, p. 205.
10. See Jenny Sharpe, 'The Violence of Light in the Land of Desire; Or, How William Jones Discovered India', *Boundary* 2, Vol. 20, No. 1. (Spring, 1993), pp. 26-46.
11. Ranajit Guha, '*Dominance without hegemony: history and power in colonial India*', Harvard University Press, 1997, p. 155.
12. See Claude Marcovits, 'Some Trends in European (Mainly British) Historiography of Modern India', *Economic and Political Weekly*, Vol. 22, No. 10 (Mar. ', 1987), pp. 416-418; See also S. Bhattacharya, Paradigms Lost: Notes on Social History in India, *Economic and Political Weekly*, Vol. 17, No. 14/16, Annual Number, (Apr., 1982), pp. 690-693+695-696; also see Eugene F. Irschick, 'Order and Disorder in Colonial South India', pp. 460-461 and 476-480.
13. Deepak Kumar, 'Medical Encounter in British India, 1820-1920', p. 166.
14. Ann Stoler, 'Perceptions of Protest: Defining the Dangerous in Colonial Sumatra', *American Ethnologist*, Vol. 12, No. 4 (Nov., 1985), p. 648.
15. David Scott, 'Colonial Governmentality', p. 192.
16. See for an elaborate explanation and review of the works on the concept of 'Resistance', Jocelyn A. Hollander and Rachel L. Einwohner, 'Conceptualizing Resistance', *Sociological Forum*, Vol. 19, No. 4 (Dec., 2004), pp. 533-554.

17. Rosalind O'Hanlon, *op.cit*, p. 215.
18. Mridula Mukherjee, Peasant Resistance and Peasant Consciousness in Colonial India: 'Subalterns' and Beyond', *Economic and Political Weekly*, Vol. 23, No. 41 (Oct. 8, 1988), p. 2114.
19. David Featherstone, 'Specialities of Transnational Resistance to Globalization: The Maps of Grievance of the Inter-Continental Caravan', *Transactions of the Institute of British Geographers*, New Series, Vol. 28, No. 4 (Dec., 2003), p. 405.
20. David Featherstone, pp. 408.
21. Rosalind O'Hanlon, *op.cit*, p. 216.
22. Joanna Liddle and Rama Joshi, 'Gender and Imperialism in British India', *Economic and Political Weekly*, Vol. 20, No. 43 (Oct. 26, 1985), p. WS73; Note: " ...the Indian system of male domination was one of the main pillars on which the British founded their rule..."; Note also: "...Under the social structures preserved, augmented or spawned by colonial systems, numbers of actual or potential employees are subordinated to their masters not just within their working hours, not just as individual workers but as families, members of a class, caste or community", see Amiya Kumar Bagchi, Colonialism and the Nature of 'Capitalist' Enterprise in India', PE-44.
23. See for details on the contradictory approach of the British government to the liberation of women in India, Joanna Liddle and Rama Joshi, *op.cit*, pp. WS72-78.
24. Note: "The colonial state, while it adopted the rhetoric of freedom and individual dignity, was reluctant to dismantle social structures like slavery that would involve both a loss of revenue as well as the allegiance of the landed groups who were their bulwark." See Dilip M. Menon, 'Religion and Colonial Modernity: Rethinking Belief and Identity', *Economic and Political Weekly*, Vol. 37, No. 17 (Apr. 27 – May 3, 2002), p.1666.
25. Joanna Liddle and Rama Joshi, *op.cit*, p. WS73.
26. Susan Bibler Coutin and Susan F. Hirsch, 'Naming Resistance: Ethnographers, Dissidents, and States', *Anthropological Quarterly*, Vol. 71. No.1 (Jan., 1998), p. 1.

27. Jocelyn A. Hollander and Rachel L.Einwohner, *op. cit.*, p. 534.
28. *Ibid.*, p. 538.
29. James C. Scott, *Weapons of the Weak: Everyday Forms of Peasant Resistance*, OUP, Delhi, 1990, p. xvi.
30. *Ibid.*, p. xvii.
31 Note: "Historical-structural" approaches "show ideology, values, traditions, and rituals to be of consequence and trace the importance of culture to group, organization, and community dynamics and to other features of social structure. Yet they never presume that protest is mechanically determined by social structure. They show the patterning of defiance to be contingent on historical circumstance." Eckstein S, ed. *Power and Popular Protest: Latin American Social Movements*, Berkeley, University of California Press, 1989, p. 3, quoted in Marc Edelman, ' Social Movements: Changing Paradigms and Forms of Politics', *Annual Review of Anthropology*, Vol. 30 (2001), p. 291.
32. Rosalind O'Hanlon, *op.cit*, p. 213.
33. Jocelyn A. Hollander and Rachel L. Einwohner, *op. cit*, p. 548.
34. Bharat Patankar and Gail Omved, *op.cit*, p. 2171.
35. L.S. Vishwanath, 'Peasant Movements in Colonial India: An Examination of Some Conceptual Frameworks', *Economic and Political Weekly*, Vol. 25, No. 2 (Jan. 13, 1990), pp. 118-122.
36. Rosalind O'Hanlon, *op.cit*, p.195.
37. Ghanshyam Shah, *Social Movements in India: A Review of Literature*, Sage Publications, New Delhi, 2004, pp. 94 & 108.
38. See David Arnold's 'Rebellious Hillmen: The Gudem-Rampa Risings, 1839-1924.' in *Subaltern Studies-1:Writings on South Asian History and Society*. Edited by R. Guha, Delhi: Oxford University Press.
39. Ghanshyam Shah, *op.cit*, p.108.
40. Shine Varghese, 'Women, resistance, and development: a case study from Dangs, India', *Development in Practice*, Vol. 3, No. 1, February 1993, p. 3.
41. Shine Varghese, 'Women, resistance, and development', p. 12.

42. Note: "The beginning of the organized women's movement was in 1904, when the National Social Conference, whose aim was to explore social issues including women's emancipation, set up a separate Indian Women's Conference. Then in 1917 the Women's Indian Association, which had links with the British suffragette movement, was formed. In 1925, a branch of the International Council of Women was started, known as the National Council of Women in India. And in 1927 the All India Women's Conference was founded, which stressed the political goal of self-government as a means to achieve women's aspirations." Joanna Liddle and Rama Joshi, 'Gender and Imperialism in British India', *Economic and Political Weekly*, Vol. 20, No. 43 (Oct. 26, 1985), pp. WS75.
43. Joanna Liddle and Rama Joshi, *op.cit*, pp. WS72.
44. Ghanshyam Shah, *op.cit*, p. 140.

1

Dominance and Resistance in Colonial India

The Theme

The Colonial State which gained political dominance through coercion had subsequently encountered a series of resolute resistance from the colonized in India. The Colonial State was thus formed in the crucible of resistance. Therefore, the resistance of the oppressed against the multiple forms of exploitation by colonial, landlord and capitalist masters has thus a long tradition. So, throughout the period of British colonial rule in India, the process of interrogating and confronting the existing and also emerging social, religious, political, economic, and cultural systems, had become manifest in the varied forms, i.e., in the form of the social and religious reform movements, the popular revolt of 1857 by Indian sepoys and many tribal, peasant and working class struggles throughout the late eighteenth century, through nineteenth century to the second half of the twentieth century. The tradition of resistance and protest was thus not sporadic in the history of colonial India.

This process of resistance signified blistering protest against the prevailing regimes of dominance and the emerging value systems. The struggles articulated the growing or failed aspirations of diverse social groups representing varied identities like caste, class or gender. These resistance movements by their critical interrogation and intervention in colonial India threw very serious and at times determined challenge to hegemony of colonial State and also other hegemonic socio-cultural practices. The chief thrust of the book is therefore to deliberate and discuss the nature of transformation triggered by the Colonial State in varied fields and the beginning of resistance against the different forms of entrenched dominance buttressed by colonial penetration in India. It focuses on the multiple zones of conflict and collective actions of the diverse social groups in colonial India.

Therefore the impact of the colonial policies, transformations in social, economic, and political realms, the peasant resistance against the dominance of the landowning classes and the colonial State, the Tribal revolts against the multiple forms of exploitation and the intrusion of the colonial State through its interventionist forest policies abridging their traditional and customary rights, working class movements against the capitalist exploitation whether Indian or European, the anti-Caste movements interrogating the established forms of dominance and seeking social justice and equality are the chief themes of critical interrogation.

Therefore the book chiefly focuses on the interrogation of the anatomy and the internal dynamics of the resistance movements in colonial India. While focusing on the multiple sites and the sources of resistance of the oppressed, it also aims to explore and debate the plurality or myriad forms of resistance and the nature of their manifestation. It also attempts to articulate on the need to look for new sources i.e., non archival sources to construct or reconstruct the genealogy of the resistance movements in colonial India. It re-examine the 'politics of the people', the common people or the masses and the paradigms of resistance movements. It also focuses on the process of spontaneous and organized expressions of discontent against oppression, domination and marginalization and how the protests turn into institutionalized movements. It also addresses the issue of how new identities were forged among the oppressed and how they came out with new strategies for survival and resistance. It aims to address the emergence of alternative perspectives on history and historiography of the oppressed and the marginalized in colonial and post-colonial India.

The book debates the Indian experience on the formation of identities and resistance against the multiple forms of oppression. It seeks to focus on the issues that are of enduring relevance to the perception of the resistance movements in colonial and post colonial India.

Contributors and the brief abstracts of their papers

1. The introduction to the book is presented by the Editor on the theme of 'Dominance and Resistance' locating its significance in colonial context exploring the multiple layers of resistance and decoding myriad structures of dominance in modern India.
2. Dr. Devireddy Subramanyam Reddy in his paper on 'Andhra Pradesh in 1857' discusses the revolt of 1857 in colonial Andhra and Nizam Andhra tracing its critical significance to the establishment of British rule in India. He explores the nature of indigenous resistance involving diverse social groups to the expansion of British dominance particularly in colonial Andhra in 1857.
3. Dr. Mohammed Mustafa in his paper on 'Dominance and Resistance in Early Colonial Rule: The Company and the Chittoor Palegars During 1802 – 1805' traces the factors, which critically contributed to the emergence of native resistance to the colonial dominance in Chittoor. He locates the resistance of Palegars against the British East India Company in the loss of traditional power held by them. He argues that the Chittoor palegars' revolt presents a classical example of the beginning of the penetration of Company's domination in the interior regions.

4. Dr. Shri Krishan, through his contribution on 'Drug-use in History, Colonial Dominance, and Resisting Drugs: Some Implications for Contemporary Social policy' locates the significance of Drugs in the enterprise of empire building by the western powers, the evolution of a modern drug policy in India, and the resistance to the policy of colonial government by the Indians with focus on revisiting post-colonial context and continuities.
5. S. Mahaboob Basha in his paper on "Ending up Making a Monkey While Intending to Portray a Gentleman" Controversy in a Women's Organisation in Colonial Andhra– Story of the *Shri Vidyarthini Samajamu*, 1902-1947' makes a study of women's organizations in different parts of colonial Andhra. It narrates the story of the *Shri Vidyarthini Samajamu*, also known as the *Kakinada Vidyarthini Samajamu*, which emerged at the very beginning of the twentieth century. It also presents in detail the eruption of controversy surrounding the *Samajamu*. In focusing on the functioning of the *Samajamu*, it offers a systematic analysis of the nature and limitations of the Womens' organization in colonial Andhra.
6. Dr.G. Samba Siva Reddy in his paper on 'Non-Brahmin Movement in Colonial Rayalaseema, 1916-1937' traces the emergence of Non-Brahmin movement in colonial Rayalaseema between 1916 and 1937. He probes the failures and successes of the movement in countering the hegemony of the Brahmins in different realms. He argues that the Non-Brahmin movement fizzled out primarily due to the failure of elite Non-Brahmin upper castes to develop a coherent policy of inclusion of other lower castes in the society.
7. Dr. B. Rama Chandra Reddy in his paper on 'A Messianic Movement among the Tribals of Andhra in 1900' traces the emergence and course of a messianic movement among the tribals in the Vizagapatam District of Madras

Presidency (presently Andhra Pradesh) in 1900. He analyses the movement in the light of Stephen Fuchs ideas on messianic movements in India. He explains that the political subordination, economic exploitation and social degradation of the tribals during the British colonial regime paved the way for the revitalization movement. Subsequently, the movement had metamorphosed from the religious into a movement with political overtones. The leaders vainly tried to enlist support of a deposed and a reigning Raja of the locality. However, the British suppressed the movement promptly. Curiously, it had occurred only months after a similar well recorded Birsa Munda movement took place in Chotanagpur area. The paper mainly used the primary data collected from the archival sources.

8. Dr. M. Lakshmanan in his paper on 'Contractual Work And Fragmented Social Security' discusses the various methods that the employers had used to recruit workmen. He articulates on the methods of work organized in various firms and the sort of authority that the employers had possessed over their workmen in legal terms. Contextually he focuses on the attitude of the employers to social security measures in colonial Madras. He argues that social security measures cut across caste / community differences among the workers and were administrated within the framework of the low level of industrial development.

9. Bibin Kuriakose in his paper on 'Working Class Resistance in Travancore: A Study of Punnapra Vayalar Struggle of 1946' discusses the emergence of working class movement in the erstwhile princely state of Travancore. The efforts of the left parties to protect the interests of the workers against the onslaught of the capitalist class and the Princely state and also the struggle of the workers for the introduction of responsible government and the loss of lives by the workers are important aspects, which are focused in the paper.

10. Paper by Dr. B. Krishnamurthy on 'Colonial Dominance and Constitutional Resistance in French India' aims to explore the uniqueness of the case of French India, where the colonized people resisted the colonial as well as elitist class dominance through constitutional means and tries to draw some lessons to present day impasse.

2

Drug-use in History, Colonial Dominance, and Resisting Drugs: Some Implications for Contemporary Social Policy

Shri Krishan

Drugs in Contemporary Society

Drug abuse is a social evil. It destroys not only the vitals of the society but also adversely affects the economic growth of the country because this is a trade which generates large unaccounted money which, in turn, leads to adoption of several means of money laundering. The money generated is used for various purposes including anti-national and terrorist activities and even clandestine trading in arms and ammunition. Drug trafficking activities have sharply increased over the years and unscrupulous persons dealing in drugs have flourished despite hard punishments provided under the law because they have been able to evade the process of law. Unfortunately, the kingpins and the carriers of these drugs at the international and national level are concerned with only large undue financial gains and not with massive ill effects of use of drugs on society. In recent times, there has been significant development in the communication systems and means of transportation. This has also led to considerable increase in Narcotics drug trafficking. The drug traffickers have been able to flourish despite stringent punishments provided under the 'Narcotic Drugs and Psychotropic Substances Act'. They are able to evade the process of law and cause great harm to the social and economic growth of the country and particularly the young generation. This resulted in serious hampering of the socio-economic growth and multi-dimensional development of the country. The punishment for drug trafficking became more and more stringent by the passage of time, but it has not been able to provide real solution to the basic problem. Drug problems are part of the larger problems of disease, poverty, unemployment, violence, economic disparity and styles of living. In this paper we wish to highlight some important facets of history of drug-abuse and its implications for a consistent and viable public guiding principle on drugs.

Recently, the ministry of social justice and empowerment of the government of India and UN office on drug and crime conducted a joint study of the extent, pattern and trends of drug abuse in India. The basic objective of the study was to put in place a drug abuse monitoring system and remove the bottlenecks in system and address issues relating to institutionalization especially of the training of professionals and sensitization of institutes. It used the profile of drug addicts from various governmental, private and NGO's and found that drug abuse vary across socio-economic groups and across time and regions. In a sample of 16,942 drug addicts, it was found that 97.2% were male and 71.9% were married and 51.7% were from rural background. Furthermore, 15% were illiterate, 12% were graduates, 7.4 % were currently unemployed and 12.4% were never employed. The average income of users was only Rs. 3408/- per month while mean expenditure on drugs was Rs. 1653/- per month.[1] This clearly indicates the financial costs for the individual family apart from the emotional costs of drug addiction for the family of the victim. The women in such families are the worst sufferers who carry the entire burden of torn families on their shoulders. They suffer from cruelty, violence and maltreatment of male drug addicts. There are other reports that point towards growing menace of drug addiction, which is cutting across new spectrum. For instance, increasing number of women are taking to drugs and intravenous usage of heroin, morphine and opiate drugs is also increasing. Himachal Pradesh has emerged as a major centre of cultivation and international trafficking of *hashish*, although most cannabis and *hashish* trafficked into India come from Nepal, which because of its strategic location between Southeast and South-west Asia has emerged as a chief heroin transshipment area.[2] International Narcotics Control Board, a quasi-judicial body monitoring the implementation of the UN International Drug Control Convention, also expressed concern over access to drugs in Asia and Africa, given the proximity of the region to major opium production centers such as the Golden Crescent and the Golden Triangle and widespread cultivation of cannabis. Apart from the growth of intravenous drug abuse, there is also increase in the abuse of pharmaceutical products such as codeine-based cough syrups and anxiolytics in tablet form and injectable analgesics. It has been estimated that about 2.58% of AIDS patients were intravenous drug users. The lack of proper state control and failure of enforcement agencies are seen as the real culprits in preventing its growth.[3] There are others who stress problem families and broken homes along with peer group associations for the growth of drug addiction.[4] Whatever be the reasons, one thing is certain that illicit trafficking and consumption of drugs is on rise. According to the World Drug Report (2004) of the UN office on Drug and Crime, 185 million people or about 30% of world population in the age group 15-64 had used illegal drugs in the previous one year and cannabis consumption was on top of the list, followed by amphetamine type stimulants.

What are Drugs?

When we talk about drugs and drug-culture, we are referring to psycho-active substances which alter the states of consciousness of the user. But not all mood-altering substances are characterized as 'drugs'. Tea, coffee, cocoa, and tobacco contain chemical like nicotine and caffeine that affect our mood. But they are legal substances although the use of Tobacco recently has been restricted. When we refer to drugs, it is generally the illicit commodities that alter the state of our consciousness. It has to be pointed out, however, that the categories of legal/illegal have been changing historically and they are not rigid or static categories. Many commodities like opium, cannabis, cocaine and LSD (Lysergic Acid Diethylamide) were earlier legal but many states have now banned their use. Similarly alcohol is legal in many countries but forbidden in some Islamic countries. In other words, we want to stress that there has been a shifting and negotiable boundary between licit and illicit commodities. It has political and cultural meanings. Secondly, these are non-food items of consumption which are consumed by human beings either for hedonistic purposes or for medicinal purposes. In either case they are legally controlled through medical prescription or legal proscription. It is only in non-medical context that we term their use as drug-abuse. We also popularly use the term narcotics for them which refer to substances causing sleep or insensibility but generally it has implications of illegality about them. Such usages or descriptions are of recent origins. They have emerged within the context of modern capitalism which as we would wish to emphasize as a kind of narco-capitalism which potentially created new dangerous modes of use or consumption, in societies with the technical capacity to produce chemically refined products and their circulation in global markets as commodities. The earlier folk usage gave way to use of more potent and purified substances unconstrained by traditional social practices and cultural context of consumption. This rupture also marked the naturalization of certain products such as tea, coffee and tobacco as intermediate goods between food and drugs but which had addictive or 'habituative' qualities about their use. We all are aware of the role of tea, coffee and wine in setting the moods in balance in modern society.

Traditional Patterns of Drug-use

The contemporary drug policy seeks to control demand and supply of drugs through the declaring the production, trafficking and consumption as illegal activities. The uniform UN Control Convention also ensures that most states adopt a similar prohibition-oriented bureaucratic approach. Such a punitive approach ignores the socio-cultural context of traditional drug use in different societies and cultures. The use of drugs has not been confined to any particular time or culture. People used drugs for transcendence and visionary experience or what is termed as the 'altered state of consciousnesses' since the beginning of human civilization. The Aztecs used peyote and *ololiqui*, a small lentil like seed containing lysergic acid. The aborigines of Australia chewed *pituri*, a desert shrub. The indigenous people of upper Amazon had *yage*, a telepathic vine and there is evidence that ergot, from which LSD is derived, was the mysterious *kykeon* used by the ancient Greeks in the annual Eleusinian mysteries. Often those who partook of these substances to float into a sacred space projected sacred qualities onto the plants themselves. A variety of hallucinogenic compounds survived in the Middle Ages in Europe despite the attempts of Christianity and the Holy Inquisition to stamp out the pagan cults and their visionary experience associated with drugs. The European colonizers of the New World also tried in some cases to eradicate and banish the use of these psychedelic substances as a sort of madness or possession by evil spirits. However, they re-entered the metropolitan countries as a project of romantic rebellion signifying a return to the repressed psyche. Incidentally, this was also the age of discovery of synthetic chemical industries in Europe.[5]

Similarly, the use of alcoholic beverages was common to virtually all cultures through most of their recorded history.

This was also linked to early man's desire to achieve altered state of consciousness through use of intoxicants. The human nervous system's limbic system has sites for natural pleasure, which are essential for our survival. Drugs create intense feeling of pleasure for the first time users, as the limbic system is flooded with dopamine, a neurotransmitter. However, continuous use and unnatural flooding of brain ultimately reduces the number of dopamine receptors resulting in less and less production of dopamine and even causing death of some neurons. Thus, the use of drugs changes the basic biochemistry of brain. The contemporary functionalist anthropology of drinking behaviour focuses on the symbolic and cultural specific aspects of alcoholic consumption. In this approach, cultural mores are linked to the basic functional needs of a society. Mandelbaum (1965) related changes in drinking customs as clues to basic social changes.[6] The production of alcoholic beverages is a simple organic process of fermentation, by which sugar is transformed by the action of yeast to produce ethyl alcohol. Sugar for this process can be easily obtained from honey, fruits, sprouting grains and milk. Hence, the early Bronze cultures of the Eastern Mediterranean and Mesopotamia harnessed the process of fermentation to produce beer quite early. Some scholars believe that the fabled *Soma* of the Vedic period was a psychedelic mushroom, amanita *muscaria*[7] In Sumerian culture, we have documentary evidence and pictograph of beer as early as 3200 B.C. and there is evidence of use of beer in temple rituals.[8] In these early cultures, it was realized that excessive use of intoxicants was dangerous and could pose problems for social cohesiveness. Therefore, consumption was made a social and group activity and it was integrated into the core system of myths and ritual practices of the emergent culture. Such cultural traditions and normative order prescribed the use of intoxicants for social and ceremonial functions and proscribed excessive solitary consumption. The contemporary ethnographic research findings also demonstrate the role of socio-cultural factors in determining the use of various types of intoxicants and this could have serious implications for making of a social policy. There are about 4,000 species of plants on earth that contain psychoactive substances and about sixty species have been used throughout the human history. The most common of these are Opium poppy (*Papaver somniferum*), Cannabis (*Cannabis sativa*) and Cocoa (*Erythroxylum*). There have been a variety of causes for using such drugs. Because of their pain-relieving property, cannabis and opium were often used in the traditional medicinal system. They also provided physical and psychological stimulation to workers engaged in arduous employment. As natural gift of nature or God, they were also used in religious or cultural ceremonies and played a key role in maintenance of culture and community traditions. In such pre-modern forms of use their consumption was regulated, their production was limited and cultural mores checked their abuse. Drugs also functioned as a medium of relaxation for the members of elite class. From the beginning of commercial activities, such drugs and psychoactive plants also earned a good amount of money for the peasant cultivators. In some cases, they were also source of calories and nutritional values. For instance, Hemp and its seed oil was a source of rural staple diet in some parts of India and rural communities also used it to tide over the demographic crises in eighteenth and nineteenth centuries especially during famine periods.

Drugs in the Commercial and Industrial Age: New Patterns of Global Dominance

According to Court Wright (2001), a fundamental change took place between 1500-1800 in the pattern of use of drugs or means of altering waking consciousness due to the rise of transoceanic trade and empire-building. As there were enormous profits and revenues involved in the marketing of psychotic resources and products, European merchants, planters, and governments encouraged their production and exchange on a global scale, the use of which was restricted and confined geographically and in some cases democratized their consumption as the use of such substances was a privilege of the affluent sections only. The selection of commodities for commercial global exchanges was based on the shelf-life as well as the cultural biases of the European merchants. Certain substances like *kava*, *betal*, *qat* and *peyote* failed to become commodities but the big three, alcohol, tobacco and caffeine, which have become so 'naturalized' that we do not even consider them as drugs, were the deliberate choice of the profit-driven process.[9] Viticulture or selective cultivation of grape vines for making wines was an old practice in Europe but use of sugar and the Baltic grains and subsequently conversion of perishable potatoes into spirits as cheap source of calories and intoxication made it possible to mass-produce the spirits and exacerbated drunkenness and alcoholism in both European and Non-European societies. The modern technology also raised the potency of the drugs. The pre-modern fermented beverages had low-alcohol content and they spoiled early but the modern techniques made it possible to add heavy ethanol punch to the alcohols. The economic and social use of wines also changed with this. The use of tobacco also spread after its discovery by the Portuguese in the late fifteenth century, it was already a global crop by the seventeenth century and it spread cutting across social categories although the mode of consumption varied with class, gender and locality. The triumph of cigarettes in twentieth century with clever use of advertising, rapid urban social pressures and changing gender roles marked the process of switch-over from shag-tobacco to a more convenient mode of consumption.[10] The Contemporary drug problem is a by-product of nineteenth century Chemical Revolution and it is closely intertwined with the rise of modern chemical industries in the Western world. German chemist Friedrich Sertuesner had isolated morphine from opium in 1803 and its commercial production started in 1827 by Merck and Co. The drug was used in a number of morphine based medical products. C.R Wright produced Diacetylmorphine from boiling morphine in1874 and the drug was ten times more potent. The German company Bayer started its production in 1898 under the brand name

Heroin and it too was widely utilized in pharmaceutical sector and its markets. Albert Niemann isolated cocaine from the leaves of Coca plant in 1859 and German firm Merck and Co. and American company Parke Davis specialized in the manufacture of cocaine based patented medical products. French Wine Coca was a popular beverage and a mixture of Coco and Wine, which had to be re-launched in American markets as Coco-Cola after Prohibitionists objected to the wine content in it.[11]

Role of Drugs in the Empire-Building

Drugs were at the heart of the empires of the modern period. Sales of opium in China, of alcohol in Africa, of tobacco grown in the Caribbean, of tea planted in India and of cannabis across South Asia all provided the financial resources to build administrations and the economic impetus to open new markets and to control ever wider areas. While significant economically, drugs were also central to the politics of empires; Europeans drew up treaties and fought battles in Asia in order to compete for drugs routes long before the Opium Wars of the nineteenth century. The relationship between consciousness altering commodities and imperialism was significant in cultural terms too. The image of the dissolute Asian addict, or the helpless African or Australasian lost in alcohol, was a recurring theme in the 'Orientalist' construction of Western superiority that legitimated empire; it was also at the centre of debates about the 'civilizing' nature of imperialism as liberals and missionaries decided that these victims were in need of salvation.

The Portuguese brought Tobacco to India and also discovered the use of opium in India where it had been used for pain-relief in medicinal contexts along with cannabis. The European trading interests, driven by economic gain, changed the very context of drug use from medicinal use to recreational/ intoxication leisure use. The Dutch and the British were to radically change the use of opium in Asian cultures. There was a huge demand for Asian goods like spices, silk, cotton textiles, silk and ceramics in Europe and the Dutch and British often had a substantial trade deficit with India and China. The Dutch company started opium exports from Bengal to the Far-East and it rose from 0.6 metric ton in 1660s to 89 metric tones in 1699. They re-exported it to China also, sometimes earning as much as 400 percent profit. When the East India Company took control of Bengal, it introduced a kind of syndicate system and monopoly rights over the trade of opium in Bengal. The Company made advances to zamindars for production and procurement of opium and apart from exports, also encouraged the domestic consumption through about 10,000 state owned shops. The drug traffic also increased with the global exchanges of capital, people and ideas in the context of an uneven and hierarchical modernity. The imperial expansion of European powers since 15th century was based on disruption of traditional patterns of consumption and production as well as increasing movements of narcotic substances in the global commercial networks. We know the role of opium in the grand commercial design of the British Empire. According to Trocki, the administrative and military costs of the empire were met by this opium trade and 'super-profits' associated with it. Opium paid a substantial part of the cost of colonial administration. The East India Company and its successor, the British Indian Government, reaped significant profits both from producing and exporting the drug, and also by selling it to its own colonial subjects. It was like a cash-cow for the most Asian state administrations in the 19th and even early 20th century. The drug was also important for the development of both European and Asian capitalism as its trade created first large scale accumulation of capital without which reproduction of capital would not have been possible. The great British Managing houses, the banks and insurance companies, the financial sinews of modern capitalism had their own roots in the Asian trade and all had a start in the opium. It fuelled commercialization as it acted as a commodity that created other commodities.[12] Amar Farooqui also points out the role of opium trade as a source of revenue for the colonial state in India as it provided about 6 per cent of total revenues in the period 1789-90 to 1838-39 and about 15 per cent of the total revenues between the period1839-40 to 1888-89. Secondly, it paid for the Chinese goods imported into Britain especially tea and it created a mechanism for remitting colonial plunder to the metropolis.[13] In Bengal, the East India Company established its monopoly over opium trade from the beginning of its rule and forced the unwilling farmers to accept advances of money to grow poppies instead of other crops. The colonial administrative hierarchy over opium cultivators included the village *muttus* or *khatadars*, the agents of the villagers, the *sunder muttus* or the members of landed aristocracy, the Company *gumastas* or local commercial agents of the Company and the Collector at the top. As a result of government's promotion the land under poppy cultivation increased tremendously and by the mid-1850s, the total area under opium cultivation in Bengal was about 31 million hectares where under licensed system about 1.25 million peasants were involved in it.[14] There was no malicious intent behind promotion of opium trade except for profit-making and getting wealthy if we could call that a 'crime'. The British traders and colonial administrators knew that it was a poison; it was addictive and did no good to its users but it made the invisible hand of capitalism to work.[15] The Opium grown in Malwa, being cultivated by independent farmers emerged as a threat to the Company monopoly of opium trade and the British government invaded some of the strategically important areas, secured greater control over the Western Coast and started levying a heavy transit duty on the opium passing through its territories. However, the local princes, indigenous traders and cultivators resisted the British administration over the share of profits in the trade.[16]

In Malwa region, the bulk of opium was produced in princely states from where it reached Bombay port for export. It had to pass through the British-controlled territories there and the Company state earned huge revenue by charging transit duties on its passage through its territories. The export from Bengal had grown from about 127 metric tones in 1800 to 6.372

metric tones in 1857. In 1830s the revenue from opium accounted for 11 per cent of the total revenues of the East India Company but they rose to 17 percent in 1850s.[17] There was a lively debate on the morality of opium trade and evangelical current of ideas thought it to be an impediment in spreading Christianity and its values in the East. The drawing of revenues from the 'vice'–the flowing poison was considered to be respons ble for the enfeeblement of consumers who were depicted as more 'effeminate than the women' and it was a loss bigger than the one that could be counted in dollars and cents as 'figures and language utterly failed to portray its magnitude and extent' as there were many religious and moral bearings of the trade. The opium trade was held accountable for all the social ills like loss of health, waste of property, moral degradation, and imbecility.[18] However, Royal Commission on Opium (1895) advocated continuation of free opium trade as it was found to be highly lucrative one. Therefore, it is not only necessary to keep in mind the historical role of Imperial centre of modern global capitalism in order to work out a viable drug policy but it is equally pertinent to draw from the experience of our society under colonialism.

The evolution of a modern drug policy in India dates back to 1770's. The East India Company was on the verge of financial bankruptcy in 1770 and asked for a parliamentary loan. The British Parliament, while agreeing to grant such a loan, was also worried about the repayment of the loan by the private company and it was suggested that a tax be directed at India's intoxicating hemp drugs namely *bhang*, *ganja* and *charas*. A law was enacted in 1778, according to which no one was permitted to manufacture or sell hemp drugs without obtaining a proper license from the district authorities. The objective of the law was to 'increase the public revenues' as well as to control 'immoderate consumption'. This law also included tobacco and toddy in the list of taxable drugs. While the colonial state professed altruistic motives, the real consideration was economic gain. Initially the Ilberian doctors who accompanied the Portuguese had made some observations regarding hemp. Subsequently, William B. O'Shaughnessy, professor of chemistry and medicine at the Medical College, Calcutta experimented with the effects of cannabis or hemp. The Company administration found another source of revenue in cannabis trade. The use of this drug was quite widespread among all classes and strata of society and the British raised the duties on the consumption of *ganja*. In the beginning, the wholesaler was taxed on his holding of *ganja* and the tax was collected at the point of trader's purchase from the peasant. There was large scale evasion of tax in this system as the traders or *byavapris* made clandestine dealings and transactions with the cultivators. The colonial state, therefore, strengthened the surveillance machinery and system of taxing the traders at the point of selling was instituted. The cultivator who wished to produce hemp crop had to approach the authorities to obtain a license to produce the drug in his fields and this provided the information about the cultivators who were producing the drug and made surveillance easier. The surveillance staff made tours of cannabis-producing areas to make estimates of production and when the crop was ripe, the wholesalers were issued permits to store a specified quantity of the drug.[19] Subsequently, many British administrators voiced the concern over violent intoxication prevalent among indigenous population and stressed the need to impose prohibition. Apart from the public order, the colonial authorities also linked drugs with poverty, ignorance, disease, crime and other problem that were endemic to the country. These problems were attributed to drug abuse especially to consumption of *bhang*, *ganja*, and *charas*. In 1890s, there was intense debate in the British parliament and statistics of lunatic asylums were quoted to show a causal link between cannabis-consumption and insanity.[20] The Board of Revenue was against prohibition and advocated a policy of control through taxation. At this stage, England was emerging as the major drug supplier but cannabis was only a minor revenue-generating resource. The big money lay in opium and its trade and Indian peasants were the main producers of that profitable commodity. The opium trade with China helped the British to erase the huge trade deficits it had with that country.[21] It also makes it clear that revenue, not altruism, was concern of British colonial rulers. They were equally concerned with the spread of drug habits in their armed forces, which would have undermined the efficiency of the force. The Indian Hemp Drug Commission (1893-94), after examining a number of witnesses, which included English and Indian physicians, civil and medical officials, magistrates and policemen, traders and farmers as well as a number of Christian missionaries, concluded that *bhang* was the cheapest and the most popular drug in use and it had no unpleasant effects. Ganja was the main source of revenue for the state and use of *charas* was more prevalent among the wealthier Indians where it was being substituted by alcohol. The Commission also noted the socio-religious usage of *bhang* and *ganja* and concluded that these drugs did little harm to the society as such.[22]

Third major source of revenue for the colonial state was liquor. The excise regulations of the Government of India began in Bombay in the year 1790. It was claimed that the people began to develop a taste for liquor, and that the cost of a quart of *mowali spirit*, made of the juice of the palm, was so low — only a half-penny — that anybody could get drunk on it. The argument used was that putting a tax on the tree, would make people drink less. However, the real motive, at least according to some contemporary observers, was "to grind money out of a vice, and not to pulverize the vice".[23]

The system initially adopted by the Government, was to restrict manufacture by licensing Government distilleries - The distillery system was designed ostensibly for controlling the traffic in liquors and the strength of country spirits (which it may be noted is the same noble aim that current excise policies in independent India follow today), but in reality for enhancing the revenue and assuring maximum profit to government. However, the Indian Excise Committee of 1905-06, reported that: "The consumption of all classes of foreign liquors has largely increased...the consumption of country beers is causing much drunkenness in certain areas.....Between 1901-02 and 1911-12 the issues of country spirits in distillery areas rose in Bombay from 1,792,618 proof gallons i.e. about 117 gallons per 1,000 population, to 2,705,567 gallons, or about 168 per 1000; in Sind from 52 per 1000 to 55 per thousand; and in Madras the increase in consumption of country spirits was from 24 gallons to 41 gallons per thousand".[24]

Under a system where liquor manufacture was in the hands of the people, it was not possible to regulate the manufacture and consumption of alcoholic drinks effectively. Proper control was only possible if liquor was made in a limited number of factories under the close supervision of excise officers. In this wish for central distilleries, the moral ideals of the colonial administrators, turned out in best Victorian fashion, to be in complete accord with their financial needs. The response of the government, to further these noble aims, was to recommend that customary drinks such as toddy and locally made arrack be replaced by a mass produced commodity in central distilleries for supply to liquor shops throughout each district. This would, it was envisaged by the Abkari Commission in 1869, produce more wholesome spirits at less cost than the village distilleries and that the excise rates could be raised as a result. As the liquor trade became a monopoly, the tax on drink increased by leaps and bounds and the price of alcoholic beverages soared over the years. The Bombay Excise Administration Report of 1927-8 reported that, in parts of Gujarat, before the 1878 Act a quart bottle of *mahua daru* cost five to six annas. By 1928 it cost Rs. 2-8-0 which represented a fivefold increase in price. A contemporary account notes that 'throughout a great part of the Bombay Presidency the native of India now pays as much, relatively, for common country liquor as the Englishman does for champagne'.[25]

Resisting Drugs and Colonial Policy

According to Amar Farooqui, in Malwa region, the bulk of the surpluses which accrued from opium production were appropriated by non-company participants in the enterprise in this period. He suggests that attempts by the British to control the supply of Indian opium to China were unsuccessful. In India, for example, the amount of opium exported increased 12-fold in the 1820s; this provided profits for those involved in rural production, for the merchants who shipped the product, for the elites who acted as bankers and invested in the trade and for the state itself, which developed comprehensive systems for gathering duties on movements of the drug. As the British tried to tighten their grip on opium trading in the west of the region, the stakes grew higher, as profits from contraband carried with them the risk of detection. To avoid British interference, opium routes moved through Rajasthan and as far north as Sind. By the 1830s, up to 1000 chests of opium a year was making the journey to Karachi, where almost a third of customs duties were taken from opium shipments alone by the end of the decade. Even where the British did assert some sort of control over the movements of Malwa opium, it seems that the bulk of the profits remained in Indian hands. The British skimmed off revenue by imposing a system of licensing that controlled the movement of the drug into the port city of Bombay. However, it was local merchants who bought and sold it, and as such they retained most of the spoils to be had from speculation and trade. Farooqui shows how important opium trading was to Indian agents, and argues that the British annexation of Sind and indeed the decision to embark upon the First Opium War in 1839 were closely related to the resentment of colonial administrators towards the wealth being accrued from opium by local groups in western India. Farooqui further argues that it was a kind of intense struggle and negotiation between the colonial state and indigenous participants over the extent and manner of colonial control and the indigenous social groups including cultivators, merchants, zamīndars and princes kept the system of clandestine operations alive by holding back the information about the exact trading activities and feels that this subversion of colonial control through large scale smuggling was a type of 'everyday form of resistance.'[26] James H. Mills also outlines similar autonomous strategies and designs made use of by the cultivators of hemp drug crop which consisted of unspectacular methods of avoidance, sabotage and sly land encroachment. According to him peasants in Ganja mahal of Bengal resisted the colonial state intervention in monitoring the trade in preparation of hemp crop. This they did because of their knowledge of eco-environment and local geographies. They did so not by physically changing their environment but by using these local landscapes in surreptitious ways. According to him, the cultivators could do so by exploiting and manipulating the sheer extent of suitable land available to them to grow hemp and their knowledge that the apparatus of colonial state for enforcing its policies was limited. The British had only a rough estimate of how much hemp was grown in a year through their 'out door enquiries'. There always remained a substantial gap between the cultivated areas peasants declared as set aside for hemp cultivation and actual area they b ought under such cultivation. This was because peasant producers brought supplementary areas taking advantage of fertility of soil, the geographical extent of their fields and peasant's knowledge that the British government's surveillance capacity was limited. In other words, according to him the regional environment and local geography contributed mainly to this politics of resistance pursued by the cultivators and these strategies of defiance, land-encroachment and undeclared land-use were commonly used by the peasants. Secondly, Mills argues that river system and waterways especially river Jabuna in Ganja mahal provided the opportunity to smuggle illicitly produced hemp narcotics by evading colonial state surveillance.[27] This type of analysis of popular resistance is based on anarchist-inspired valourization of covert and unorganized, the so-called 'every day forms of protests' as the viable form of resistance available to the subordinate and exploited people because they are incapable of counter-hegemonic spectacular open rebellion. The traditional 'sub-culture' theory of delinquency, which was the political offspring of functionalist anomie theory and the end of ideology era in the Western World, had long back celebrated and glorified symbolic and magical forms of resistance. Individualistic attacks, subversions in any form, defiance and violation and contempt of dominant values were overemphasized in such resistance and any source of collective identification based on class and with a goal of emancipation was deserted.[28] James C. Scott defines the disguised, unobtrusive forms of resistance at the material, status and ideological realm as 'infra-politics' which involves acts of avoidance, escape, dissimulation, slander, pilferage, foot dragging and so on, forms in which resistance is expressed obliquely or ironically.[29] We feel that Gramsci's notion of hegemony and counter-hegemony are essential to understand the notions of dominance and resistance and Scott's notion is based on the rejection of Gramsci's notion of hegemony but at the same time he retains his notion of the autonomous, self-determining subject and the role of human agency. Moreover, the protest and counter-hegemonic gestures of the oppressed and exploited strata are also based on moral and ethical languages and belief in such moral-ethical normative order. What Scott and these historians call the 'every day form of resistance' might be survival strategies of individuals or even attempt to get rich where smuggling of narcotics is involved and as such individualized acts hardly in any way empowers members of the oppressed sections. Trocki, in fact, has shown convincingly how it was the merchant capital which benefited from the opium trade in the Western India and the peasant producers gained very little.[30] Amar farooqui argues that there was hardly any effective discourse within India questioning the propriety of opium use except for moralistic contentions of the Christian missionaries and even the Nationalists were not inclined to oppose the opium trade. According to him, only Dada Bhai Nauroji consistently opposed opium trade.[31] However, apart from Christian missionaries, opposition to Government's drug policies also came from professional groups. In 1892, a declaration signed by about 5000 medical professionals demanded that the government of India should prohibit the growth of the poppy and manufacture and sale of opium, except for medicinal purposes.[32] Initially there might have been no organized protest or agitation on trade in narcotic substances but voices were heard even in the nationalist circles against it. Romesh Dutt, in his famous work, India in the Victorian Age: An Economic History of the People, argued that the poppy cultivators had continuously, year after year, protested to the authorities against this cultivation, but their protests were frequently ignored. Gopal Krishna Gokhale also denounced the opium revenues derived from the moral degradation of Chinese people as a stain on India while speaking in the Indian legislative council in 1907.[33] There was also some organized resistance to government's drug policy and some 301 temperance associations met in Bombay in 1904 under the All-India Temperance Conference and demanded complete prohibition.[34] There were stray cases of resistance to the policy of colonial government by the villagers. In March, 1935, some Thakarda tribesmen killed the village headmen of Chamasa near Ahmedabad as he had spotted them distilling illicit liquor.[35] Similarly, the raid by an excise party at Narangi village under Virar police station to detect illicit distillation on 12 September infuriated the villagers who beat the sub-inspector leading to his death subsequently. It happened to be an auspicious day of celebration of Gauri Ganpati festival.[36]

Another radically different solution to the problem brought about by British abkari policies was to give up drink altogether. In the Brahmanic Hindu culture abstention from spirituous drinks was considered a great virtue, and even before the colonial era there were certain tribal and low-caste peasants who refused to drink in the belief that this would raise their status in the wider society. These families tended to be the more prosperous ones which were trying to distance themselves from other members of their community, for refusal to drink together in a community in which such drinking represented a symbol of mutual solidarity could be considered a gesture of renunciation of membership of that community. Food is an important identity symbol in South Asian society – as elsewhere - and is related to issues of purity and impurity as well as to issues of status and social mobility. Food symbolizes identity at the same time as it marks boundaries. The boundaries drawn by the discourse and practice around food deal with questions of status. In the caste system, the hierarchy of foodstuffs attributes to each stratum's diet its hierarchical value. A change in dietary practices has frequently been described as a means for the lower strata to acquire a higher social status. In South Gujarat, the collector of Surat noted in 1895, the formation of total abstinence leagues almost through the district. The movement began in the towns of Surat and Nowsari and spread to the outlying villages. An organized crusade against drink was carried on for a while by means of public meetings and caste pressure. The great mass of those who joined did so under the persuasion that they would force down the prices of liquor and toddy while a few were roused by a sincere desire to diminish drunkenness. This particular movement was short-lived, collapsing rapidly after several influential caste leaders were found to be drinking secretly, however many such movements were recorded in Gujarat, ultimately culminating in the famous Devi movement of 1922-23. This anti-liquor movement represented a major attack on the abkari system throughout south Gujarat, as well as on the much hated Parsi liquor and toddy dealers. The movement forged an alliance between the peasants and tribals and the middle class Gandhian nationalists of Gujarat.The common platform was that of abstention from liquor and toddy.[37] In his preaching, Viswanath Maharaj, who was an influential religious leader in South Gujarat in 1930's, asked his Dhanka and koli and other followers to give up drinking.[38] The emergence of Gulia Maharaj and later his brother Ramdas in West Khandesh district also proved important in weaning Bhil adivasis from drinks and it was the popularity of these Bhagats that compelled the Congress ministry to declare West Khandesh as a dry area in 1938.[39] The Indian National Congress had from its earliest years put forward the view that the chief concern of the British in their excise policy was to raise as much revenue as possible in a manner which went against the best interests of the people. It was argued that although officials claimed that high prices discouraged drinking, in practice the local revenue officers did their utmost to stimulate the consumption of liquor.

The nationalist intervention was basically confined to promotion of temperance movement although the nationalist also agreed with the colonial administration about the moral impact of drugs. This aspect of social history has not well been investigated. Gandhi encouraged the temperance movement although he neither planned it nor anticipated it during the Non-Co-operation days. According to Judith Brown, a combination of factors contributed to its emergence such as the antipathy of orthodox Hindu as well as Muslim to alcoholic drinks, the inducement of claiming a higher ritual status for the backward castes, shortage of money after the war and its efficacy as a political weapon because this could impact the governmental revenues from excise. Bombay Provincial Congress Committee launched a vigorous campaign in June 1921, forming vigilance committees and a number of volunteer groups to enforce picketing of liquor shops and even social intimidation was used to put into effect the decisions.[40] The picketing of liquor shops found the most enthusiastic support during the Non-Cooperation campaign as the foreign liquor shops symbolized wealth and were readily identified with the customs and habits of colonial rulers in the popular imagination. Secondly, in the context of Khilafat wrongs, the theme of colonial injustice was infused with religious prohibitions on the consumption of liquor. Both the Hindu and Muslim volunteers participated in this campaign. There were instances of communalized abuse of customers and they were taunted if Hindus, whether they had gone to drink cow's blood and if they were Muslims, if they were to liquor shops to drink pig's blood.[41] The anti-liquor campaign also provoked communal antagonisms and tensions as the November 1921 riot between the Parsis and Muslims in Bombay city was result of this.[42] During the Civil Disobedience movement, Gandhi specifically asked the women volunteers to engage in activities like picketing of liquor and toddy shops. In a Pamphlet entitled 'How to do Picketing?' Gandhi outlined the tactics to be followed during picketing. The women volunteers were advised to first appeal to the owner, and then the potential customers. They were also advised to dress in a recognizable dress, carry banners and sing *bhajans* or devotional song when picketing. In order that women volunteers appeared 'respectable', Gandhi prohibited the practice of obstructing customers and the use of abusive language by the volunteers. Thousands of Gujarati women were involved in the Bombay Presidency in this work of picketing liquor and toddy shops during Civil Disobedience. In Bombay city itself, the number of women volunteers organized under the banner of Desh Sevika Sangha peaked at 560 but remained stable around 300. However, only women of 'good classes' were recruited in the work. The membership was strictly controlled and the suggestion of leftist that women volunteers should lay on the floor of doors of liquor shops was found to be against the innate modesty and dignity of women.[43] The women were supposed to be the symbols of the purity and respectability of the nationalist movement. Favouring women for the job, Gandhi wrote, "... If men approach drunkards, the latter will resort to obscene language; however, if young girls approach as to why they drink, ask them what indeed they are up to, whether it befits them under drink to fail to recognize a mother or a daughter, then hearing such words steeped in affection, even the worst drunkards will hang his head in shame..."[44]

There was intense picketing of liquor and toddy shops in some parts of Agra. There both male and female volunteers sat on *dharna* during Civil Disobedience movement before the liquor shops in Firozabad and Sevikas disrupted the normal business by persuading customers not to buy drinks. In Pinhat, Dhimishri, Fahaibad and Samshadbad volunteers destroyed toddy trees and in Sikanderpur zamindars pledged not to lease their toddy trees. There was also some disruption in the auction of toddy shops during the Civil Disobedience movement and Toddy Bacha Hai Hai (the toddy babies, be doomed, be doomed) became a popular slogan. The British were called toddies because of the revenue the colonial state earned by encouraging liquor sales.[45] The Colonial state dependence on revenue from liquor was so important that that the authorities were not willing to tolerate even the most peaceful resistance. In Delhi, the Chief Commissioner was advised by the Home secretary to introduce, as a legal technique of discipline, the Prevention of Intimidation Act Ordinance in Delhi Province to deal with the liquor-picketers. There was a debate among the official as how to apply such a measure in dealing with non-violent picketing. The Delhi Public Prosecutor stated on 21 April, 1930 that the system of picketing was mostly peaceful and non-violent and confined to free persuasion. He lodged a dissent that law would make such a non-violent act of persuasion an offence. The Deputy Commissioner also commented that if 'molestation' were defined as 'attempt to stop someone doing or not doing an act or loitering near a place where someone resides or works' then the law would effectively ban people from standing around in public. Despite these protests, however, the Ordinance was made available to deal with picketers in Delhi on 30 May, 1930.[46]

Revisiting Post-Colonial Context and Continuities

We observe some continuity with the colonial drug policies after independence as the Gandhian programme of prohibition was sidelined on the plea that the state could not take the steps in this direction due to potential loss of revenue. The loss of revenue would have hurt the government's action in volatile Kashmir and Hyderabad. So the satanic influence of drugs continued so as to protect excise revenue of the government. Some of the states did introduce prohibition especially Bombay, Madras and Saurashtra after the independence but it failed miserably due to continued trade of all intoxicants in the adjoining states.[47] Subsequently, some Gandian workers and followers of Vinoba Bhave launched agitations in some parts of country but again it was confined to sale of liquor. One was led by Sunder Lal Bahugana in Uttarnchal area in 1966 which continued till women activists were successful in getting enacted a law banning liquor in the state in 1972. The environmental Chipko movement later marginalized this campaign. The *adivasi* women also led a similar movement in 1973 in Dhule district of Maharashtra when they indulged in large scale destruction of illicit distilleries. The anti-liquor agitation resurfaced in Uttaranchal again in 1984 and in Andhra Pradesh in early 1990's.[48] However, despite these isolated movements, the drug use patterns and governmental policies have not changed much.

Scholars have highlighted the socio-cultural context of traditional drug use and how such use contains within it a strategy of harm reduction for the potential users. For example, there were a variety of purposes for use of cannabis in Indian context. Firstly, it was used for medicinal purposes along with other ingredients in treatment of rheumatism, migraine, malaria and cholera. Secondly, it was used at the time of Shivratri, Krishnashtami, Holi and Akha Teej and other festive occasions. Thirdly, holy men used it to attain altered states of consciousness. The culturally ingrained drug use patterns prevented non-cultural excessive use despite easy availability and local cultivation of such drugs. The imposition of state controls and attempts at eradications, therefore, only resulted in more harmful modes of consumption (injecting, for example) and popularity of non-traditional forms of drug use. The Narcotics Drugs and Psychotropic Substances Act (1985) took away the responsibility of drug abuse control from community norms to near defunct legal establishment and criminalized socio-cultural and recreational use of cannabis and opium. The result was that instead of bringing under control, the legislation promoted the proliferation of alcohol, heroin and other more harmful pharmaceutical drugs.[49]

It is also quite evident that drug production and drug dealing have been a substantial source of revenue especially since the commercialization of drug trade on a global scale. It has made up budget deficits and enriched individuals, social groups, business firms or even the whole countries. Drugs also involve economically marginalized sectors of population such as peasant cultivators or small-scale drug peddlers.[50] It also breeds organized criminal gangs as closely knit sectors of society in the world of business or state institutions. The modern drug economy is a growth in the sectors of illegal activity and is interpenetrated with the official sectors of the society.[51] Molly and his other research co-workers (2002) investigated this marriage of legal and illegal in their study of growth of Bombay's underworld and its role in drug trade. They outline the broad map of activities and nexuses at the structural level that supported the growth and operations of underworld in the city and scanned the lives of gangsters. They linked this to the various governmental policies, unmet needs of the citizens due to various system failures in governance as well as socio-economic changes in the city especially the demographic profile of city's population. A special emphasis has been placed by them on the stagnation of manufacturing sector and creation of a very large sector of unproductive employment in service sector relating to trade, hotels and restaurants, bars and so on.[52] Buxton points out how the UN bureaucracy and its model of drug-control for elimination of production, distribution and consumption of drugs that has been expressed in a number of Conventions draws heavily from the ideology of prohibition and its worldview as developed in USA. It is often a tool of American foreign policy goals and how such universalized policy framework is inappropriate in national context of many countries.[53]

On the basis of above observations, a number of inferences can be drawn that would be useful for the policy makers. First of all, it is clear that a purely punitive approach that tries to outlaw drug trade is bound to prove futile and is likely to create a network of smugglers and illicit drug trafficking. The attempts to introduce prohibition in the United States in 1920's had encourage d more alchohalism. Since the drug trade is highly profitable business, vested interests involved in this will not care for the legal or moral angle. The nature of state in the developing societies is also such that it gets entangled in the activities of underworld. Therefore, some sorts of community control and culturally sanctioned pattern of drug and alchohal use, which reduces the harmful effects of excessive consumption of drugs, will ensure a better implementation of the objective of a society free from drug-addiction.

References

1. See Ministry of Social justice and Empowerment, Govt. of India, and UN office on Drug and Crime, Drug Abuse Monitoring System: A Profile of Treatment Seekers, New Delhi, 2002.
2. Indo-Asian News Service, March 6, 2006.
3. G. Srinivasan, "Drug abuse: Asia on a new high" in The Hindu Business Line, March 11, 2006.
4. S.S. Shastri and K.P. Kolhatkar, "Socio-Demographic Features of cannabis and heroin abuse in Bombay", in the Journal of Postgraduate Medicine, Vol. 35(4), 1989, pp. 196-98.
5. See Martin A. Lee and Bruce Shlain, Acid Dreams: The Complete Social History of LSD, Grover Press, 1985 for details.
6. David G. Mandelbaum, "Alcohol and Culture", Current Anthropology, Vol.6 (3), 1965
7. See R. Gordon Wasson, Soma: Divine Mushroom, Mouton, 1968.
8. See R. Rudgley, The Alchemy of Culture: Intoxicants in Society, 1993 for more details.
9. David T. Court Wright, Forces of Habit: Drugs and the Making of the Modern World, Harvard University Press, Cambridge and Massachusetts, 2001, pp. 2-9.
10. *Ibid,* pp. 9-19.
11. Julia Buxton, The Political Economy of Narcotics; Production, Consumption and Global Markets, Zed Books, London, 2006, pp.14-16.

12. See Carl A. Trocki, Opium, Empire and the Global Political Economy: A Study of the Asian opium Trade, 1750-1950, Routledge, London and New York, pp. 9-10.
13. Amar Farooqui, Smuggling as Subversion: Colonialism, Indian Merchants and the politics of Opium, 1790-1843, Lexington Books, 2005, p. 2.
14. M. Emdad-ul-Haq, Drugs in South Asia: From Opium Trade to the Present Day, Macmillan Press Ltd, Basingstoke, Hampshire and London, 2000, pp. 19-23.
15. Trocki, *op. cit.*, p. 32.
16. Emad-ul-Haq, Drugs in South Asia, pp. 29-31.
17. Julia Buxton, *op. cit.*, pp. 8-9.
18. Natham Allen, The Opium Trade: Including a Sketch of its History, Extent and Effects, 1858, digitalized by Google from Harvard University copy, pp. 44-63 and also R. Alexander and others, The Rise and Growth of British Opium Smuggling, 1856, Digitalized by Google from University of California copy, pp.2-6.
19. James H. Mills, Cannabis Britannica: Empire, Trade, Prohibition, Oxford University Press, Oxford, 2005, pp. 2-6 and his paper "Cannabis in Colonial India: Production, State Intervention, and Resistance in Late Nineteenth Century Bengali Landscape", in Michael K. Steinberg, et al, eds., Dangerous Harvest: Drug Plants and the Transformation of Indigenous Landscapes, Oxford University Press, Oxford, pp. 221-26.
20. *Ibid.*, pp. 4-5.
21. David Owen, British Opium Policy in China and India, Archon Books, London, 1968 B.Inglis, The Opium War, London, 1976 and Timothy Brook Takashi Wakabayashi, Opium Regimes, China, Britain and Japan: 1839-1952, University of California Press, Berkeley, 2000 for more details of British colonial policy regarding opium trade.
22. Indian Hemp Drug Commission (Vol. 1-7), Shimla, 1893-94.
23. The Indian Excise Committee of 1905-06.
24. *Ibid.*

25. The Bombay Excise administration Report,1927-28, Maharashtra State Archives, Bombay.
26. Amar Farooqui, Smuggling as Subversion, pp. 5-11.
27. Mills, "Cannabis in Colonial India", pp. 226-30.
28. See Stanley Cohen, Folk Devils and Moral Panics: The Creation of Modes and Rockers, Oxford, 1980, S. Hall and T. Jefferson, eds., Reistance through Rituals: Youth Sub-cultures in Post-War Britain, London, 1976, Paul Willis, Learning to Labour, London, 1978 and D Hebdige, Sub-culture: The Meaning of Style, London,1979 for a variety of such stylistic and symbolic protests.
29. See James C. Scott, The Moral Economy of the Peasant: Rebellion and Subsistence in South-East Asia, New Haven, 1976, The Weapons of the Weak: Everyday Form of Resistance, New Haven, 1985 and Domination and The Art of Resistance: Hidden Transcripts, New Haven, 1990 for such an approach.
30. Trocki, Opium, Empire and Global Political Economy, pp. 58-87.
31. Farooqui, Smuggling as Subversion, pp. 4-5.
32. M. Emdad-ul-Haq, Drugs in South Asia, p. 4931 *ibid*, p. 52.
33. Romesh Dutt, India in the Victorian Age : An Economic History of the People, 1904, pp. 155-56.
34. M. Emdad-ul-Haq, *op. cit.*, p. 52.
35. Bombay Chronicle, 24 March,1935.
36. Bombay Chronicle, 1 October, 1937 and also Annual Police Administration Report, Maharashtra State Archives, Bombay, 1937, p. 15.
37. David Hardiman, Coming of Devi, Oxford University Press, Delhi, 1987.
38. P.G. Shah, Tribal life in Gujarat, Bombay, 1964, pp.72-74.
39. Home/Special file No 982, 1938-43, Maharashtra State Archives, Bombay.
40. Judith Brown, Gandhi's Rise to Power: Indian Politics 1915-1922, Cambridge University Press, Cambridge, 1972, pp. 315-16.
41. Chief Excise Inspector, Bombay to The Superintendent of Salt and Excise, Bombay, November 7, 1921, Govt. of Bombay, Home (Special) File 355(21) F of 1921, MSA.

42. Rajnarayan Chandravarkar, Imperial Power and Popular Politics: Class, Resistance and State in India, Cambridge University Press, New Delhi, 1998, p. 315.
43. Geraldine H. Forbes, Women in Colonial India: Essays on Politics, Medicine and Historiography, Orient Black Swan, Delhi, 2005, pp. 46-48.
44. Mahatama Gandhi, Collected Works, Vol. XLIII, pp. 154-55.
45. Suruchi Thapar-Bjorkert, Women in the Indian National Movement: Unseen Faces and Unheard Voices, 1930-1942, Sage Publishers Pvt.Ltd., New Delhi, India, 2006, pp.116-17.
46. Stephen Legg, Spaces of Colonialism: Delhi's Urban Governmentalities, Blackwell Publishing, 2007, p.112.
47. M. Emdad-ul-Haq, Drugs in South Asia, pp. 107-11.
48. David Hardiman, Gandhi: In His Times and Ours, Orient Blackswan, Delhi, 2003, pp. 216-18.
49. Charles Molly and Gabriel Britto, "Culture and Drug Scene in India" in Guilham Fabre and Michel Schiray, ed., UNESCO Report on Globalization, drugs and Criminalisation, Part III, 2002, pp. 4-30.
50. The profitability of drug cultivation is clear even to illiterate peasants as shown by the demand of debt-ridden farmers of Vidharbha region of Maharashtra where recently the villagers of Naigaon from Dhamangaon *taluka* of Amraoti district sought permission from the authorities to start cultivation of marijuana (*ganja*) to repay their debts. (The Times of India, January 24, 2006.)
51. M.L. Smith, et al, Why People Grow Drugs: Narcotics and Development in the Third World, London, 1992 for an analysis of political economy of drugs.
52. Charles Molly, K.S. Nair, Gabriel Britto and A.A. Das, "The Bombay's Underworld: A Descriptive Account and its Role in Drug Trade" in Guilham Fabre and Michel Schiray, ed., UNESCO Report on Globalization, Drugs and Criminalisation, 2002, pp.7-50.
53. Buxton, The Political Economy of Narcotics, pp.1-2.

3

Andhra Pradesh in 1857

Devireddy Subramanyam Reddy

The British India was never free either from armed rebellions or non-violent movements. There had been continuous and formidable resistance to British rule from its very inception in India. In fact, the first hundred years of British rule from 1757 to 1857 and even the post-1857 period witnessed outbreak of innumerable armed struggles for 'independence' from foreign rule and thereby established local traditions of anti-colonial armed struggles[1]. The first of such insurrections was of the Hindu Sanyasis and Muslim Fakirs during 1768 and 1800. The greatest and the most wide-spread of the armed struggles, comparable with the Taiping Rebellion of the same phase in China, was the Great Uprising of 1857-1858 which shook the British authority to its very foundations, and became a tool for early nationalist mobilization and non-violent, some times even violent, movements during 1885 and 1947, to which the British power had to succumb, finally, in 1947.

The Uprising of 1857 meant different things for different men at that time. And different causes were at work in mobilisation in different places. The causes of one community were different from another community. The causes of one caste were different from another caste. The causes of one class were different from another class. The causes of one section were different from another section. The causes of one region were different from another region. In otherwords, the causes of Generals and other Officers were different from the causes of common soldiers. The causes of rulers, ex-rulers, their successors and talukdars were different from the causes of the other sections of the society. The causes of every section of the society such as the peasantry, artisans, small business men and traders, tribals, labourers etc., were different from each other. And there was no common cause. For sepoys it was loss of privileges etc., which made them to revolt against the British rule. For rulers, ex-rulers and talukdars it was loss of power, pension, territory and privileges. For peasants it was loss of land and income. For artisans it was loss of professional profits. For tribals it was loss of forest rights, land and income. For Hindus and Muslims it was danger to customs, religion and caste, and conversion to Christianity. But, interestingly personal grievances gradually converted into larger causes to eliminate the British colonial rule which was considered to be responsible for exploitation and oppression of the native rulers and the ruled, both Hindus and Muslims. The above discussion also reveals that there were different identities at work in 1857 uprising. In otherwords, there were Muslims and Wahabis, Hindus and Sanatanis, sepoys and peasants, artisans and small business and trading communities, tribals and labourers, rulers and ex-rulers, descendents of ex-rulers and adopted sons of ex-rulers, talukdars and zamindars, upper caste and lower caste people, rich and poor, North Indians and South Indians, Hindi speaking people and people speaking other Indian languages, and there were also female war-lords and non-combatant women considered to be coarse, vulgar, loud, morally degraded and sexually promiscuous or courtesans[2]. Thus, the rebels included people of different identities - community (Hindu and Muslim), caste, tribe, class, region (kingdom or pre-modern nationality) class, profession, language etc. But, at the same time, we find unity in diversity or diverse interests and identities. In the battleground all the rebellious natives with different causes and different identities were one - fighters for 'freedom' from colonial rule, despite communal flare-ups in certain localities of United Provinces where the uprising of 1857 had in fact turned into a mass movement. For the rebels 1857 was a battle against the common enemy the *firangi* or foreigner. It was a *Gadar* (revolt) of the *Balwai* (people) against the *firangi* (foreigner) or *Kaffur* for the 'freedom' of their *mulk* (pre-modern mother land/ kingdom)[3]. No doubt the rebels were great patriots and they were for ending British colonial rule. But their fight was not for the freedom of the whole of the country as we see in the Phadke and Alluri Sitaramaraju movements of later period. Their fight was for the freedom of their kingdom and reestablishment of native rule but with nominal monarchical authority, as in England, under a democratic and republican constitution as was to be seen in Delhi, Bareilly etc., during 1857[4]. Their patriotism confined to the goal of achieving freedom for their kingdom which they considered in those days as their nation (in the political sense), not the whole of India that came into existence after 1947. Hence, self-interest of individuals, classes, communities, states etc., dominated the field. The preference for native rule, whether Hindu or Muslim, was mainly because it was less exploitative and oppressive compared with the British colonial rule.

Further, the Uprising of 1857 was not an isolated and sudden outbreak. It had been long preparing. Rather it was the culmination of accumulated discontent in various quarters for which the new rulers of the country were responsible. It was a continuation of earlier traditions of armed struggles as is evident from the innumerable movements and mutinies of pre-1857 period[5]. Moreover, the sepoy mutinies and civil commotions of pre-1857 period had run on two parallel lines. It was only the revolt of 1857 which brought about a link-up of many of these elements on a massive scale with a formidable challenge to the alien rule.

It is also interesting to note that in Punjab and a greater part of Madhya Pradesh the Uprising of 1857 was purely a mutiny. In western part of Bihar, a greater part of United Provinces and a small part of Madhya Pradesh the mutiny was succeeded by a general revolt of the people including the dispossessed chiefs, ejected landlords and tenants. In Rajasthan and Maharashtra there was discontent against the British and passive, even active, sympathy with the mutineers among the civil population, but no overt acts of rebellion could be found among them. In the whole of Bengal, Assam, eastern Bihar, Orissa, small part of Madhya Pradesh, and South India, excepting pockets of Nizam Andhra and British Andhra, practically remained almost unaffected by the Great Outbreak. In otherwords, there was the greatest dislike of British authority where it had not yet been long established and there was the least effort to overthrow British rule in those parts of India which had longest been subject to British rule i.e., outbreak of revolts in new territories and near absence of revolt in the old possessions. It points to a state of acclimatization and adjustment coupled with the experience of frequent suppression that had broken the spirit of many men which prevented the people of the old possessions from renewing their offensive in the year 1857.

Broadly, the uprising was against the external (colonial) order of exploitation and oppression, as well as the internal (banias, usurers, etc.) order of exploitation and oppression, but primarily against the former as it was indirectly responsible for the latter's exploitation and oppression. It must also be noted here that no community, class or caste as such was entirely for or against the British colonial rule. Only a determined minority took active part in the rebellion while the overwhelming majority remained passive.

The events of 1857 in India have been variously described by writers as a Sepoy Mutiny, a Feudal War, a Peasant or Peoples War, Religious War (or Jehad or a "just war") and The Indian War of Independence. The labels or words used about 1857 contain interpretations. To elaborate, the first description suggests a revolt confined to the army. The second description suggests a rebellion confined to the feudal classes such as rulers, ex-ruler, successors of ex-rulers, adopted children of ex-rulers, talukdars and zamindars. The third description suggests a broad based and a much larger mass uprising involving the peasantry, artisans, tribals and all other classes. The fourth description suggests a revolt confined mostly to the Muslim community (against British political domination, not against the religion of the British race, and jehad included non-Muslims also). The fifth description suggests a nation-wide upsurge of people for independence of the whole country. Similarly, the first, second, and fourth descriptions diminish the events of 1857. The third description gives a more or less balanced position of the event. The fifth description magnifies the events. But, all the labels or words unmistakably suggest a bitter resistance and hard fight for 'independence' from colonial rule.

The uprising began on 10 May 1857 and ended in April 1859. It began, at first, in Meerut in the North and then spread like wild fire to Murshidabad, Kanpur, Lucknow, Delhi, Punjab, Central India etc. Thus, the movement at first confined to the North. But very soon it gripped many parts of India, even where the agitation was not violent there was unrest in the peoples minds. In otherwords, it was not uniform throughout the country as has been noticed earlier. It began originally as a revolt of the discontented sepoys. Gradually, it turned into a kind of major mass uprising of the Hindus and Muslims, involving even the tribal communities[6]. The prime aim of the rebel natives was the overthrow of the British rule and protection or reestablishment of native authorities (and thus to some extent nativistic in outlook). The rebels also aimed at establishing a different political system; a democratic and republican form of government in a crude form or in embryonic stage. This became possible because the native rulers or erstwhile rulers as of Delhi, were prepared to be contented and live with nominal authority as in the case of the Queen of England and like the Nizam of Hyderabad and other native chiefs than to live under colonial rule, but unhesitatingly along with the titles, paraphernalia of royalty, personal properties, income for maintenance and certain other privileges[7]. Among the ruling classes who were actively involved in the uprising included Nana Saheb (Dhondopant), Tantya Tope (Ramachandra Panduranga), Rani Lakshmi Bai, Kunwar Singh, Hazrat Mahal, Azimulla Khan, Bahadur Shah etc[8].

It is interesting to note that no community, caste or class was entirely for or against the British. As noted earlier different sections of the society fought against the British. Similarly, the others supported the British. For example, the sepoys of the Madras and the Bombay Armies remained loyal to the British and fought for the Government even in the worst affected areas although a section of the Bengal Army fought against the British. Similarly, the English educated classes almost kept aloof from the mutinous sepoys[9]. Even, public meetings were held in many parts of India condemning the mutiny, and congratulatory addresses, even illuminations, followed notable British victories in 1857[10]. The associations like the British Indian Association and the Mohammadan Association of Calcutta passed resolutions on the outbreak of the mutiny, denouncing it and trusting that it would meet with 'no sympathy, countenance or support from the bulk of the civil population....'[11] Even leaders like Syed Ahmed Khan who became the undisputed leader of Muslims in Uttar Pradesh in the post-1857 period was a staunch supporter of the British during the mutiny[12]. Prominent rebel leaders like Bahadur Shah, Nana Sahib, and Rani Lakshmi Bai also denounced the sepoys at the beginning of the revolt. In fact, it was the natives who had at first called the uprising of 1857 as a sepoy mutiny.

Other prominent classes or groups who kept aloof from the revolt included the great ruling chiefs such as Sindhia, Holkar, Gaekwar, the Nizam, and the historic ruling houses of Rajasthan, Mysore, Travancore and Kashmir. (As soon as the news of the uprising of 1857 reached Kashmir on 11 May 1857 John Lawrence informed his allies and asked for help. Meanwhile, rebellion of Indian soldiers at Lahore and Sialkote also came. Maharaja Ranbir Singh of Kashmir and his Diwan Hari Chand (who died outside Delhi on August 1857) sent a contingent of 3000 soldiers to Lawrence, under the command of Diwan Nihal Chand. It consisted of 2000 infantry, 200 cavalry and six guns. Due to his help he was appreciated by Governor General. Presents were sent to him by the British Queen. His loyalty and sincerity was commended by the Queen. He was offered Rs. One Lakh and a Jagir in Oudh which of course he politely refused to take. He was granted right to adopt a son on failure of having male heir to succeed him. He was conferred the title of 'the Star of India'. He was so loyal that he held a darbar to commemorate the success of the British. He asked the Queen, in a letter, for a life size statue of the Queen of England[13]). The Sikh chiefs such as those of Jhind, Patiala and Nabha and other loyal elements of population actively helped the British. Even the Gurkhas offered their services to the British in 1857. In the region south of the Yamuna particularly at Nasirabad and Neemuch order was restored with the help of troops of Jodhpur. The ruler of Orchcha and other chiefs fought against the rebels of Lalitpur etc. As noted already, the upsurge of the people was limited to a comparatively narrow region of India, comprising at best the greater part of Uttar Pradesh and a narrow zone to its east, west and south. The whole of Bengal, Assam, Orissa, Rajasthan, and greater parts of Punjab, Bihar, and Madhya Pradesh, as well as the whole of India, south of the Narmada, hardly witnessed any overt act of rebellion on the part of the people except in British Andhra and Nizam Andhra. Even within the narrow zone where the civil population revolted, there were considerable sections who were friendly to the

British. The ruling chiefs in East Punjab and the entire landed aristocracy of Bihar with very few exceptions, firmly and consistently stood by the British Government. Even in Avadh and Rohilkhand, several chiefs, including the Nawab of Rampur supported the British. One of them Derigbijah (Digbijay?) Singh gave shelter to Mowbray Thomson, one of the survivours of the Kanpur massacre, at a considerable risk to himself. It may be noted here that even the talukdars of Avadh were not hostile to the British. They became hostile only after the Confiscation Proclamation was issued by Lord Canning on 20 March 1858 which threatened practically the whole body of talukdars with the confiscation of their 'ill-gotten' gain[14]. The talukdars made it their first business to recover the estates they had lost and, therefore, they fought against the British. The Banias and Mahajans who were benefited by the British rule also supported the British[15].

But, it must be noted that the support of certain sections of the society to the colonial rulers in their conquest, expansion, consolidation and administration was not new in 1857. It was there since the inception of British rule and continued to be there even after 1857 till India got Independence in 1947. Thus, the reestablishment of British rule in 1857 and continuation of its authority till 1947 was made possible more by the Indian collaboration with the British Government rather than by British repression. It is to be noted here that the might of the British was magnified and Indian collaboration with the British Government was minimized. The truth was that there were more than two thousand Indians to each Britisher in India even by 1939.

As a result, repression and suppression became easier. The British followed indiscriminate, ruthless and brutal methods to suppress the uprising which demonstrate the popularity of the rebellion. The suppression included large scale destruction of villages, public hangings, and blowing off people from canons, long term imprisonments, transportation for life, forcible realization of collective fines from the rural folk, confiscation of properties for damages - all in a desperate effort to restore colonial authority. Indiscriminate slaughter of men and burning of whole tracts of inhabited country became general. Whole lines of villages in the track of the army were burnt down and for miles corpses hung from trees[16]. Brigadier Neill's course from Benaras to Allahabad was particularly marked by corpses of villagers, and the riversides for miles presented an array of demolished houses. In fact Neill's excesses earned him the epithet, "A monster in human form". He had put people to death in the most reckless manner which made Satyamurthy call him "a monster miscalled man" and that in the matter of terrorism, "General Neill to General Dyer was an apostolic succession". The war of mutinies was thus turned into a war of revenge and extermination. Terror-stricken, the populance even migrated, especially for Mauritius. In 1850, they numbered 12,562, but at the end of 1857, the Indian population of the island was 1,07,072 males and 30,462 females[17].

In this connection we may note that for getting independence for the entire country three things are required. Firstly, the effort of the whole population of the country. Secondly, the positive attitude of the native rulers, ex-rulers and other ruling classes for the independence of the whole nation and not for their own kingdom. Thirdly, the operation of world events in favour of the country desiring to get independence. Unfortunately, none of these existed in 1857. They existed only in 1947. Therefore, India could get independence only in 1947 and not in 1857-58.

British Andhra in 1857: While the North witnessed an open rebellion against the British colonial rule, the South appearing to be peaceful at first, had seen silent as well as violent struggles as could be observed in British Andhra and Nizam Andhra. Many instances of sepoy mutinies as well as civil and tribal insurrections could be seen in Andhra during 1857. As soon as the news of the Revolt of 1857 in the North spread like wild fire in the South the "native" press was quick to respond to it. The serious discussion in the Government of Madras on the insurrection in the North, as is evident from its resolution dated 3rd September 1857 and as reported in the vernacular news papers of the day, shows that the insurrection had extremely worried the Government of Madras Presidency[18].

That the total number of men tried by courts martials in the Bengal Army, the Bombay Army and the Madras Army during the disturbances of 1857-58 were 1954, 1213, and 1044 respectively[19] shows that the Madras Army as compared with the Bengal and Bombay Armies, did not lag behind in respect of participation of Madras Army in the Revolt of 1857.

In fact, the anti-British sentiment was wide-spread in the South including British Andhra and Nizam Andhra. The resolution of the Government of Madras, in the Judicial Department, dated 3rd September, 1857 observed: "Hyderabad is always inflammable and was sure to be deeply excited.... Our provinces of Kurnool, Kadapa and Malabar contain a large number of Mussalman population which would participate in these feelings, and at Madras itself and the towns of Arcot, Vellore, Trichinopoly animosity was felt in consequence of extinction of the nawabship of the Carnatic"[20]. The popular sentiment in places like Triplicane, the erstwhile headquarters of the Carnatic Nawabs became so "suspicious" that military posts were established in different parts of the town on 29 June 1857[21]. The European volunteers were enrolled and other precautions taken. Triplicane was the centre of the Muslim population connected with the nawab of Carnatic whose territory included even the present Chittoor and Nellore districts of British Andhra[22]. Thus, the conditions required for a major uprising existed even in the South, including Andhra. Only a leader had to emerge as in different regions of the North. Naturally, measures were taken to check the spread of anti-British feelings as well as activities[23]. But, they could not stop the latter as is to be observed hereunder.

In North Arcot, including the present Chittoor district of British Andhra, plans and secret meetings were held for organizing a revolt against the British, from as early as January

1857, probably in anticipation of the uprising of 1857. It is on record that one Syed Kussa Mohammed Augirzah Hussain held talks in this connection with the Zamindars of Punganur (now in Chittoor district of Andhra Pradesh) and Vellore (now in Tamil Nadu). But he was apprehended by the British, in March 1857, and a security was demanded of him[24].

In February 1857 a regiment in Vijayanagaram in British Andhra which was ordered to march to Kurnool refused to go on the pretext of lack of carriages for moving their families along with them[25].

In another instance a cavalry regiment refused to do service in Bengal unless they were guaranteed the old rates of pay and pension which had been altered long back in 1833[26].

In Bellary, "seditious rumours unfavourable to" the British Government began to be spread abroad in June, and fires of grain stacks along the frontier were reported on 10th June 1857[27].

Similarly, in the middle of June 1857 bands of armed Rohillas who proclaimed that they were the servants of Nana Saheb Peshwa crossed from the Nizam's territory, into Kurnool and Kadapa districts "with a deeper object"[28]. It was these bands which had later joined the party that made the attack on the Hyderabad Residency on 17th July 1857[29]. The Rohillas as well as the Arabs from the Nizams dominions raided the border districts of British Andhra on several occasions. They made raids into Kurnool and Kadapa districts. They raided Rudravaram[30] in Koilkuntla taluk. They also attacked the taluk treasury at Jaggaiahpeta[31] in Krishna district. The Madras Government suspected some connection between these raids and the uprising in the North.

In Machilipatnam a green flag and a proclamation urging the slaughter of the English were seized on 10th July 1857[32] and it was reported on 15th August 1857 that prayers for the success of the Mughal emperor of Delhi were offered in the mosques[33].

On 28th July 1857, "a conspiracy was discovered, the ramifications of which extended (from Belgaum) to Mysore, Kurnool and Madras generally"[34]. In fact, two emissaries had left for Madras (Presidency). Therefore, directions were given to apprehend them and also to take precautionary measures[35]. Meanwhile, the British Resident at Hyderabad sent one of the emissaries intercepted letters to the Madras Government.

There were strong rumours that the tribals round Narasapatnam in Visakhapatnam district were organizing a rebellion in 1857. Therefore, the Government took necessary precautions against it[36].

A Telugu placard was also found at Visakhapatnam calling the local Muslims to raze the town to dust and rename it Muhammadpatnam during the Moharrum[37], indicating involvement of Muslims in the Uprising of 1857 in British Andhra.

Proclamations and "seditious" letters urging the Nizam and his Diwan to begin the holy war (as in the North) against the British were seized on 28the June 1857[38].

In Madras and surrounding provinces correspondence was going on about the fall of the British power during the coming Moharrum festival in 1857[39].

To incite the sepoys a large number of disbanded sepoys and also emissaries of prominent leaders of the neighbouring provinces particularly of Maharashtra entered the Madras Presidency and also the Nizams dominions[40].

On 28th August 1857, a Muslim by name Sheik Peer Saheb suddenly appeared in Kadapa and began preaching Jehad against the British; while the other Muslims of Kadapa (in the Ceded Districts of Madras Presidency) also started offering prayers in the mosques of Kadapa for the success of the Mughal emperor. Sheik Peer also met the native officers and men of the 30th Regiment (on 28th) in the Cantonment of Kadapa and told them that during the coming Moharrum festival the British Government would cease and the Mughal dynasty would be reestablished. He was also said to have excited sedition amongst them[41]. He condemned the Nizam for his pro-British policy. He seemed to have secretly met Varadarajulu (Havaldar), Parasuram (Lans Naick), D. Veeraswamy (Sepoy), Yellappa

(Dalayat), Mohammed Ashraff (Subedar Major), Satvaji (Dalayat), C. Jaggaiah (Jamedar), Mohammad Ghouse (Havaldar), Moulvi Abdul Ajij, Hussain Saheb etc. of the 30th Regiment stationed at Kadapa[42]. Sheik Peer also appeared to have met the Mohammedan Law Officer and the Chief Mohammedan Officer of the 30th Regiment[43]. When he met the Havaldar, the latter heard all that he had to say, but finally placed him in custody, and reported the matter to the Commanding Officer. Sheik Peer was sentenced to ten years imprisonment and kept in confinement in Tirunelveli[44] in the present Tamil Nadu state. The others whom he met earlier were awarded other punishments. Then, a moveable column was formed and a squadron of cavalry was sent to Kadapa, in addition to other local arrangements. All this seemed to have damped the ardour of all those who might have felt some advantage possible out of a state of riot and confusion[45].

It is interesting to note that it was the tribal communities like the Savaras, the Koyas, Konda Reddies, Bhagatas, Khonds etc. of Ganjam, Visakhapatnam and Godavari districts in British Andhra who had actually turned more violent and fought against the British during the Uprising of 1857. They were led by Dandasena of Gaiba of Parlakimidi Zamindari in Ganjam district, Sanyasi Bhupati of Gudem in Visakhapatnam district, and Korukonda Subba Reddy of Koratur in Godavari district.

The Savara tribals of Parlakimidi Zamindari rose in revolt against the British under Dandasena, the chief of Gaiba in the then Ganjam district of British Andhra. He was an old offender. He escaped from British custody. He had exercised wide influence with the Savaras. His followers burnt and plundered the Sarkar villages. As a result the British authorities sent Captain Wilson to suppress the revolt. The troops under Wilson penetrated into the Savara 'country' and put down the rebellion. The rebel Dandasena was caught and hanged to death. The suppression of this revolt had a great effect in preventing such uprisings, in future, in the Savara 'country'[46].

Similarly, Sanyasi Bhupati of Gudem in Visakhapatnam district had also raised the banner of revolt against the British with the support of the tribal people[47].

Of the three tribal movements in British Andhra, during the Uprising of 1857, the rebellion of Korukonda Subba Reddy was the most important one. It was also known as the Yernagudem tribal uprising since it had occurred in Yernagudem of Godavari Agency area. This had taken place during 17th September 1857 and April 1858. Subba Reddy was a petty hil chief of Koratur which was on the banks of river Godavari. The rebellion originally started from a private dispute between Korukonda Subba Reddy and one Sankara Swamy, the village Munsiff of Buttayagudem, who had a large number of Koya followers[48]. Gradually, it turned into an anti-colonial movement of the tribals just as the personal issues of most of the leaders of the Uprising of 1857 in the North led to the rebellion against the colonial rule.

The hurdles created by the British in the collection of tolls on the river Godavari and the revenue collections in several villages, the prospect of becoming the Zamindar of Polavaram with the help of Nana Saheb and lastly the personal dispute (between Korukonda Subba Reddy and Sankara Swamy) over the marriage of Subba Reddy's his son Munga Reddy with Sitamma, one of the two young widows of Gurugumalli Muthyala Reddy, the Nagavaram estate holder[49] - - - all together made Korukonda Subba Reddy to start a rebellion against the British on the pretext of dispute over the marriage with Sitamma and also, more probably, over the control of Sitamma's estate and its revenue through marriage with Sitamma. Subba Reddy's rebellion lasted for 8 months from September 1857 to April 1858. He was supported by the tribals like Savaras and Konda Reddies, followers and relatives. But, the tribal rebellion was suppressed by April 1858[50]. The rebel leaders were captured and punished. Subba Reddy was captured on 11th June 1858 due to the treachery of Chintapalli Dasi Reddy[51]. Subba Reddy and many of his followers were awarded death sentence[52].

It is interesting to note that the civil population of British Andhra, in general, excepting the tribal communities expressed its loyalty to the British Government. In important places like Bezawada[53] (Vijayawada), Guntur, Nellore[54], Chittoor[55], Rajahmundry, Visakhapatnam, Dhavaleswaram[56], Madras[57], Zamindar of Chundi[58], Kalahasti etc; public meetings were held and address of loyalty were submitted to the Government. The Muslims also equally participated in these public meetings[59]. The people of Chittoor, in their address of loyalty, had declared that they not only abhor the proceedings but also would continue to be firm and loyal to the British Government. They continued in their address that "the security of person and property, the efficient and important administration of justice, the establishment of educational institutions for the Hindu mind and other solid advantages"[60] made them express their gratitude and loyalty to the British Government.

Even most of the educated natives excepting a few also rivalled each other in expressing their loyalty to the British[61]. More than the intelligentsia it was the folklorists who had played key role in arousing anti-colonial sentiment through various folk forms.

The Kings, Nawabs, Zamindars, Jagirdars, Palegars etc., to whom the people of the region could express their loyalty and follow them in their revolt against the British, as during the late 18th century and early decades of 19th century, had already been eliminated by the British. The moneyocratic Zamindars created under the Permanent Settlement in the place of the earlier aristocratic Zamindars, or acceptance of the latter as the former, under the same Permanent Settlement were, however, contented with the proprietary rights conferred upon them by the Permanent Settlement and therefore rarely thought of raising the banner of revolt. They remained loyal to the British. This was probably, because of their earlier experience with the British or because they were witness to the suppression of numerous Zamindari, Palegari etc., rebellions before 1857. Hence, the Uprising of 1857 had a limited impact on British Andhra.

The loyalty of the sepoys in British Andhra, as in other regions of South India including Nizam Andhra, too saved India for the British. In fact, Major General Beresford in his minutes of 17th July 1857 had praised the loyalty of the Madras Regiments[62].

Although the harsh measures adopted by the British served as a warning to the rebels and brought the revolt to a halt the rebellious atmosphere continued to exist even after the so-called suppression of the revolt in Andhra. There occurred, for example, two rebellions,one in Rampa, a small village in the Chodavaram division of the Godavari district and the other in Rekapalli, a village in the Bhadrachalam taluk of the same district in the year 1879[63].

Nizam Andhra in 1857: The Uprising of 1857 in North India had its immediate impact on the kingdom of the Nizam of Hyderabad. The main reason for this was total domination of the British in the Nizams territory, as in Delhi, and the existence of a good per centage of Muslim population who were unhappy with the growing British power and declining Muslim power in the Nizams kingdom as also in the other parts of the country. Most of the people here, particularly Muslims were waiting for an opportunity to overthrow British rule and reestablish the real authority of the Mughal ruler in Delhi and of the Nizam in Hyderabad. Such an opportunity came in the form of the Uprising. Naturally, the people of Nizams territory showed keen interest in the developments and also in the fortunes of rebels in the North[64]. They also decided to show their solidarity with the rebels of the north. The net result was the outbreak of a number of rebellions against the British in places like Aurangabad, Hyderabad etc., in spite of the pro-British policy of the then Nizam Afzul-ud-Dowla and his Diwan or Prime Minister Salar Jung I.

As noted already the anti-British feeling was roused in Hyderabad by the events in North India. The elements of insurrection here were as rife as in many other parts where it actually broke out. Analyzing the current feelings of the Muslims in Hyderabad at that time Col. Davidson, the Resident of Hyderabad wrote : "Every eye was turned towards Delhi and Lucknow, and the news of every kind was eagerly sought and paid for. Disastrous rumours of the wildest kind, hostile to the British Government, were prevalent and always acceptable to the fanatical and seditious character were intercepted from Aurangabad, Bhopal, Ahmedabad, Belgaum, Kurnool, and Mysore; and there cannot be a doubt that had a popular leader arisen, Hyderabad would have been speedily in a state of insurrection as it had already been of sedition, but fortunately no one of rank, wealth, and position could arise after the unsuccessful attack on the Residency in July 1857, which was the culminating point of our troubles in Hyderabad, and also as it was plain to all that the British Government were determined to fight the battle to the last and at all hazards, wherever insurrection showed itself"[65].

But, (1) the imposition of the Subsidiary Alliance of 1798 and the Subsidiary Treaty of 1800 on the Nizam, (2) the control of Nizams relations with other countries, (3) the stationing of a big British force in the Nizams capital, (4) the insistance on the payment of money to meet the expenditure on salaries of the British forces stationed in the capital, (5) the appointment of British Resident in the Nizams Darbar and establishment of indirect rule through the Resident[66], (6) the appointment of pro-British people as Diwans and other higher Officers, mostly from outside the Nizams kingdom, (7) the neglect of locals in the appointments of the Nizams Government, (8) gradual reduction in the number as well as in the importance of the Arabs and Rohillas who played key role before the establishment of the British indirect rule[67], (9) the arrest and confinement of the Wahabi supporter Prince Mubariz-ud-daula in Golkonda fort and his final death in the fort[68], (10) the increasing opposition to the British domination from the ruling family, army and people at large, (11) the lending of money to the Nizam by British financial companies and pressurizing of the Nizam to hand over revenue right over valuable lands[69], (12) the British take over of Berar,

Raichur and Osmanabad in 1853 (in spite of the opposition of the then Nizam Nasir-ud-daula and his Diwan Siraj-ul-Mulk) for meeting the expenditure on the British subsidiary force stationed in Secunderabad under Subsidiary Treaty of 1800[70], (13) the increasing influence or domination of the British in the kingdom, not allowing even Moharrum processions as at Bolarum[71], (14) the total cooperation of the new Diwan Salar Jung with the British, (15) the total surrender and slavish behaviour of the new Nizam Afzul-ud-daula with regard to the British, and later, (16) the propagation of anti-British sentiment in the Nizams kingdom by prominent Maratha leaders like Tantya Tope, Nana Saheb etc., and their agents, (17) the anger of Moulvis leading to attempted declaration of Jehad against the British, (18) the sticking of innumerable posters at several places in Hyderabad, particularly on the walls of Mecca Masjid, Charminar etc., with appeals to the Nizam and his Diwan to declare war against the British and also to the people of all sections, both Muslims and Hindus, more particularly to the Muslim community to revolt against the British, remove British rule in India and reestablish the real authority of the Muslims in all the Muslim kingdoms, more particularly in Delhi, and (19) the increasing anti-British sentiment among the people of different sections and communities of the society[72] served as a fire to lit the fuel (national as well as regional level causes) for the anti-British movements in the Nizams kingdom.

While this was the unhappy situation in the Nizams dominions which was generating strong anti-British feeling among the people the Uprising began in North India on 10th May 1857, first, in Meerut, and then spread like wild fire to Muradabad, Kanpur, Lucknow, Delhi, Punjab, and Central India. Kunwar Singh in Bihar; Begum Hazrath Mahal in Oudh; Holkar, Sindhia, Tantya Tope and Nana Saheb in Maratha territories; Ranajit Singh in Punjab; and Rani Lakshmi Bai in Jhansi rose in revolt against the British to put an end to their rule.

The news of the Uprising in the North quickly reached the Nizams dominions as also the other native kingdoms and

British territories in the South and inspired the lovers of freedom from alien rule. In the Nizams kingdom the Mullas, Mashayaks, Pesh Imams and several others began propagation of anti-British feelings. Slogan bearing wall-posters began to appear on the walls in the city of Hyderabad. "Ijahar Nama" proclamation appeared everywhere. People were asked to participate in this sacred war, the Jehad. The slogans included: "Jamedars and Khajis should come forward and declare war against the Christian Kafirs". "If it is not done in an year or two Afzal-ud-daula and Salarjung would have to work in the street roads"[73]. To the Hindus also the appeal was made in the name of their religion by pointing out how "the British Government defiled it by introducing the remarriage of widows, the abolition of Suttee, etc., and that they would put an end to your religion". In another poster an appeal was made to the effect that "all the Muslims must assemble in Mecca Masjid on 1273 Hijiri Shavvad 25th[74].

Religious divines like Alla-ud-din, also called Moulvi Ibrahim incited people to revolt against the British. He had even delivered sermons at Mecca Masjid in Hyderabad city, branding the British as the enemies of Islam and exhorted the Muslims to drive them out. Diwan Salar Jung called him to his presence and severely warned him to desist from indulging in seditious activities. Later, he was banished from the country and was kept in confinement in the isles[75]. Similarly, Moulvi Akbar tried to declare jehad against the British by hoisting the flag of Islam at the Mecca Masjid in the presence of the Muslims who congregated there to offer prayers[76]. Attempts were made to undermine the loyalty of the army personnel of the Company posted at Secunderabad and Bolarum.

While great tension prevailed at Hyderabad other developments took place at Aurangabad. There was great disaffection among the Company troops. The news of the early successes of the rebels and reverses of the British in the North generated great excitement among the Company troops at Aurangabad. (1st & 3rd battalion artillery, 2nd battalion infantry,

3rd battalion). They feared that they would be asked to proceed to Delhi and fight against the rebels. They refused to leave the borders of the Nizams kingdom stating that they would not fight against their own co-religionists in the North[77]. The disaffection in Aurangabad troops took a serious turn on 23 June 1857. About 90 sepoys whose loyalty was suspected were disarmed and arrested[78]. The arrest of their comrades increased the anti-British feeling of the sepoys. A Jamedar Amir Khan revolted against the British. A Daffedar Mir Fida Ali tried to shoot Captain Abbot. Mir Fida was caught, court martialled and hanged. Amir Khan escaped[79]. But, a number of sepoys suspected to be involved in the affair were arrested. Many of the 1st & 2nd Cavalry of the Hyderabad contingent troops stationed at Aurangabad were disbanded. This was however, put down easily[80]. This outbreak which took place within a few weeks of the developments in the North was the first serious incident in the Nizams kingdom in 1857.

Similarly, the Hyderabad contingent troops stationed at Budlana in Aurangabad were also affected by the revolt in the North. They revolted against the British under Jamedar Chhidda Khan. But their revolt was suppressed. Their leader Chhidda Khan along with his 12 followers left Buldana and arrived in Hyderabad with the hope of getting protection from the Nizams Government (instead, a reward of Rs.3000/- was announced for his arrest). But, Chhidda Khan and his followers were arrested (by Salar Jung's men) and were sent to the British Residency (now housing Koti Womens College and Osmania Medical College) on 17th July 1857 for confinement and trial[81].

But, Salar Jung's arrest of Chhidda Khan and his followers created a great commotion in the city of Hyderabad. The agitated people congregated at the Mecca Masjid on 17th July 1857. They decided to send four Moulvis to the Nizam with a request that Chhidda Khan and his associates be released. They also resolved to attack the British Residency in case the Nizam were to refuse the request[82]. The Moulvis gave inflammatory speeches. They highlighted the Nizam Afjul-ud-daula's slavish mentality. They blamed the Diwan Salar Jung for his treachery. On hearing the congregation at the Mecca Masjid on 17th July 1857 and sticking of posters Salar Jung sent a body of Arab guards to disperse the crowd. He also assured the Resident that he need not apprehend any danger from the rebels.

But, shortly after this, the dispersed people gathered again and a crowd of about 5000 mostly consisting of the Rohillas moved towards the British Residency under the leadership of a Jamedar of the Rohillas Turre Baz Khan (also called Kurre Paz Khan) along with Moulvi Alla-ud-din[83]. They reached the Residency's western gate, the turning point from the present Osmania Medical College to the Musi river. Meanwhile, Salar Jung sent a message to the Resident stating that the Residency was in danger. He also desired the Resident to defend himself till such time as he would be able to send a body of the Nizam's troops to the assistance of the Resident. As a result the Resident alerted his forces. Turre Baz Khan, meanwhile, began his attack on the Residency around 4 'O clock on the evening of 17th July 1857[84]. The rebels took shelter in the residences of two businessmen namely Ubban Saheb and Shahukar Jayagopal Dass, just opposite to the Residency gate and then began their guerilla warfare against the British forces till the sunset of the same day. While the British forces fought with modern weapons, the Rohillas used only the traditional weapons like swords, talwars etc. Naturally, the British forces under the Resident Colonel Davidson repulsed the attack and ably defended the Residency (now known as Koti in Sultan Bazar of Hyderabad) and also brought the situation under control by around 4 O' clock in the early morning of 18th July 1857. During the attack, Davidson said to Salar Jung "I have come prepared to die here. I will fight till my last breath". In fact it was not a big fight. The official figures show that four Rohillas had died in the fight. But, in reality 25 armed men died. There was no casualty on the British side[85]. Turre Baz Khan and Moulvi Alla-ud-din escaped from the place. But, in a couple of days Turre Baz Khan was arrested with injuries in police firing at Satkalwa at

Mogiligidda[86] near Shadnagar in the present Mahaboob Nagar district. A few months later Alla-ud-din was also arrested at Mangalapalli[87] near Hyderabad in the present Ranga Reddy district. Alla-ud-din was tried and given life imprisonment with banishment from the country. He was sent as prisoner to the Andaman islands on 28th June 1859. While he was still in prison in Ándamans he died in 1884[88]. He was the first and the only prisoner from the Nizams kingdom to undergo imprisonment in the Andamans jail which was newly built for the criminals of 1857. With regard to Turre Baz Khan he was also tried and sentenced to transportation for life. Though the British Resident recommended death penalty to Turre Baz the Governors-General refused to increase his punishment. However, Turre Baz escaped from prison on 18th January 1859. As a result, an award of Rs.500/- was announced to those who could hand over him to the British authorities. Meanwhile, information with regard to his whereabouts came through a person named Kurbani Ali. The British forces immediately rushed to the place called Toopran. In the fight between Turre Baz and the British forces Turre Baz was short dead. His body was brought to Hyderabad and hanged to a tree in the Sultan Bazar near the British Residency in Hyderabad so as to create terror among the people of the city[89], as was done in the case of Narasimha Reddy of Koilkuntla, Velu Thambi of Travancore etc. With this the last major trouble or tension ended in the kingdom of Hyderabad, although some minor anti-British revolts continued to take place here and there as is to be noted hereunder.

Raja Venkatappa Naik was one among such people. He was the proprietor of the Surapuram estate in the erstwhile territory of the Nizams-Karnataka bordering on the present Mahaboobnagar district. Unfortunately, while he was being taken to the prison with a halt at Secunderabad Venkatappa suddenly took the gun from a nearby security man, shot himself and died heroically[90]. On knowing this, his friend Bhaskar Rao Baba Saheb, the Narugonda estate holder also rose in revolt against the British. But, he was caught and hanged to death.

Similarly, Rukma Reddy and others also indulged in anti-British activities[91]. Very soon after the outbreak of the Mutiny on 10th May 1857 a number of Maratha leaders began entering the Nizams kingdom to instigate people against the British so as to overthrow the British rule. One such Maratha leader was Rao Saheb Peshwa, a relative of Nana Saheb and close associate of Tantya Tope[92]. He was the earliest Maratha leader to establish contacts with the people of the Nizam's kingdom and to mobilize them for a movement to overthrow the British rule. Rao Saheb was also caught in Kanpur and was hanged to death on 20th August 1862.

But the situation in the kingdom continued to be critical as the emissaries of Nana Saheb, Tantya Tope etc; were actively moving and inciting the people to create trouble to the Nizam and the British. The discontent against the British rule, in fact, took a more concrete form in the shape of rebellion in various parts of the kingdom such as the Rohilla and Bhill rebellions in the Nirmal and Ajanta regions, the rebellion of Ramji Gond in Adilabad, Ranga Rao Patwari in Kawlas etc[93]. Revolt of Bhimrao Desai of Koppal in the present Karnataka, Gonds and Rohillas of Nirmal in Adilabad district of A.P; Kulkarni Narsinga Rao of Palamur in Mahaboobnagar district. Bhills under Sivaji Naik in Aurangabad district, Sonaji Pant in Raja Rayarayan estate, Patwari Ranga Rao Pagay, Jahangir of Nizams Palace who fired at the Resident, Raja Balakrishnan in the Nizams palace and firing of a cavalry man at Captain Mechintire and the latters death on 18th April 1858, sacrifice of ordinary men Tatya Mudgal and others are some other incidents in the Nizams territory[94].

It may be noted here that almost all the incidents which have taken place in the Nizams kingdom either before or during the Uprising of 1857, including the attack on the British Residency on 17th July 1857, were not very significant events. In fact, they had little face value compared with the mutinies, revolts, movements and battles of the same period in the North. But, if we understand the importance of the support of the

Nizams kingdom for the very survival of the British rule in India we come to know of the real value of the incidents, under the existing limitations, in the Nizams kingdom during the Uprising of 1857. At a time when a greater part of the nation had turned into hot-bed of violent or non-violent or silent movements of different sections and communities of the society, which aimed at the overthrow of the British rule in India the Nizam's timely support and loyalty to the British saved the British empire in India. But for the help, sincerely extended, by the Nizam Afzal-ud-daula and his Diwan Salar Jug either in detecting conspiracies or in suppressing every violent and serious outbreak of anti-British rebellions the British empire would not have survived in India. Had the Nizam allowed the uprising of the North to spread into his own kingdom and to the South the British empire might have disappeared from the political map of India during the Uprising of 1857 itself. His loyalty to the British was so strong that in appreciation of his services the British restored Raichur and Osmanabad (Dharashiv) territories to the Nizam, gave him assurance of continuation of his authority (although nominal) and scrapped the heavy debt of Rs.50,00,000/- that the Nizam had to pay to the British Government[95] and also made over to the Nizam the Samsthan (estate) of Shorapore which had lapsed to the British after the death of Raja Venkatappa Naick, and the title of the "Star of India" was also given to him besides several presents. The kingdom of Hyderabad and the friendship and good will of the Nizam was so important to the British that the Governor of Bombay wrote to the Governors-General stating : "If the Nizam goes, all goes"[96].

As noted above the Nizam and his army were always ready to take the field in favour of the British during the Uprising of 1857 in the North. The Nizam was wholly convinced that his fate depended totally on the British and any attempt to deviate from the provisions of the subsidiary treaty concluded in 1800 would only result in his losing his position as well as his kingdom, and the establishment of the British direct rule. He was also convinced that the Mughal emperor whose kingdom confined just to the boundaries of Delhi and who had, like him, already become a puppet in the hands of the British or nominal head of the state and facing even the risk of losing even this nominal authority would never come to his rescue in the event of his revolt against the British. He was also sure that the native Hindu rulers of Maharashtra, Rajasthan and Punjab were only waiting for an opportunity to conquer Muslim kingdoms, either at Delhi or at Hyderabad or at some other place, and not to help him in the event of his revolt against the British. Moreover, the Marathas, Rajputs, and Sikhs were not in favour of the restoration of the Mughal or Muslim authority because they had in the past suffered a lot in the hands of the Mughal rulers or other Muslim rulers and some of them had even lost their kingdoms. In fact, the Marathas, Rajputs and Sikhs along with Gurkhas had already been offering their services to the British Government, considering the 1857 event as a grand opportunity for taking full vengeance against the Mughals[97]. That the Maratha, Rajput and Sikh leaders or rulers were against the restoration of Mughal / Muslim rule is supported by the conduct of Nana Saheb, first in inducing the sepoys not to proceed to Delhi and then in proclaiming himself as Peshwa[98]. None of the Rajput and Maratha chiefs responded to the invitation of Bahadur Shah. All the propaganda in Maharashtra was carried on in the name of Nana Saheb[99]. This was the situation which made the Nizam not to respond to the appeals of Bahadur Shah or any other Muslim ruler or leader to revolt against the British. As a result, a great part of India including Nizams kingdom was almost free from any overt acts of hostility against the British, excepting smaller incidents.

References

1. For more details see : S.B. Chaudhuri, *Civil Disturbances during the British Rule in India (1765-1857),* The World Press Ltd; Calcutta, 1955, A.R. Desai (ed); *Peasant Struggles in India,* Oxford University Press, New Delhi, 1979, Narahari Kaviraj,

Wahabi and Farazi Rebels of Bengal, People Publishing House, New Delhi, 1982, K. Rajayyan, *Rise and Fall of the Foligars of Tamil Nadu*, University of Madras, 1974, Devireddy Subramanyam Reddy, *The Struggle for Independence in Andhra*, Sree Chandana Haritha Publications, Tirupati, 1998, Sunil Sen, *Agrarian Relations.* Peoples Publishing House, New Delhi, 1979.

2. Lata Singh, 1857 Visibilising the 'Other' in History : Courtesans and the Revolt, in *Economic and Political Weakly*, 12 May 2007, p.1677.
3. Badri Narayan, Popular Culture and 1857 : Memory Against Forgetting, in Biswamoy Pati (ed), (hereafter referred to as Pati), *The 1857 Rebellion*, Oxford University Press, New Delhi, 2007, p. 273.
4. Talmiz Khaldun, *The Great Rebellion*, in Pati, *op.cit;* pp.123-131, K.M. Ashraf, *Muslim Revivalists and the Revolt of 1857*, in Pati, *op.cit;* pp.151-158.
5. S.B. Chaudhuri, *op.cit;* A.R. Desai, *op.cit;* Sunil Sen, *op.cit.*
6. K.S. Singh, *The Tribals and the 1857 Uprising*, in Pati, *op.cit;* pp. 262-71.
7. Talmiz Khaldun, in Pati, *op.cit;* pp.123-131.
8. S.B. Chaudhuri, *Theories on the Indian Mutiny*, in B.Pati, *op.cit.*
9. R.C. Majumdar, *The Character of the Outbreak of 1857*, in Pati, *op.cit.*
10. *Ibid.*
11. C.J. Griffiths, *Siege of Delhi*, London, 1910, p. 259.
12. R.C. Majumdar, *op.cit;* pp. 40-41.
13. F.M. Hassnain, *British Policy Towards Kashmir* (1846-1921), Sterling Publishers Pvt. Ltd., New Delhi, 1974, pp. 38-39, Prithvi Nath Kaul Bamzai, *A History of Kashmir*, Metropolitan Book Co. (Pvt.) Ltd., New Delhi, 1973.
14. Rudrangshu Mukherjee, *Awadh in Revolt*, in Pati, *op.cit;* pp. 221-234.
15. R.C. Majumdar, in B.Pati, *op.cit;* pp. 23-52.
16. S.B. Chaudhuri, in B.Pati, *op.cit;* pp. 53-92, K.K. Datta, *Reflectionson the Mutiny*, in Pati, *op.cit;* pp.112-119.
17. *Hindu Patriot*, 29 April, 1858.

18. *Judicial Consultations*, Fort St. George, Madras, G.O.No.1081-A, dated 3 September 1857.
19. *British Parliamentary Papers, 1859*, Session II, Vol.23, Tamil Nadu Archives, 467 cited by N. Rajendran, The Revolt of 1857: Rebellious Prelude and Nationalist Response in Tamil Nadu, in Subyasachi Bhattacharya, *Rethinking 1857*, Orient Longman, New Delhi, 2007, p.193.
20. Document Nos. 42 & 17, in M. Venkatarangaiya, (hereafter referred to as M.V.R.), *The Freedom Struggle in Andhra Pradesh* (Andhra), Vol.I (1800-1905 A.D.), A.P. State Archives Publication, Hyderabad, 1997, Judicial Consultations, Govt. of Madras, G.O.No.1081-A, dated 3 September 1857.
21. Document Nos.42 & 17, in M.V.R. *op.cit.*
22. *Judicial Proceedings, September 1857*, Tamil Nadu Archives. (hereafter referred to as T.N.A.)
23. *Judicial Consultations*, Fort St. George, Madras, No.38, dated 30 June 1857, T.N.A; Notification dated 27 July 1857, in *Fort St. George Gazette*, dated 7 August 1857, T.N.A.; *Circular Order* No.733 dated 27 June 1857 and No.798 dated 10 July 1857, T.N.A.
24. *Frontline*, 29 June 2007, p. 22.
25. Document Nos. 16 & 42, in M.V.R.; *op.cit; Administrative Report of Madras Presidency, 1857-58,* in M.V.R.; *op.cit.*
26. *Administrative Report of Madras Presidency, 1857-58,* Infra Document No. 42.
27. *Judicial Proceedings,* September 1857, T.N.A.
28 *Ibid;* M.V.R.; *op.cit;* P.60, Document Nos. 11 & 42, in M.V.R.; *op.cit.*
29. Document Nos. 17 & 42, in M.V.R.; *op.cit.*
30. Document Nos. 23 & 42, in M.V.R.; *op.cit; Administrative Report of Madras Presidency, 1857-58,* M.V.R.; *op.cit;* p. 60.
31. Document Nos. 21, 22 & 42, in M.V.R.; *op.cit.*
32. Document Nos. 30 & 42, in M.V.R.; *op.cit.*
33. Document No. 42 in M.V.R.; *op.cit.*
34. *Judicial Proceedings,* September 1857, T.N.A.; Document No.42, in M.V.R.; *op.cit.*

35. Document No. 42, in M.V.R.; *op.cit.*
36. M.V.R.; *op.cit;* p.60.
37. Document Nos. 31 & 36, in M.V.R.
38. Document No. 17, in M.V.R.
39. *Ibid.*
40. *Ibid.*
41. Document No.29, in M.V.R.; op.cit.
42. *Ibid.*
43. *Ibid.*
44. *Ibid.*
45. *Ibid.*
46. Document Nos. 18, 19 & 20, in M.V.R.; *Ganjam District Manual,* pp.195-96, M.V.R.; *op.cit;* pp. 59-60.
47. Document Nos. 18, 19 & 20, in M.V.R.; *op.cit;* pp. 59-60.
48. *Ibid.*
49. *Ibid.*
50. *Ibid*; For more details of Subba Reddy's revolt see : *Letter from Purvis to Byley*, dated 7 October 1857, Fort St. George, *Judicial Consultations,* Nos. 55-56, dated 13 October, 1857, *Letter from Purvis to Pycrofts,* dated 30 April 1858, Fort St. George, *Judicial Consultations,* Nis. 9-10, dated 18 May 1858, Case No.9 of 1858, *Judicial Consultations,* Nos. 5 67-68, dated 8 August 1858, ChristaphVon Furer, Haimendorf, *The Reddies of the Bison Hills,* Macmillan, London, 1945, p.144, Case No.7 of 1858, *Judicial Consultations,* Nos.36-37, dated 21 September 1858, Case No. 5 of 1858, *Judicial Consultations,* Nos. 67-68, dated 24 August 1858, Deposition of Mohammed Saheb, *Judicial Consultations,* Nos. 39-40, dated 8 January 1858, Case No.8 of 1858, *Judicial Consultations,* Nos. 67-68, dated 24 August 1858, *Judicial Consultations,* dated 8 January 1858.
51. *Judicial Consultations,* Nos. 18-19, dated 14 December 1858.
52. Letter from Capleston to Pycroft, dated 31 July 1858, *Judicial Consultations,* Nos. 36-37, dated 21 September 1858, *Godavari District Manual,* pp. 299-302.
53. Document No. 36, in M.V.R.; *op.cit.*
54. Document No.37, in *Ibid.*

55. Document No.38, in *Ibid.*
56. Document No.39, in *Ibid.*
57. Document No.40, in *Ibid.*
58. Document No.41, in *Ibid.*
59. M.V.R.; *op.cit;* p. 63.
60. *Ibid*; p. 63.
61. Frontline, *op.cit,* p. 20, S.N. Sen, *1857 A Review,* in Pati, *op.cit;* p.101, previously published as Chapter Eleven, A Review in S.N. Sen, Eighteen Fifty-Seven, New Delhi, Publications Division, 1957.
62. Minutes of Major General Beresford, dated 13 July 1857, Document Nos.32, 24 & 42, in M.V.R., *op.cit., Administrative Report of Madras Presidency, 1857-58.*
63. Devireddy Subramanyam Reddy, *Restorative Movements in Modern and Contemporary Andhra Pradesh, 1766-2006,* Presidential Address, Modern Andhra History Section, Thirty First Annual Session of Andhra Pradesh History Congress held on 6th & 7th January 2007 at Govt. College for Men, Kadapa, pp. 32-33, Arnold David; *Rebellious Hillmen : The Gudem and Rampa Rising (1839-1924),* in Ranjit Guha (ed), Subaltern Studies, Vol.I, Oxford University Press, Delhi, 1982.
64. M. Venkatarangaiya, *The Freedom Struggle in Hyderabad*, Vol. II, A.P. State Archives Publication, Hyderabad, 1956, pp. 6-7, H.G. Briggs, *The Nizam,* Vol. II, pp. 84-86.
65. Letter from Colonel Davidson, the Resident of Hyderabad, quoted in M. Venkatarangaiya, Vol. II, *op.cit;* p.7.
66. Veldurti Manikya Rao (hereafter referred to as Manikya Rao), *Hyderabadu Swatantrodyama Charitra* (in Telugu), Swatanthrodyama Charithra Parisodhana Samstha, Hyderabad, 1992, pp.16-27.
67. *Ibid.*
68. *Ibid,* M. Venkatarangaiya, Vol.II, *op.cit;* p. 2.
69. Manikya Rao, *op.cit;* pp.16-27, M. Venkatarangaiya, Vol.II, *op.cit;* pp.1-3.
70. Manikya Rao, *op.cit*; pp. 24 & 103.
71. *Ibid;* pp.16-27.
72. *Ibid.*

73. Extracts from documents, in M. Venkatarangaiya, Vol.II, *op.cit;* pp. 8-10.
74. *Ibid;* p. 9.
75. *Ibid;* p. 11.
76. *Ibid;* p. 21, *The Englishman,* Calcutta, dated 27 June 1857
77. Documents in M. Venkatarangaiya, Vol.II, *op.cit;* pp. 24-43, Manikya Rao, *op.cit;* pp. 32-33.
78. *Ibid.*
79. M. Venkatarangaiya, Vol.II, *op.cit;* pp. 36-37.
80. *Ibid.*
81. Documents, in M. Venkatarangaiya, Vol.II, *op.cit;* pp. 24-43, Maikya Rao, *op.cit;* pp. 32-33.
82. Documents, in M. Venkatarangaiya, Vol.II, *op.cit;* p. 50.
83. *Ibid;* pp. 50-55, Manikya Rao, *op.cit;* pp. 34-36.
84. *Ibid.*
85. *Ibid.*
86. Documents, in M. Venkatarangaiya, Vol.II, *op.cit;* p. 56.
87. For more details about the attack on the Residency see documents in M. Venkatarangaiya, Vol.II, *op.cit;* pp. 44-83. Manikya Rao, *op.cit;* pp. 36-38.
88. *Ibid.*
89. *Ibid.*
90. For more details about revolt of Venkatappa Naick see documents in M. Venkatarangaiya, Vol.II, *op.cit;* pp. 84-103, & also p.VIII.
91. Manikya Rao, *op.cit;* pp. 52-53.
92. *Ibid.*
93. M. Venkatarangaiya, Vol.II, *op.cit;* p.IX.
94 *Ibid;* pp. XI-XVI, Manikya Rao, *op.cit;* pp. 40-51.
95. M. Venkatarangaiya, Vol.II, *op.cit;* p. 193, Hastings Fraser, *Our Faithful Ally, the Nizam,* p. 492.
96. Letter from Governor of Bombay to the Governors-General of India cited in Y. Gopal Reddy, *A Comprehensive History of Andhra,* Victory Publications, Hyderabad, 1990, p.193.
97. R.C. Majumdar, in Pati, *op.cit;* pp. 35-36.
98. *Ibid.*
99. *Ibid.*

4

Swami of Korravanivalasa: A Messianic Movement Among the Tribals of Andhra in 1900

B. Rama Chandra Reddy

A messiah, in its literal sense, is an 'anointed one' sent to bring about a new age and an 'expected deliverer' of the people, who will release them from their misery and realize a hope of a better world. The original and traditional belief of a messiah and saviour is originated and greatly strengthened by the Jewish and Christian religious teachings. A messianic movement is a politico-religious movement promising deliverance from deprivation, the elimination of foreign domination, and a new interpretation of the human condition based on traditional cultural values. It is typically associated with deprivation and an effect of the alienation of aboriginal people in the colonial context. Though some messianic movements among Indian primitives may owe their origin to Christian influence, others found their inspiration in Hindu messianic beliefs of Lord Vishnu's incarnations, more precisely the *Dasaavatara* (ten reincarnations) concept, from time to time when the evil is at its height.

Norman Cohn, perhaps the pioneer in the field, identifies five characteristics of millenarian movements after his study on the Western Europe during the Middle Ages (11-16th Century). He says that they are : (a) Collective, in the sense that it is enjoyed by all the faithful as a group; (b) Terrestrial in the sense that it is realized on this earth rather than in some other worldly heaven; (c) Imminent, since completely transforms life on earth and brings complete perfection rather than some lesser improvement; (d) Total because it completely transforms life on earth than some lesser improvement; and (e) Miraculous, in the sense that it is accomplished by or with the help of super natural agencies.[1] Peter Worsley in his study on the Melanesian cargo cults, says that the millenarian movements were so called because the suffering people believed that their ancestors or a culture hero were on their way back to the world in a magic ship with material goods for their happiness. He also opines that they were not irrational madness but are the results of frustrations caused by colonialism. He further stresses that they were basically opposed to imperialism by using religious idioms and were a last resort after the failure of political opposition.[2] His depiction of messianic movement holds relevance ground for the Indian context.

Stephen Fuchs in his seminal work on messianic movements in India argues that the origins of the movements are 'often conditioned by peculiar economic and social situations which are causing severe mental tension and material distress. Such situations are mainly the result of exposure to strong influence and overpowering interference by alien civilizations'. He also says that 'unable to continue their life in these distressing circumstances, but equally unable to escape their predicament, they find ultimately, often after repeated failures of flight or rebellion, their last hope in a charismatic leader or saviour' who is to lead them out of their unbearable situation and to an earthly paradise or heaven by more or less supernatural and miraculous means.[3]

Fuchs identifies fourteen important characteristic features of Messianic movements in India. They are : (One) society intensively dissatisfied with the social and economic conditions which the society is forced to accept; (Two) The existence of emotional unrest in this society displaying certain hysterical symptoms; (Three) The appearance of a charismatic leader; (Four) The leader demanding implicit faith and obedience from his followers; (Five) The test of the unquestioned faith and obedience consisting either in a radical change of life (cessation of cultivation of their land, change of employment, etc.), even destruction of their property (furniture, houses, livestock); (Six) Rejection of the established authority and call for rebellion; (Seven) Threat of severe punishment for opponents and traitors of the movement; (Eight) "Revivalism", i.e., the attempt at reviving certain important elements of the ancient traditional culture which have disappeared under the influence of the alien civilization; (Nine) "Nativism", i.e., the attempt of a primitive people to restore its whole pristine culture and to reject all alien elements assimilated from foreign cultures; (Ten) "Vitalism", i.e., the desire of the members in the movement, for alien goods, especially spiritual ones, from "heaven", through superhuman powers or through magic; (Eleven) "Cargo Cult", i.e., the expectation of alien goods, especially material ones, by boat from distant countries, provided for and sent by the ancestors; (Twelve) "Syncretism", i.e., the indiscriminate adoption of various cultural traits of modern civilization by a primitive people; (Thirteen) "Millenarism" or Chillianism, i.e., the hope and expectation of a paradise on earth; (Fourteen) "Eschatologism", i.e., the expectation of a world renewal and improvement through world-wide catastrophic revolutions and upheavals.[4]

Messianic movements were reported among the tribals of India. The important among them were the Santhal Rebellion of 1855-56 under Siddhu and Kanhu,[5] Birsa Munda Revolt of 1895- 1909, [6]the Bhil movement under Govindagiri in 1911-12,[7] the Oran Tana Bhagat Movement of 1914-25 under Jatra Bhagat,[8] Devi (Salahibai) Movement in Gujarat 1922-23,[9] the Naga Zeliangrong movement of Jadonang and Rani Gaidinliu in 1925 and after,[10] the Warlis,[11] the Grasias[12] etc. to cite a few during the colonial period. It should be noted that Stephen Fuchs considers some of the movements as messianic though they are fulfilling only three of his fourteen characteristics.

Fuchs saw only one millenarian movement in the plains of Andhra under Virabrahmam among the untouchable community (Madigas) in the Cuddapah district and none among the tribals of Andhra.[13] Fuchs observes that "the primitives in South India are divided into numerically small tribal groups; they have been decimated and scattered and so completely subdued by the superior cultivating castes that no fighting spirit is left in them. No messianic movements are reported from the South Indian primitives."[14] However, we identified two such movements among the tribals of Andhra region during the course of our study. The first one took place among the Konda Dora tribe in the Vizagapatam district. During the year 1886, it was a propagated in the Gudem agency that it was the decree of God, that the British be driven out from that part of the tribal area. Sriramulu, one of its leaders assumed himself to be Rama and Rajana Anantayya, the self styled Hanuman, promised a Konda Dora Raj for the tribals.[15] The second one took place in a small village consisting of two huts only, of the same district in 1900, which is the theme of the present paper.

The present paper in this context chiefly attempts to trace the emergence and course of a messianic movement among the tribals in the Vizagapatam District of Madras Presidency (presently Andhra Pradesh) in 1900. The tribals of Vizagapatam felt the impact of colonialism when their area was exposed to the domination of the British. The political subordination, economic exploitation and social degradation of the tribals during the British colonial regime paved the way for a revitalization movement which subsequently metamorphosed into a movement with political overtones.

Loss of Political Power

The tribals were masters of their own areas before the advent of the British. Most of the Hill Rajas also referred to as zamindaries in the colonial records, owed their origin to King Visvambara Deo I (1672-76) of Jeypore (presently in Orissa). He divided his possessions and placed under some of his faithful tribal retainers on service tenure conferring them with high sounding titles. They were entrusted with the task of keeping peace and order in their respective areas. They were also expected to supply armed forces in times of need and had to pay a small tribute.[16] Thus he formed the hill principalities of Andra (Konda Dora), Salur ("Konda Razu"), Pachipenta ("Konda Razu"), Chemudu ("Konda Razu"), Sangamvalasa ("Konda Razu") 6. Belgam (Hill Raja (Konda Razu)), Merangi ("Konda Razu"), Kurupam ("Konda Razu"), Palakonda (Jatapu) Golugonda ("Konda Razu"?) and Madgole ("Konda Razu"?)[17] However, slowly the Jeypore Raja began to loose his grip on his subordinates wherefore the hill rajas became independent. In turn the Raja of Vizianagaram became supreme in the district politics and most of the hill chiefs came under his control, often after using force. When the Vizainagaram zamindari was sequestered after the battle of Padmanabham in 1794, these hill principalities automatically came under the control of the English East India Company. The British executed permanent settlement system of land revenue with them in 1802-3 at a higher rate payable in cash. The sources of revenue like *sayer* (internal duties and collections like customs, transit duties, market tax and the like) were resumed without any consequent remission in the tribute (*jama*). The semi- independent Rajas became the zamindars under the control of the British land revenue officers.[18] The tribute payable was fixed at a high rate with 'sunset laws'. Before permanent Settlement these zamindars were treated as feudatories rather than as mere farmers of revenue, 'rather as captains of the boarders, lords of the marches, chiefs of the hills, than as private landholders and the government was conducted through them, some of them having the responsibility for (good behaviour of) the hill tribes'. But they were stripped off the ruling powers, their estates were liable to attachment for default of *peshkash* (tribute), the British police system substituted the zamindari one and civil and criminal judicatories were set up which were complex and vexatious with the hardships unknown in the 'good olden days'.[19] They were frequen+ly in arrears and debts due to the heavy tribute and rigorous collection. Hence some were mortgaged or leased out and still more were sold in public auction for paltry sums. The hill zamindaries of Merangi and Madgole were purchased by the British Government in public auction for Rs. 500[20] and Rs.1000[21] respectively in 1833 and Golugonda for Rs.100 in 1837.[22] Chemudu was under the mortgage of Bobbili zamindar for a loan.[23] After the Palconda zamindari was forfeited for the Raja's complicity in a revolt in 1833, his estate was leased out to a British company Arbuthnot & Co, who introduced cash crops like sugarcane, Mexican cotton and indigo.[24] In brief, the entire political fabric of the tribals was so badly disturbed, that by and large, they were annoyed with the policy of the British.

There were frequent revolts at least from 1770 to drive away the coercive English authority from the hills. The revolts were so endemic during 1832-34 that the Madras Government appointed George Russell as special commissioner with extraordinary powers to suppress the revolts and to ascertain the causes. On Russell's recommendations the hill areas of Vizagapatam were declared as Agency giving extraordinary powers to the Collector.[25] In Vizagapatam there were revolts in 1845-48, 1858, 1886 and 1891-92 in Gudem area, the 1879- 80 revolt in the entire hill areas of the district and 1864-69 in the Savara locality. All of them were suppressed by the British with brute force.[26]

Economic Deterioration

The economic activity of the tribals was of the subsistence type and was totally dependent on the utilization of forest resources. It involved the slash and burn cultivation (*podu*), hunting and food gathering in the forest and collection of minor forest produce to barter for necessities in the weekly markets (*santhas*). The advent of the British completely changed their way of life. The colonizer introduced money economy in the tribal society. They designed their economic policies in such a way to cater to the imperial interests, which were detrimental to the tribal economic life style.

The Madras Forest Act of 1882 came into force in 1883.[27] Nearly 928 sq. miles of forests came under the act. It laid restriction on free movement of tribals into the forests for their survival. The entry of tribals into the forests for the collection of minor forest produce was barred, 'unauthorized' felling of valuable trees was prohibited, *podu* cultivation was restricted to the confined areas and their cattle were not allowed to drift into the forests.[28] After firmly establishing them ,elves, officials of the forest department began to exact *Vetti* (compulsory free labour) service from tribals.[29] After the reservation of forests, the forest contractor entered into hills, and soon he tamed the tribals. The restrictions on *podu* cultivation transformed the agricultural class of people into wage earners under the newly entered forest contractor.

The Opium Act (No.1 of 1878) came into force in the Vizagapatam district in 1880.[30] Opium was made available to people through vendors to whom licenses were sold by the government. To promote the consumption of opium, its price in the tribal areas was considerably reduced. The hill men got five to three *tolas* (a traditional Indian weight) of opium for a rupee, whereas in the plains a rupee fetched only two *tolas*.[31] Opium acted as a prophylactic drug against malaria fever and dysentery, when used as a medicine. But the hill men were addicted to it and they consumed the drug at the cost of their regular food and the consumption was very high. Both men and women commence to eat opium from the age of ten or eleven and continue it for life gradually increasing the doses.[32] The habit weakened their system and reduced their inclination to eat; making most of hill men by thirty five dried up and withered.[33] The collector reported that 'the habit was so universal that nursing mothers even rubbed the drug on their nipples before giving their babies the breast'.[34] However, the price of the drug was slowly increased from 5 to 2 ½ *tolas* a rupee between 1880 and 1900 to augment the revenues from the cannabis, perhaps due to its reduced export to China.

The tribals knew the manufacture of liquor at home from *ippa* flowers *(Bassia latifolia).* They also drink toddy extracted from palm *(Borassus Flabellifer)* and jilugu (*Caryota Urens*) trees. The British allowed home manufacturing of liquor only after a payment of a fee of two *annas* (an *anna* was 1/16 of a rupee) a head per annum. Restrictions on their entry into forest forced them to seek other avenues like the strong rice beer prepared by the Sondi community. Taking advantage of the habit the Sondis gradually grabbed their money, crops and finally their land.[35] It was admitted later: "Drink is one of the great obstacles to progress among hill men; it ruins their agriculture, results in alienation of land and incites to crime of all kinds".[36] In the agency of Vizagapatam liquor was readily available in 2,826 shops in 1893.[37] The Akbari revenue of Vizagapatam Agency alone was Rs. 1,84,522 in 1901.[38] On account of the availability of liquor at their door steps and market places, the hill men could not resist the temptation for the drink. Every paisa they earned was spent on drink, and they generally fell into the clutches of the low country money lender who, as a rule, was the *Abkari* (revenue from liquor) renter of the shop.

The British introduced money economy in the tribal areas. Slowly the traditional barter system disappeared and even the most primitive economies came gradually within the operation of the market system. The plain traders were the people with whom tribals interacted for the first time in the shandies, locally called *santhas*, to barter their products. These shandies, in fact, served as the intra-tribal and inter-tribal meeting places.[39] The traders gave advances and loans for certain quantity of forest produce to be delivered at the time of season. In course of time they extended their activities to money lending. The tribals took loans at exorbitant rates of interest ranging on occasions to 300%.[40] During the harvest seasons, the money lenders descended like 'a plague of locusts', taking away all the grain from the threshing floor, making the tribal to further depend on them.[41] Within a few years, the small loan rapidly mounted due to the higher rate of interest and false calculations. After some years, the money lender brought pressure on the debtor either to sell or mortgage his land. The mortgage debt was never cleared and the money lender (*sowcar*) would ultimately become the virtual owner of the land. Not infrequently they used the colonial machinery like the police and the judiciary in their transactions. Harris observed: "If ever these people do air so called grievances or give trouble, it is morally certain that the *sowcar* is at the bottom of it".[42] The economic measures adopted by the colonial rulers snatched away the tribal means of livelihood and disturbed the entire fabric of tribal economy.

Social Degradation

There was hierarchy among the tribal groups. In the hills of Vizagapatam the hierarchy was Bagatas, Kottiya, Konda Dora, Muka Dora, Manne Dora, Gadaba, Porjas, Khonds, Savara and Jatapu in the descending order. Konda Mala, Domb, Paidi and Ghasis were the untouchable groups which later came under a common sanskritised name Valmiki from 1920s.[43] Sondis were plain Oriya caste of rice liquor brewers migrated to the hills. The British considered the tribals as uncivilized barbarians and took up the mission of civilizing them, giving credence to Whiteman's Burden theory, like stoppage of human sacrifice among Khonds. The Konda Doras and Bagatas lost their preeminence in the tribal society due to the political policies of the colonial masters. Their estates were confiscated by some pretext or the other. Some of the tribes were forced to change their occupation due to British economic policies. For Example, the Gadabas were a tribe of agriculturists and hunters. They also acted as palanquin bearers. Due to the introduction of railways and forest reservation, they were forced to fell trees for forest contractors and acted as guides to sportsmen and later they migrated to Assam tea gardens as coolies in the early part of twentieth century.[44] During the British rule, the plains people entered into the hills in the guise of forest contractors to exploit and extort the tribal people. Another important aspect was the rising power and influence of the untouchable groups and outsiders on the self dignified tribals. The Konda Malas, at first acted as a middleman to plain traders, slowly switched over to trade and money lending. They advanced loans to Bagatas and Konda Doras and resorted to oppression to get back the loan with interest. They often maintained false accounts and usually cheated the illiterate debtors. Their rapidly acquired wealth, their exalted notions, their arrogance and their attempts to defile the social status of the higher social groups came to be hated by the tribal groups.[45] So anger quickly flared up on account of the rich Konda Mala insolent behaviour. In 1886 in a local market, the Konda Malas were threatened by Konda Doras in course of a quarrel that 'in six months time they would be cut into pieces like *calabashes*'.[46] In 1900 some envious Bagatas looted Jerrala, one of the Konda Mala villages, on the ground that the latter were becoming unduly arrogant and the immediate cause being that at a cock fight their bird defeated that of the Bagatas. It was reported that "Bagatha, who regard themselves as the lords of the hills are beginning to regard with envious eyes the growing prosperity of the Hill Malas. The dacoit was infact, nothing but a loot of a rich pariah village by some fifty or sixty Bagathas".[47] The Sondi liquor brewers cum moneylenders recollected their debts by an exasperating method. They send untouchables like Dombs and Ghasis 'to haunt the house of the debtor who will not pay, insult and annoy him and his family and threaten to drag him forcibly before the Sondi'.[48] The Dombs and Ghasis living by cattle lifting, theft and extortion annoyed the tribals and frequently their houses and villages were attacked. In one such incident sixteen tribal headmen made a joint attack on the houses of Dombs in 1899 'in the most deliberate manner, they razed and destroyed in some fifteen villages'.[49] They planned another in the next year and 'sent round a jack branch, a well recognized form of the fiery cross, summoning the villagers other than Dombs to assemble at a fixed place on a fixed date'.[50] Thus with the influx of the British, their social system was disrupted in such a way that tribal self-respect was hit hard.

Thus the tribal life was affected during the colonial rule in such a way that they lost their power, influence, superiority and means of livelihood. The British rule resulted in affecting drastic changes in their polity, economy and society and made them subservient.

Emergence of Swamy

Around August- September (*Sravana*) 1899, Korra Mallayya, a young man of twenty five belonged to Muka Dora community,[51] and a resident of Korravanivalasa, an insignificant hamlet comprising only two houses at a distance of one and a half miles away from Pachipenta (presently in Vizianagaram district), claimed that he was religiously inspired and was the incarnation of God. He said that God had told him that Dharma Raja, the eldest of the five Pandava brothers, the heroes of Maha Bharata, would be born again at that place. About March, 1900 he prophesied that a large town, a tank, and a temple would come into existence out of God's will by April, 1900. He promised that, he would perform all sorts of miracles.[52] Later, he claimed himself to be the reincarnation of Dharma Raja. He also stated that, his infant son who was born in October, 1899 was Lord Krishna Murti,[53] and hailed himself as 'Veera Bahu Vasantarayaloo'.[54] He induced the hill people to believe him. His followers reverently called him as 'Swami' and offered him small presents. This Swami forbade the so called Pandava communities (Konda Doras, Muka Doras, Manne Doras,

Gadabas, Gaitas, Savaras and Jatapus) from eating fish and flesh. They were strictly prohibited from eating black gram, cucumber, ash coloured pumpkins, tamarind, and even mangoes.[55] He ordered the tribal people not to slaughter cattle. He also promised that ambrosia would be served to the Pandava communities soon. Further, the Swami used to give on auspicious days the chanted grain. He instructed the tribals not to plough the land,[56] and said that the grain blessed by him would grow and ripen independent of rain and Sun.[57] This promise attracted the people to him in large numbers since there was a failure of monsoon in 1899- 1900. Giving weight to his word, the fields were left fallow by the peasants of the hill areas, from Paduwa and Pottanghi to Paderu.[58] Tribal people flocked from allover the hill areas of Vizagapatam and parts of Ganjam districts. Around two to five lakhs of people expected to have visited the Swami at one time or the other. The people who came to visit him offered a copper coin, a little quantity of oil in a hallow bamboo, a piece of new cloth, grain, fruits, gourds, and even cattle.[59] About five thousand people, all adult males, built two to three thousand temporary thatched and bamboo huts, and began to reside in Korravanivalasa. The Komatis (traders) of Pachipenta were forced to come out, and sell grain to meet the daily needs of the new settlers in Korravanivalasa.[60]

Political Overtones

Until the beginning of April, 1900 Mallayya's preaching remained purely religious and his activity did not cause serious concern to the authorities. Thereafter, it took a political turn and assumed new dimensions. On 23rd April, 1900 some peons of the Salt and *Abkari* Department were assaulted resulting in the breaking the arm of one of them and rescued some tribal people who were arrested by them for an offence under the *Abkari* Act. When the Sub Inspector and peons of the Department went for enquiries, they were also warned and told that if they did not go back, 'they would also be treated the same way; the salt peons had been treated the previous night'.[61] Some hill men were stated to have assaulted some salt officers, who were carrying liquor into Korravanivalasa.[62]

After these developments, the Swami went a step further and promised that a Konda Raj would emerge under his hegemony, and supersede the existing British authority. He also stated that he would drive away the Whiteman and rule the country himself.[63] The definite date of the emergence of the Konda Raj was not given and it probably became a motivating factor for the tribals to come within the religio-political fold of the Swami, even though he already gained much fame with the chanted grain.

On 28th April, all the inhabitants of Korravani-valasa were assembled and were addressed by the Swami and his brother Kantam Dora asking the mob to go to the forest, without taking any food, on *Adivaram Amavasya* (Sunday that falls on a new moon day) i.e. 29th morning and arm themselves by cutting bamboo clubs with hallow ends.[64] It was said that these bamboos cut down on that auspicious day would turn into new guns, the sand gun powder, and the stones bullets; and while fighting with these clubs against the British government authorities' guns would become water.[65] As per their instructions, the bamboos were cut on that auspicious day with the root attached, which resembled at one end the butt of an ordinary native cap gun.[66] Every man provided himself with one of the formidable weapons. On 30th April, the Swami put them through a military drill, in which the clubs were used as guns and they were taught how to use the clubs. Then the Swami called on a ryot belonging to Pachipenta, and told him that they would loot Pachipenta on 3rd May, 1900 and asked him to communicate the same to the zamindar of Pachipenta.[67] There were two causes for the threat of looting Pachipenta. The first cause was the family dispute that Kantam Dora, brother of swamy, had with the zamindar. He thought that it was the opportune time to settle scores with him.[68] The second cause was that, the tribals and their leaders did not want the low country people to visit their God, that too wearing shoes and turbans. Earlier in April also it was reported that some of the Pachipenta people wanted to insult their feelings by trying to go there against their wishes.[69] As the Pachipenta people interfered with their religious scruples, the threat of plundering their village was given.

Murder of Police Personel

The zamindar, anticipating attack on his residence, complained to the Deputy Tahsildar of Salur, that the hill men, who had hitherto been quiet, were likely to give him trouble, and sought his assistance. The Deputy Tahsildar sent the letter to the Station House Officer of Salur, who dispatched in his turn, one head constable, Velugula Sanyasi, who was on good terms with the hill men and had often been to their compound, and four constables to Pachipenta to enquire into the zamindar's allegations. He went to Korravanivalasa with one constable and *munsiff* (headman) of Pachipenta. On 1st May, they went round the camp and finally came to the enclosure surrounding Swami's dwelling which was skirted by bamboo fence, and the head constable laid his hand on the fence. Kantam Dora came out and shouted at him not to touch the fence, and ordered him to take off his government turban, and salute the Swami. The head constable refused to do so saying: "I am not going inside; there is no need to take off my turban". Kantam Dora and three of his close followers personally informed the Swami of what had occurred. The Swami at once ordered: "They must not be allowed to live. Beat and kill them".[70] Then the followers Swamy 'yelled, whistled and fell upon him and the constable, beating them to death with sticks'.[71] The head constable was killed in broad daylight only because he represented the government and refused to do obeisance to the Swami. The next day the station house officer made an attempt to recover the dead bodies, but owing to the threatening demeanour of the Swami's followers, he abandoned it. Most of the villagers of Pachipenta fled from the village after the murders. Even the Raja of Pachipenta was so terrorized with the murders that he sent away his women and children to a safe place. The hill men threw the bodies of the dead into a tank nearby and were recovered only on 4th May by the District Magistrate's party in a much decomposed state.[72]

Seeking Support of Native Rulers

Swami's followers tried to secure the support of Venkatapathi Raju, a descendent of former ruler of Palakonda, a state prisoner at Vellore. A letter was written by one Wolka Tamman Dora stating that "Here...a most prodigious incarnation is born. That is to say Veera Bahu Vasanta Royaloo is born...For us a tutelary God is born. Our evil days seem to be coming to an end...They say that those who do not join them now have no share with them. We have no other support than this. He is incarnated to protect the sons to destroy the enemies. He is born as the scourge of death".[73] The Palakonda Raja was even offered half of the country by the Swami after the British were driven out.[74] The Maharaja of Jeypore was also approached on 5th May by a Gadaba woman, Manchala Papamma of Bhutadevivalsa, near Pachipenta, calling herself as Maha Raja's sister. She requested him to support the Korravanivalasa god in driving out the Europeans and to restore the Raj to the tribals. She tried to infuse a belief into the minds of people, that she was an angel sent by god to be born at Korravanivalasa. Shortly after she was arrested and sent away to her native place after the revolt at Korravanivalasa was suppressed.[75]

Suppression

After the murders, the government decided to punish the prophet and his followers. They feared the worst rising in the agency areas, if their activities were not nipped in the bud. Measures were, therefore, taken to mobilize reserves. Mr. Horne, the District magistrate, and Carmichael, Superintendent of Police, Vizagapatam, came to Salur and collected one hundred and sixteen men of three armed reserves and preceded to

Korravanivalasa on 6th May night.[76] Early in the morning on 7th May, 1900 the police party quietly surrounded the camp of the prophet. Seeing this, several thousands of infuriated hill men charged the police in the most unexpected and determined manner, rushed right upto the rifles, armed with battle axes, and bamboo clubs. So furious was the attack that several of the mob came into hand to hand conflict with the police. Upon this, the police opened fire on the assailants who, unable to withstand pressure, fled in different directions. The hill men were asked to come out and surrender assuring them that they would not be ill-treated. This had the desired effect and five hundred tribals laid down their clubs and surrendered. A systematic search of the camp was made for the Swami, who did not give himself up. During the search some sixty men came out brandishing their clubs, and behaving in a threatening manner. The District Magistrate ordered them to lay down their arms. After some hesitation and wavering, his orders were obeyed, and they surrendered. After this the Swami was betrayed to Mr. Carmichael by one of his followers, and he was arrested quietly.[77] The fight was a close one. The left arm of Mr. Pelly, Superintendent of Police, Jeypore, was nearly broken. Cunningham received a bruise on the chin and a constable's face was cut open. In hand-to-hand encounter, they had a very narrow escape. On the side of the tribals, fifteen were killed and twelve more wounded.[78] Five hundred tribal prisoners were set free with a stern warning. The authorities kept with them sixty others, who were considered the most important, as captives. The huts of Korravanivalasa were set on fire and reduced to ashes. Thereafter, the village ceased to exist.

Among the prisoners were Kantam Dora and Latchayya, important followers of Swami, who took a leading part in the murder of the two policemen. They were sentenced to death by the sessions court, Vizagapatam.[79] Out of the sixty captives, fifty three were found guilty of rioting and causing hurt to the public servants, and were sentenced to various terms of imprisonment.[80] The infant son of Mallayya, said to be the reincarnation of Lord

Krishna, died in the meantime.[81] The chief Korra Mallayya, the self-styled Swami, died of dysentery in the jail in July, 1900 before the end of the trial.[82]

An offshoot of the revolt had occurred at Gasaba in the Padwa taluk. Jangalamputti Lingam Dora of Padasa along with his wife went to Korravanivalasa god and on his return halted at Gasaba, a village twelve miles away from Araku. He professed to perform the same miracles with regard to the crops as the Korravanivalasa god. His followers numbered about 100 men. But he fled on 8th May, 1900 after hearing about the capture of Korra Mallayya, and his party in Korravanivalasa.[83]

Conclusion

Thus the millenarian movement of Swami of Korravanivalasa was ended. The intensely dissatisfied tribals found a charismatic leader in Swami claiming miraculous powers with millenarian prophesies of reviving their old glory by using tribal religion coupled with Hindu religious idioms. The movement presented several features which were unusual and distinguished it from previous outbreaks that took place among the tribals of the district. In the first place, the leader of a movement had claimed to have a divine origin or an apparently religious movement that had resulted in a revolt. Secondly, it was quite exceptional for the hillmen to assemble in a fixed camp of such a size and it grew up round the god man's own original hut. Thirdly, the rebels combined the superstitions with a very fair degree of self restraint. They devoutly believed in the prophesies about the city and temple, and the promise that the bamboos would turn into guns. The Swami also asserted that, by using the grain he had blessed, all ploughing or other cultivation would be rendered unnecessary. The tribals believed in this promise. Fourthly, there was some organization among the rebels. Almost certainly, the orders of the Swami were obeyed implicitly. Fifthly, most revolts in the tribal areas of Andhra were accompanied by looting, but there was none in the present one. The threatened loot of Pachipenta did not take place. The stated intention of the rebels was to drive out the British and handover the kingdom to the tribals. The murder of the constable was almost an accidental act of violence. It was not part of the rebel programme, but it was made impossible for them to conceal the character of the gathering any longer. They brought forward no complaint of any kind, and they were probably led into their course of resistance by the marvelous influence exercised by the Swami, who was inflated by the enormous following he had secured. In brief Korravanivalasa area became a veritable hornet's nest to the extraordinary influence which the Swami exercised over the hill people. The tribals fought bravely with the police force of the mighty British with their crude weapons, the bamboo clubs and battle axes called *thangies*. Like all the other revolts in the hill areas, this was also an unequal struggle between the British power and the tribals. Compared with the British, they were weak in the weapons of warfare, but not in the spirit of individuality, self-assertion, and courage.

It took place around the same time as that of the Munda millenarianism movement under Birsa Munda in Chota Nagpur area. Interestingly there are many similarities between the movements of Korra Mallayya and that of Birsa Munda. Nevertheless, this movement of 1900 was suppressed before it could seriously threaten the existence of the British. Birsa tabooed some kind of food and flesh to his followers, while the Swami prohibited his followers especially the Pandava castes from taking some kind of food and flesh. Both Birsa and Korra Mallayya told their followers that the bullets of the government would turn into water with their magical power. Birsa promised a Munda Raj, whereas Mallayya promised a Konda Raj. Both wielded considerable influence. No doubt the chanted grain enhanced the prestige of Swami. Strikingly Birsa Munda and Korra Mallayya mysteriously and suspiciously died in jail.

The movement fulfils at least twelve characteristics of the messianic movements as envisaged by Stephen Fuchs, if not more. Hence the Korravanivalasa movement of Korra Mallayya Swamy was undoubtedly a messianic movement.

References

Words would not suffice to express my sense of gratitude to my teacher Prof.(Rtd.) B. Kesavanarayana, Andhra University, Visakhapatnam for his unstinting support with paternal care in my research activities and in the preparation of the article.

1. See Norman Cohn's, *The Pursuit of the Millennium: Revolutionary Millenarians and Mystical Anarchists of the Middle Ages*, Oxford University Press, London, 1970.
2. Peter Worsley, *The Trumpet Shall Sound: A Study of Cargo Cults in Malanesia*, MacGibbon & Kee, London, 1968.
3. Stephen Fuchs, "The Messianic Movements in Primitive India", *Asian Folklore Studies*, Vol. 24, No. 1, 1965, pp.11-12.
4. Stephen Fuchs, *Rebellious Prophets: A Study of Messianic Movements in Indian Religions*, Asia Publishing House, Bombay, 1965, pp. 1-20; Stephen Fuchs, "The Messianic Movements in Primitive India", *op. cit.*, pp.13-14.
5. See for details Kalikinkar Datta, *The Santhal Insurrection of 1855-57*, University of Calcutta, Calcutta, 1940; W. J. Culshaw and W. G. Archer "The Santhal Rebellion", *Man in India*, Vol. XXV, 1945, pp. 18-45; L. Natarajan, "The Santhal Insurrection 1855-56" in A. R. Desai (Ed.) *Peasant struggles in India*, Oxford University Press, Bombay, 1979, pp. 136-147. Stephen Fuchs mentions that the revolt is fulfilling 11 characteristics of messianic movements. He gives a table as Appendix in which the number of characters fulfilled by each revolt is mentioned. See for the table in Stephen Fuchs, "The Messianic Movements in Primitive India", *op. cit.*, p. 62.
6. K.S. Singh, *Birsa Munda and His Movement 1874- 1901: A Study of Millenarian Movement in Chotanagpur*, Oxford University Press, Calcutta, 1983. As per Stephen Fuchs the revolt fulfills 12 characteristics. Daniel J. Rycroft "Capturing Birsa Munda: The Virtuality of A Colonial-Era Photograph" *Indian Folklore Research Journal,* Vol.1, No.4, December 2004, pp. 53–68.
7. R.S. Mann, "Structure and Role Dynamics among the Bhils of Rajasthan: A Case of Bhagats" in K.S. Singh (Ed.) *Tribal*

Movements in India, Manohar, New Delhi, 2006, Vol. II, pp. 309- 323. Stephen Fuchs says that the revolt completes 6 characteristics.

8. K.S. Singh, "Tribal Peasantry, Millenarianism, Anarchism and Nationalism: A Case of Tanabhagats in Chotanagpur, 1914-2" *Social Scientist*, Vol. 16, No. 11, November, 1988, pp. 36- 50; Stephen Fuchs, "The Messianic Movements in Primitive India", *op. cit.,* pp. 21-27. As per Fuchs the revolt is fulfilling 13 characteristics of messianic movements.
9. David Hardiman, "Adivasi Assertion in South Gujarat: The Devi Movement of 1922-3" in Ranajit Guha (Ed.), *Subaltern Studies III: Writings on South Asian History and Society*, Oxford University Press, Delhi, 1992, pp. 196- 230; R.B. Lal, "Socio-Religious Movement among the Tribals of South Gujarat" in K.S. Singh (Ed.) *Tribal Movements in India*, Manohar, New Delhi, 2006, Vol. II, pp. 285- 308.
10. Gangmumei Kabui, "The Zeliangrong Movement: A Historical Study" and D.P. Mukherjee et.al, "The Zeliangrong or Haomei Movement in K.S. Singh (Ed.) *Tribal Movements in India*, Manohar, New Delhi, 2006, Vol. I, pp. 53-66 and 67-95. Stephen Fuchs mentions that the revolt is fulfilling all the fourteen characteristics.
11. Stephen Fuchs, "The Messianic Movements in Primitive India", *op. cit.,* pp. 56-59. As per Stephen Fuchs the revolt fulfills 5 characteristics.
12. As per Stephen Fuchs the revolt fulfills 3 characteristics.
13. Stephen Fuchs, *Rebellious Prophets", op. cit.,* pp.260-264.
14. Stephen Fuchs, "The Messianic Movements in Primitive India", *op. cit.,* p.15.
15. B. Rama Chandra Reddy, "The Gudem Tribal Revolt of 1886" in Yagati Chinna Rao(Ed.), *Perspectives on Economic Development and Social Change, Essays in Honour of K.S. Chalam*, Rawat, Jaipur, 2009, pp. 214- 232; See also David Arnold, "Dacoity and Rural Crime in Madras 1860-1940", *The Journal of Peasant Studies*, Vol. 6 No. 2, January 1979, pp. 140-167.

16. W. Francis, *Madras District Gazetteers- Vizagapatam*, Government Press, Madras, 1907, p. 265.
17. D. F. Carmichael, *A Manual of the District of Vizagapatam in the Presidency of Madras*, The Asylum Press, Madras, 1869, pp. 320-332 and 341- 346. The community of the raja is given in the brackets and the exact word is taken as mentioned in the Manual. However it should be noted that Konda Dora and Konda Razu are synonymous. For details about Konda Doras see Edgar Thurston and K. Rangachari, *Castes and Tribes of Southern India*, Government Press, Madras, 1909, Vol. III, pp. 349- 356.
18. For details see M.S.R. Anjaneyulu, *Vizagapatam District 1769-1834: A History of the Relations between the Zamindars and the East India Company*, Andhra University, Waltair, 1982, pp. 33- 81.
19. Ibid., pp. 62-63.
20. As per the Permanent settlement the tribute was fixed at Rs. 18,500 in 1802. D.F. Carmichael, *op. cit.*, pp. 329-330.
21. As per the Permanent settlement the tribute was fixed at Rs. 35,000. Earlier in 1813 also it was sold for arrears in public auction for Rs. 5,000. Ibid., pp. 320-322.
22. In the permanent settlement it was fixed at 10,000 per annum in 1802. W. Francis, *op. cit.*, p. 249.
23. D. F. Carmichael, *op. cit.*, p. 326.
24. W. Francis, *op. cit.*, pp. 287-290. Nearly 700 acres under indigo cultivation.
25. G.E. Russell, *Reports on the Disturbances in Purla Kimedy, Vizagapatam and Goomsoor in 1832-36*, Vol. I, The Asylum Press, Madras, 1855.
26. B. Rama Chandra Reddy "Tribal Revolts Godavari And Vizagapatam Districts 1857-1917", Unpublished Ph.D. Thesis, Andhra University, Waltair, 1993; See also David Arnold, "Rebellious Hillmen: The Gudem-Rampa Risings 1839- 1920" in Ranajit Guha (Ed.), *Subaltern Studies I: Writings on South Asian History and Society*, Oxford University Press, Delhi, 1999, pp. 88-142.

27. For more details of the Act, see The Madras Forest Act No.V of 1882; *The Criminal Court Manual (Madras Acts)*, Madras Law Journal Office, Madras, 1953, pp.206-227; For details of British motives in reserving forests see Rama Chandra Guha, "Forestry in British and Post-British India: A Historical Analysis", *Economic and Political Weekly*, 20th October, 1983, pp.1883-1884.
28. W. Francis, *op. cit.*, pp.111-115.
29. Government (G).Order (O) .1288, *Judicial*, 27th September, 1909; G.O. 1534, *Public (Political)*, 15th September, 1939. All the archival information was collected from Tamil Nadu State Archives, Madras (Chennai).
30. Graham Dixon, *The Truth about Indian Opium*, His Majesty's Stationary Office, London, 1922, pp. 8-16; For details on British Opium policy before 1875 see F.S. Turner, *British Opium Policy and its Results to India and China*, Sampson Low, Marston, Searle & Rivington, London, 1876 ; John Richards."Opium and the British Indian Empire: The Royal Commission of 1895." Cambridge, England. May 23, 2001 http://www.drugpolicy.org/library/opium_india.cfm.
31. G.O. 235-235A, *Revenue*, 23rd March, 1888; G.O. 2822, *Judicial*, 20th November, 1885. *Tola* is a traditional Indian weight standardized as 180 troy grains. It was the base unit of mass in the British Indian system of weights and measures introduced in 1833. A *tola* was equivalent to 11.398 grams. For details see Henry Yule and A.C. Burnell, *Hobson-Jobson: A Glossary of Colloquial Anglo-Indian Words and Phrases and of Kindered Terms, Etymological, Historical, Geographical and Discursive*, New Delhi, 1986 (First published in 1886), p. 928.
32. Two small doses are taken each day to commence with and these are gradually increased both in number and quantity. Special Assistant Agent to Agent, Vizagapatam, dated 8th April, 1887, G.O. 235-135A, Revenue, 23rd March, 1888.
33. Principal Assistant Agent to Agent, Vizagapatam, dated 11th May, 1888, G.O. 1970, Judicial, 15th September, 1888.
34. W. Francis, *op. cit.*, p. 192.

35. Agent, Vizagapatam to Chief Secretary, dated 21st July, 1885, G.O.2822, Judicial, 20th October,1885; W. Francis, *op. cit.*, pp. 186-189.
36. Note on Agency Policy, G.O.1183, Judicial, 8th May, 1916.
37. *Report on the Administration of Madras Presidency for the Year 1892-93*, pp. 8-9.
38. It rose to Rs. 3,36,231 in 1914. Agent, Vizagapatam to Secretary, dated 12th May, 1915, G.O.2496, Judicial, 12th October, 1915.
39. There were 180 shandies in Vizagapatam Agency area. For details G.O. 2033, Judicial, 1st October, 1895; G.O.1434, Judicial, 8th September, 1899; G.O.1493, Judicial, 19th September, 1905; G.O.1447, Judicial, 15th August, 1907; G.O.1686, Judicial, 19th December, 1908; G.O.2339, Judicial, 19th November, 1913.
40. G.O.1540, Judicial, 16th October, 1903; G.O.1914, Judicial, 9th December, 1911.
41. G.O.1928, Judicial, 27th December, 1900.
42. G.O. 2496, *Judicial*, 12th October, 1915.
43. For details of hierarchy in the tribal areas of Vizagapatam District see A. Muniratamam Reddy, "The Bagata and the Related Tribes", unpublished Ph.D. thesis, Andhra University, Waltair, 1971.
44. Edgar Thurston and K. Rangachari, *op. cit.*, Vol. II, pp. 242-252.
45. K.E. Rajpramukh and P.D.S Palkumar, "Livelihood Challenges and Strategies: The Valmikis of Eastern Ghats", *Anthropologist*, Vol. 7, No. 2, 2005, pp. 153-160.
46. Agent, Vizagapatam to Governor dated 22nd July, 1886, G.O. 2601, Judicial, 29th September, 1886.
47. Head Assistant Agent to Agent, Vizagapatam dated 30th May, 1901, G.O. 1371, Judicial, 2nd September, 1901.
48. W. Francis, *op. cit.*, p. 110.
49. Agent, Vizagapatam to Chief Secretary, dated 15th July, 1899, G.O.1447, Judicial, 11th September, 1899.
50. Agent, Vizagapatam to Chief Secretary, dated 29th June, 1900, G.O.1173, Judicial, 22nd August, 1900.
51. W. Francis and Edgar Thurston say that Korraya Mallayya belonged to Konda Dora community. See W. Francis, *op.cit.*,

p. 304; Edgar Thurston and K. Rangachari, *op.cit.*, Vol. III, pp. 353-354. But the available archival records clearly say that he belonged to Muka Dora community. G.O.789, Judicial (Mis.) (Confdl.), 9th June, 1900; G.O.1115, Judicial (Mis.), 14th August, 1900; G.O.1371, Judicial, 2nd September, 1901. Thurston in his ethnographical report says that Muka Dora "is recorded, in the Madras Census Reports, 1891 and 1901, as a sub-division and synonym of Konda Dora, and I am informed that the Muka Doras, in Vizagapatam, hold a high position, and most of the chiefs among the Konda Doras are Muka Doras. Mr. C. Hayavadana Rao—inclines to the opinion that the Muka Doras form a caste distinct from the Konda Doras". Edgar Thurston and K. Rangachari, *op.cit.*, Vol. V, p. 103.

52. Deputy Tahsildar and Magistrate of Salur to Senior Assistant Collector dated 2nd April, 1900, G.O.789, Judicial (Mis.) (Confdl.), 9th June, 1900; S.P. to I.G.P., dated 10th May, 1900; Acting Senior Assistant Agent, to Agent Vizagapatam, dated 30th May, 1900, G.O.1371, Judicial, 2nd September, 1901.

53. Acting I.G.P. to Chief Secretary dated 29th May, 1900, G.O.789, Judicial (Mis.) (Confidential), 9th June, 1900.

54. Tamman Dora to Venkatapathi Raju, Palkonda pensioner, undated, G.O.1115, Judicial (Mis.), 14th August, 1900. Potuluri Virabrahmam, a messiah of Cuddapah district of Andhra Pradesh prophesied the intending catastrophe like Nostradamus and his prophesies were recorded in a book called *Kalagnanam* (Knowledge of time). He told his followers that he will reincarnate in the name of Vira Bahu Vasanta Rayalu to protect his believers, when the evil becomes rampant in the society. For details see R.N. Pillai, *Veerabrahmam: India's Nostradamus Saint,* Abhinav Publications, New Delhi 1991; Stephen Fuchs, *"Rebellious Prophets" op. cit.,* pp. 260-264.

55. Tamman Dora to Venkatapathi Raju, Palkonda pensioner, undated, G.O.1115, Judicial (Mis.), 14th August, 1900. The record is not throwing any light why the consumption of these items were prohibited. The official counter insurgency records are silent on this issue.

56. Deputy Tahsildar of Salur to Senior Assistant Magistrate dated 2nd April, 1900, G.O.789, Judicial (Mis.) (Confidential), 9th June, 1900.
57. Acting I.G.P. to Chief Secretary dated 29th May, 1900, G.O. 789, Judicial (Mis.) (Confidential), 9th June, 1900.
58. Special Assistant Agent, to Agent, Vizagapatam, undated, G.O.1371, Judicial, 2nd September, 1901.
59. Acting I.G.P. to Chief Secretary dated 29th May, 1900, G.O. 789, Judicial (Mis.) (Confidential), 9th June, 1900.
60. Acting Senior Assistant Agent, to Agent Vizagapatam, dated 30th May, 1900, G.O.1371, Judicial, 2nd September, 1901.
61. Acting I.G.P. to Chief Secretary dated 29th May, 1900, G.O. 789, Judicial (Mis.) (Confidential), 9th June, 1900.
62. S.P. to I.G.P., dated 10th May, 1900; G.O. 789, Judicial (Mis.) (Confidential), 9th June, 1900.
63. District Magistrate to Chief Secretary, dated 8th May, 1900, G.O. 789, Judicial (Mis.) (Confidential), 9th June, 1900.
64. Deposition of Tamman Dora, dated 24th May, 1900, G.O. 789, Judicial (Mis.) (Confidential), 9th June, 1900. *Adivaram Amavasya* was particularly an auspicious day to Hindus and especially to sorcerers. The Hindus take a holy dip on that day in the sea and sacred rivers. It is also auspicious for the deeds of lawlessness.
65. Deposition of Tamman Dora, dated 10th May, 1900; and Acting I.G.P. to Chief Secretary, dated 29th May, 1900, G.O. 789, Judicial (Mis.) (Confidential), 9th June, 1900.
66. Preliminary Register Case No.3, 1900, G.O. 1115, Judicial (Mis.), 14th August, 1900.
67. G.O. 1490, Judicial (Mis.), dated 10th October, 1900; G.O. 1115, Judicial (Mis.), 14th August, 1900.
68. Acting Agent to Chief Secretary, dated 7th July, 1901, G.O. 1371, Judicial, 2nd September, 1901.
69. Deputy Tahsildar to the Senior Assistant Collector dated 2nd April, 1900, G.O.789, Judicial (Mis.) (Confidential), 9th June, 1900.
70. Preliminary Register Case No.3, 1900, G.O. 1115, Judicial (Mis.), 14th August, 1900.

71. District Magistrate to Chief Secretary, dated 5th May, 1900, G.O.789, Judicial (Mis.) (Confidential), 9th June, 1900.
72. Case No. 15 of 1900, G.O.1490, Judicial (Mis.), 10th October, 1900.
73. Confidential No. 205 of 1900, G.O. 1115, Judicial (Mis.), 14th August, 1900.
74. Deposition of Tamman Dora, dated 24th May, 1900, G.O. 789, Judicial (Mis.) (Confidential), 9th June, 1900.
75. Acting Agent to Chief Secretary, dated 7th July, 1901, G.O. 1371, Judicial, 2nd September, 1901.
76. S.P. to I.G.P., dated 10th May, 1900; G.O. 789, Judicial (Mis.) (Confidential), 9th June, 1900.
77. Acting Senior Assistant Agent, to Agent Vizagapatam, dated 30th May, 1900, G.O.1371, Judicial, 2nd September, 1901.
78. W. Francis says that eleven of the tribals were killed. W. Francis, *op.cit.*, p. 304. This seems to be incorrect. The actual number of killed was fifteen. All were killed by bullets except one, who was bayoneted. S.P. to I.G.P., dated 10th May, 1900; G.O. 789, Judicial (Mis.) (Confidential), 9th June, 1900. G.O.1490, Judicial (Mis.), 10th October, 1900; G.O. 1115, Judicial (Mis.), 14th August, 1900.
79. G.O.1490, Judicial (Mis.), 10th October, 1900; G.O. 1115, Judicial (Mis.), 14th August, 1900.
80. Most of them were given two years imprisonment and two boys were given 20 stripes each. G.O.1029, Judicial (Mis.), 26th July, 1900.
81. District Magistrate to Chief Secretary, dated 3rd July, 1900. G.O. 1115, Judicial (Mis.), 14th August, 1900.
82. G.O. 1115, Judicial (Mis.), 14th August, 1900.
83. Acting Agent to Chief Secretary, dated 7th July, 1901, G.O. 1371, Judicial, 2nd September, 1901.

5

Colonial Dominance and Constitutional Resistance in French India

B. Krishnamurthy

French Colonisation in India

The French came to India for the purpose of trade and profit, but acquired territorial possessions in the Indian soil by exploiting the then prevailing political anarchy and instability. As a result of Dupleix's forward policy, the French had carved out "a colonial empire in India, which was twice as large as France, containing thirty million people in the early 1750s".[1]

July 1751 was the apogee of the French power in India and Dupleix's most successful and finest hour. However, the French interests suffered a serious setback when Dupleix was recalled to France unceremoniously in 1754. Moreover, the British played its game more successfully and as a result, major parts of India came under the British control and the French had lost to the British in the colonial race.[2]

Thus, the term 'French India' is being used in this paper not to suggest 'France in India', but just to denote those Indian territories which were under the colonial administration of France from early eighteenth century onwards till it was brought to an end. The French fortune with all its ebb and tide continued to be present in India under the shadow of the British colonial rule and by mid-twentieth century the French were holding in all five settlements, covering 50,938 hectares or 509 sq. kms.[3]

Name of the settlement	*Area (Hectares)*	*Population*
Pondicherry	29,145	204,653
Karaikal	13,515	60,555
Yanam	1,429	5,711
Mahe	5,909	14,092
Chandernagore	940	38,284
Total	50,938	323,295

Besides these settlements, the French were having eleven loges or sites of their warehouses at Surat, Kasimbazar, Dacca, Patna, Jougdia, Calicut, Masulipatnam, Balasor and some other places. In all, these loges were approximately covering an area four Sq. Kms. with 2000 inhabitants by mid-twentieth century.

Native Population under the French Rule

As a consequence of the French efforts to establish and extend their territorial possessions in India, thousands of natives came under the ambit of their colonial rule. Due to the political instability and incessant wars among the native states, the merchants, weavers and other people living under their rule migrated to those places which were under the French control thinking that they could gain protection and livelihood. By 1715, the Hindus lived in Pondicherry numbered from 60, 000 to 70,000; and Christians 2,500 of which about 500 were French nationals and the Eurasians.[4] By 1725, the population of Pondicherry crossed one lakh mark.[5] However, by the end of the eighteenth century, the population of Pondicherry got dwindled and by 1791, there were just 600 French, including Eurasians and 7,000 natives.[6] Thus, Indians by birth, upbringing and culture continued to live under the French rule in Pondicherry and other establishments. Native population of the French India was considered as sujet francaise (French subjects). By mid-twentieth century, the native population under the French colonial rule numbered 323,295 (refer Table).

Colonial Dominance

The rule of the European colonial masters like the French brought in a totally new phenomenon in India, as it witnessed the shifting of the political and economic decision-making power to the hands of the rulers, thousands of miles far away. The colonial political, economic and socio-cultural policies were formulated and implemented with the sole aim of protecting, promoting and enhancing the interests of the colonizers at the cost of the colonized. 'Colonies for the colonial masters' remained the guiding principle of both colonial policy and action. Dominance, practiced unabashedly in all the spheres of colonial rule, was the natural outcome of such a principle.

Political Dominance

Under the French colonial administration, the Governor was simultaneously the chief of the French East India Company as well as the representative of the French Crown in India. The Governor and the members of the Conseil Supérieur (Superior Council) conducted the political and administrative affairs of the colony. Le Second, who was next in the hierarchy after the Governor, was in-charge of the colonial judicial administration. Moreover, the European, especially French, army officers and soldiers, as well as police officials and sergeants were there for ensuring security from external threats and maintaining law and order within the settlement.

Since the number of French was quite limited, they had to depend on the natives even for running their day to day activities. From the initial stages the elite section of the native society took an active part in the colonial administration. Dubashes or the interpreters and clerks drawn generally from the native population helped the French administration in their political and economic activities. The post of the Chief of Dubashes, who was also designated as le chef de Malabar or Chief of the Natives was the highest position to which any native could aspire under the French colonial administration. Sepoys or the native soldiers, recruited and trained by the Europeans, were employed to protect the settlements from the native powers as well as from the other European competitors. Nayanar or the native police chief and other police personnel were appointed to take care of the law and order situation, especially in the native quarters, within the settlements.

The decree of August 1784 reconstituted the Conseil Superieur and permitted some Indian businessmen and important persons, nominated by Governor, to be the members of the same. However, role of the natives in the French Indian administration was quite negligible earlier and only in 1788, the Consultative Chamber, whose members were chosen from the notables among the native population, was created. Still, the native fortunes continued to be dim under the French colonial horizon.

Electoral Politics in French India

In February 1848, the Second Republic came into existence in France, which took the momentous decision to permit the French Indians to send a representative to the National Constituent Assembly. However, the elitist elements in the Karaikal region played mischief and spread a rumour that the preparation of the electoral rolls was a ploy to deceive the ordinary people belonging to the fishermen and the scheduled caste communities to identify and recruit coolies for exportation to Mayotte and la Réunion islands, where they were required in abundance. Thus misguided, these people ran away to the neighbouring British territory. On getting a report from the Governor to this effect, the authorities in Paris resolved to withdraw the offer in the very next year.[7]

By the decree of February 1, 1871 under the Third Republic of France, the French Indians were permitted to send one representative to the Assemblée Nationale in Paris. At that juncture, there were 29, 620 voters in French India and the right to vote were offered to those who were above 25 years and having some assets. The colonial administration introduced two-lists of voters – one for the Europeans and their descendants and another for the natives. Half of the members of the governing Councils were to be elected by the Europeans and the other half by the natives. The fact that a microscopic minority of the Europeans elected equal number of representatives as majority of natives clearly betrays the racial discrimination displayed by the colonial political set up. Another drawback was that though the voting age was reduced to twenty one subsequently, women were not eligible to vote.

Yet another disturbing trend was the quality of native leadership. Nadou Chanemougavelayouda-moudéliar, undisputed leader of the native population was strong enough to get any candidate of his choice elected as member of the National Assembly in Paris, but was not in favour of a local man, fearing that it might result in the creation of two power centres in the local politics. He was not equally interested in a professional politician thinking that he may out-maneuver him. In the end on the advice of his astrologer Chanemougame had chosen Pierre Alype, publisher of a weekly journal France d' Outre-mer in Paris and wrote to him proposing his candidature with the only condition that he should never visit his constituency. Alype accepted the condition and was got elected in 1881.[8] He continued to get elected as long as he enjoyed the patronage and support of Chanemougame.

In 1898, when Louis Henrique developed an understanding with the latter, Alype could secure just seven votes. This clearly shows the hold of Chanemougame over the native electorate. There was no exaggeration when Etienne Flandin's spoke in the Chambre des Députés on February 22, 1906: "While glancing through the annals of the colony, you will find that in a period of twenty-five years there were in India as many as 30 Governors, 44 Directeurs de l' Intérieur and 21 Procureurs Généraux". In the months of March and April 1905 three Governors were holding office at the same time. Flandin alleged that 'no Governor, no functionary could pull on in India, if he did not submit to the will of that extraordinary personality... Chanemougame together with his astrologer was the real ruler of French India."[9] This was the case up to 1908. Chanemougame was nicknamed as "the black Louis XI", the Hindu Machiavelli, and the 'King' of French India. It was also mentioned that he was an arch-defender of the upper castes and a status quoist and nemesis of the egalitarian and reformist Ponnoutamby Pillai.[10]

For about twenty years from 1908, Gaebelé party was in power and French India became the pocket borough of the Gaebelé family with its nepotism unrestrained, members of the family placed on all coveted posts in the colony and Henri Gaebelé himself was one time President of Conseil Général, Mayor of Pondicherry and President of Chambre de Commerce. By late 1920s, Thomas' Party or Franco-Hindu Party ruled French India for about a decade. While personal interests were taken care of unhindered, public welfare, especially the welfare of the working class was thrown to winds. Political uncertainty continued and between 1919 and 1939 there were no less than 14 Governors.

Thus, the French Indian political scenario was dominated by political jugglers or power brokers. Some individual Frenchmen held formal political power but in concert with local power brokers like Chanemougame, Vallabadasou and Nandagobalu Chettiar. Though there were attempts to introduce democratic institutions, local self-government and electoral politics, the dominant sections of the society, both European and the native elite, had seen to it that their vested interests would prevail over the common people's welfare and wellbeing.

Socio-cultural Dominance

Indian society remained divided in the name of class, caste, creed, sect, and sex and the majority of the people suffered silently under the domination of the native higher castes and elite. The caste system had reduced and relegated a majority of the Hindu society as untouchables, ignorant, hapless and helpless. The lower castes and the womenfolk lived a life of misery. The dominance of the colonial masters in the socio-cultural spheres characterized by racial overtones and religious intolerance added to their misery.

(a) Racial Overtones of Colonial Social Policy

From the initial stages of their existence in Pondicherry, the French were well aware of the racial, cultural, societal, religious and linguistic differences between them and its aboriginal inhabitants as well as recent settlers. In the French Indian settlements, social privileges were determined on the basis of colour and the majority-ruled were discriminated on every count by the minority-rulers. The French sense of racial and cultural superiority found expression in their concept and creation of ville blanche and ville noir (white and black township), which maintained the racial segregation of the Europeans as well as their descendents and the native Indians.[11]

The permission given to Ananda Ranga Pillai to enter into the fort area in the white township on palanquin and to wear footwear in the presence of the Governor as a special privilege clearly shows that other natives were denied of their basic rights.[12] At a later date, the French colonial administration issued an order preventing the native advocates from wearing footwear when they attended the courts presided over by the French judges. This order was perceived by the natives as the arrogant display of racial discrimination of the French ruling class. Promenade and clubs exclusive for the Europeans too were maintained.

Equality before law and equal punishment for same offence were not practiced and for the same offence the Europeans and the natives were punished differently and while the Whites were treated leniently, the natives were given severe punishment, thus proving the practice of racial discrimination. The case of a lower caste man who was sentenced to death by hanging for killing his wife, which was finalized in a single day, proves the travesty of justice meted out by the French colonial masters on the natives.[13]

(b) Prevalence of Slavery

In 1728, while Dumas was functioning as Governor of Ile de France (present day Mauritius) and Ile de Bourbon (present la Réunion), he paid a visit to Pondicherry ostensibly to discuss some constitutional dispute with Lenoir, the French Governor at Pondicherry, but actually to buy slaves. Lenoir bought 100 slaves, boys and girls between the ages of eight and twenty-five, who were boarded on La Sirene bound for Ile de France et Bourbon, where there was a big need for slaves for working in plantations. Slaves were available at cheap rate in Pondicherry region because of the famine that came in the wake of the Mughal-Maratha wars in the Carnatic. Later in 1736, the Directors of the French Company in Paris wrote to Dumas, who by then had become the Governor at Pondicherry, canceling the order, which had been placed earlier for slaves with the Conseil at Chandernagore, and agreeing with him that "prisoners of war would be more economical".[14] Pillai sights the case of a young boy, who was arrested in a petty case, was shipped to the Isles to serve there as plantation labour and he also talks about the activities of some tricksters and mischievous fellows who used to intoxicate the gullible by mixing some intoxicant in lime used with the betel leaf – then they were shipped to the Isles, while they still remained unconscious. Indians were sentenced in the Chaultry court with slavery for a fixed period or in perpetuity in the Isles de France et Bourbon.[15] Though in the aftermath of the French revolution and the royal decree of February 22, 1792, the slave trade was prohibited, it appears that the trade on human cargoes continued to take place unhindered in French India for some more time.

(c) Colonial Religious Policy

The proselytizing policy of the French appealed especially to the socially and economically down-trodden sections among the Hindus, who have thronged the Christian missionaries with the hope of achieving upward social movement and of taking benefit of the new opportunities thrown open by the commercial activities of the French Company. One of the prize-catches of the missionaries was Tanappa Mudaliar alias Lazero de Motta, who served the French Company as Chief Dubash and got a small but beautiful church built for the Capucins, a Christian religious order. While the native Christian population in Pondicherry numbered to some 2,000 in 1715, it almost tripled by January 1726, as a result of conversion, which went on full-swing.[16]

Hoping that the man at the helm of affairs of the natives at Pondichery being a Christian would be of immense significance to their fortunes, the Jesuits insisted that the post of the dubash should be given only to a native Christian. Nainiyappa PIllai, though was highly useful for the French Company in its dealings with the native merchants, fell from the favour of the Jesuits for his refusal to budge and this cost him his post and later his life also. His son was subsequently converted to Christianity. Ananda Ranga Pillai's confirmation on the post the Chief Dubash was delayed due to the influence of church over Dupleix and his wife.

Due to the influence of the Jesuit missionaries a policy of intolerance was followed towards the native Hindu population living in the French Indian colonies which resulted in their mass exodus from Pondicherry more than once.[17] In March 1701, François Martin, the first Governor of the French Company in Pondicherry, prohibited the ceremonies of both the Hindus and the Muslims during the fortnight of Easter and on Sundays. The last straw on the back of the Hindu population was mounted by the destruction of Vedapureeswaran temple in September 1748.[18]

Dominance in the Economic Sphere

At the advent of the Europeans, India was in higher status economically and it had remained a manufacturing country enjoying markets far and wide. It is estimated that before the coming of the Europeans to India, about 40 per cent of the population of India was engaged in handicraft industry and the rest in agriculture Enterprising Indians maintained commercial contacts with Africa, South East Asia and Far East and through the hands of intermediaries, Indian merchandise even reached the European markets.

All these changed in due course and the Indian economic scenario began to be dominated by the European capitalists. While, moneyed merchant class collaborated with the Europeans in the inland, coastal, inter- as well as intra-Asian trade and Indo-European trade and reaped great fortune, small producers and people belonging to artisan class, especially weaving community, suffered heavily and lost their livelihood. Subsequently, they were dreduced to the status of industrial workers and daily wage earners.

Industrialisation of France in the mid-nineteenth century influenced French India as well. Usine Gaebelé, a textile mill, was established in 1892 at Mudaliyarpettai in Pondicherry and Rodier Mill was founded in 1898. Savana Mill owned by a company in Bordeaux in France followed suit. The Gaebele mill was later acquired by Ehny and came to be known as Ehny Mill. All these mills belonged to the French and British capitalists. Gondalpara jute mill in Chandernagore too came into existence in due course of time. Big export enterprises like Ralley Brothers, Volkar and East Asiatic Company too were present at Pondicherry. However, in the other French Indian Settlements like Karaikal, Yanam and Mahe, there was no industrialization of significance.

French Revenue System

At first, the French used to collect land revenue directly from the people but it proved to be a hard task for them due to the fraudulent, insincere and evasive tactics practiced by the native clerks, who were employed by the Company in assisting it in tax assessment and collection. Moreover, direct tax collection called for show and at times, use of force towards poligars, the local chieftains, demanding huge expenses and fraught with other complications. Thus, to ensure a fixed income, the French took to ijara or putting-out system of farming of its territories to the chosen one, naturally the highest bidder.[19] Anyhow, in case it could not get a handsome offer, the Company resorted to direct collection appointing its own clerks and peons.[20] Moreover, stipulated amount was also collected from the peasant community towards expenses to be incurred on maintaining irrigation canals and roads. Bellecombe, the Governor of French India, laid down certain regulations in 1777 relating to this payment. Besides land revenue, customs duties, sales taxes, especially on the sale of monopoly goods such as tobacco and betel leaf, income tax, and several other such taxes were collected from the native population.[21]

Initial Resistance

From the beginning there were popular movements against the French colonial rule and its socio-economic policies. Especially its religious and taxation policies and practices were stoutly opposed by the native population whenever they crossed the limit of tolerance.

(a) Resistance to Colonial Religious Policy

Those native people who came under the jurisdiction of France were not always happy under the French colonial rule and occasionally they have displayed their displeasure in an organised way. Reference has already been made to the intolerance shown by the French to the native religion, rituals, customs and traditions. During 1701 and the following years, due to continued intervention of the French in the religious life of the native people, some 2000 families left their colonies.[22] The French Governor had to use force as well as persuasion to retain in/ bring them back to their settlements. Agriculture suffered in the Karaikal region and much of the lands remained uncultivated for lack of population, due to the religious intolerance displayed by the French to the native population.[23]

(b) Resistance to the French Taxation Policy

The French Indians were quite discontented with the tax system implemented by the French. Whenever new taxes were imposed upon without taking note of the economic deprivation of the populace, the latter resorted to mass exodus from the French establishments. For instance, in 1785, when taxes on the monopoly goods like tobacco and betel leaf as well as nut were introduced, disregarding the voice of the people against such a step, the natives of Karaikal fled away from the French settlement and took asylum in the villages under the native rule.[24] In many a case the tax-farmer turned out to be the villain, who benefited at the cost of both the French Company as well as the local taxpayers. There were series of mass protests and unrest, whenever the problem created by a tax farmer crossed the tolerance level of the peasant population.

In mid-1780s, the French authorities rented out the collection of taxes in Karaikal and its dependencies to one Savarimuthu Pillai. The rentier reduced the varom or expenditure stipulated for rice cultivation and tried to pocket the amount. In 1787 widespread agrarian unrest broke out in Karaikal and its dependencies on this count and farmers abandoned their land and evacuated from their villages. The French Governor Comte de Conway dispatched de Fresne to Karaikal to bring round the farmers to amicable settlement and this produced desired effects.

In 1791, once again there was a general uprising of farmers against Arokiam, the rentier, who had taken some arbitrary decisions harming the interests of the farming community. In this struggle, the visiadars (local constabulary) and toll collectors too joined hands with them. M. de Espinasse with his 53 European soldiers and 260 sepoys was hard put against the rebels and the French Governor had to send Touffreville with 100

European soldiers to suppress the popular rising, which, it was perceived correctly, had thrown a challenge to the French authority. Touffreville was later appointed by the French Indian authorities as Commandant of Karaikal, as a reward for his success in quelling the mass resentment.[25]

After some time, the problem once again resumed with greater rigor. Vilvendra Pillai and Savarimuthu Pillai, the tax-farmers, who had secured the right to collect land revenue quoting higher rates, created fresh problems to the native population. The latter joined together and manhandled them and then, went to Touffreville to demand the cancellation of their license to collect the taxes. In stead, they promised to pay the taxes directly, which was earlier practiced and was known as kudi kuththagai. On getting a stern reply that the license to collect taxes would be given to the highest bidder and so, direct tax collection was not feasible, the natives withdrew from the town in great numbers. They got support from some neighbouring poligars as well. Some 10, 000 people with arms blockaded the town and prevented entry of rice, vegetables and fire-wood into Karaikal. When they came to know that the French had arranged for the supply of food-materials from Nagour through sea route, they attacked the boats and confiscated the materials from them. A letter was also written to the people of Nagappattinam against the dispatch of food-materials to Karaikal on the name of the people of Karaikal.

The popular movement became so severe that Touffreville had to plead for help from de Fresne, the French Indian Governor in Pondicherry. The latter, on the one hand dispatched military reinforcement to quell the movement and on the other had sent Nainathai Mudaliar, a notable resident of Pondicherry, to convince the people and to settle their problem.[26] Still, the problem continued to rage for some more time and only in April 1792 the farmers and the visiadars returned to their work.[27]

In Pondicherry also in 1791 peasants rose against the tax collector Abira Mudali, who arbitrarily collected half of the produce from them. Keeping Léger, the Intendant of

Pondicherry, in good humour and securing the support of local bigwigs, he even went to the extent of harvesting the crops in their fields employing his own goonda elements. The peasants complained to the higher authorities against his activities and demanded to cancel his license to collect the taxes with immediate effect. They promised that they would pay the taxes directly to the French by way of kudi kuththagai. Initially, the French higher-ups tried to avoid taking any serious action against the tax collector. Later, on seeing the determination of the people, the French authorities decided to cancel the arrangement with him.[28] This incident clearly shows that the peasant community of Pondicherry too did not hesitate to agitate against the injustice meted out to them.

Constitutional Resistance

Mention has already been made about the racialist overtones of the French colonial politico-social policy and its manifestation in the administrative order to the effect that any Indian advocate had to remove his shoes whenever he appeared before a European judge. As a mark of protest a native advocate Ponnuthamby Pillai attended the court presided over by a French judge wearing the suit and shoes. When the judge ordered him to remove the shoes, Pillai tried to reason with him that his shoes go with the suit and so need not be removed. The French man got offended and temporarily debarred him from attending the court. Pillai appealed to the cour de cassasion in Paris and won the case. However, the fact that an Indian lawyer should have to fight in the first place for the right to be shod in court is indicative of French "assimilationist ambivalence".[29]

The socially down-trodden sections of the people of Pondicherry were discontented with the age-old caste system which had always placed them at a disadvantageous position. Under the French colonial dispensation they came to witness the racial discrimination, which had placed the whole native society in a disadvantageous position. The higher strata of the native society reacted to the new situation with contempt and indifference. But, the lower strata of the society viewed that as an opportunity and light at the end of the tunnel. The leaders of this section, who already got converted to Christianity but continued to face the disadvantageous position due to their caste origin, found an ingenious plan to transform their double disadvantage (due to their birth on the one hand and their being native on the other) into singular advantage.

As mentioned elsewhere, the European residents formed only a very small part of the population, and the formation of the two lists led to rather acrimonious disputes as to the rationale of the distinction. A clamour was raised against it, especially among the Christian converts of the colony, who, having adopted the religion and many of the social customs of the Europeans, naturally desired the same privileges. This led to another decree in 1881, which provided a certain method, Renonciation au Statut Personnel, by which all inhabitants were permitted, by the observance of certain formalities, to renounce their indigenous status and their personal law, and be governed, to all intents and purposes, by the laws applicable to Frenchmen.

Taking benefit of this order a progressive group of people led by Ponnoutamby devised an ingenious plan for the emancipation of the lower castes from the caste tyranny on the one hand and the racial discrimination followed by the French colonial rulers on the other. Jules Godin, the representative of French India in the French National Assembly, was called upon to persuade the French Government to bring in the required legislation to enable the Indians to renounce their personal laws and opt to be governed by French civil laws. The decree of September 21, 1881, offered all natives above the age of twenty-one, irrespective of caste and religion, the option to renounce their personal laws. Those who have opted for this and their descendants came to be governed by civil laws, which were so far applicable only to the French citizens and hence forth, they came to be known as renonçants. This decree also provided several other concessions to those who secured French citizenship.

Soon the renoncants started clamouring for the inclusion of their names in the first list of voters along with the Europeans and their descendants. However, the French Government was not prepared to include them in the first list, as it would have jeopardised the influence and interests of the 'whites' in French India. Instead, it conceded to list them separately and in all, three lists of voters - for the Europeans and their descendants numbering 572, of about 2,000 renoncants, and the natives comprising 68,000 - came into existence in 1884. Each group was supposed to elect equal numbers of the members of the Superior Council, Local Council as well as the Municipal Council. This was the quality of democracy that was introduced into French India by France. Any how, the second list for renonçants was a major step towards the legal assimilation of individuals and their families in French India.[30]

Elitist Backlash

The privileged position of the renonçants with a separate second list was not of the liking of both the first and the third lists of electorate comprising the Europeans and the majority of natives. The Europeans aligned with Chanemougame and with the blessings of the Congregation des Missions Etrangères formed a new party- Parti clerico-brahmanique to fight against Ponnouthamby.[31]

As a result the second list was abolished by the French Government in 1899. Severe conditions were introduced so as to prevent the beneficiaries of the arrangement of renunciation, from entering into the first list meant for the Europeans. This was to protect the interests of the Frenchmen whose numerical strength was quite minimal in comparison to the natives.

Thus, the protest of a group of the native population against the racial discrimination followed by the alien regime and the rigid and inhuman caste system followed by the Indian upper class, through constitutional and legal means, failed to bear fruit and left that section of the society, which was educated and intellectually oriented, discontented. Moreover, the policy of allotting higher posts only to the Europeans and not to the educated class of the native population, added fuel to the fire.

Resistance from the Working Class

The industrial developments in French India brought in its wake an industrial working class in Pondicherry, who were treated by their employers as bonded labour.[32] The workers were given a paltry sum by way of wages. They had neither job security, nor compensation in case of accident and were forced to work daily for about twelve to fourteen hours without even weekly holidays, under poor and unhygienic working conditions. Child and female labour was also widely prevalent in the French Indian colonies benefiting the capitalist class. In brief, the labour laws, which protected the interests of the working community in France, were deliberately not extended to their colonies in India.[33]

In any society, the youth and the working class always spearhead any political and socio-economic movement and the labour population of French India was no exception to this general rule. In 1908, the workers of the Rodier Mill organised strike in support of their demand for a slight increase in their wages and against retrenchment of some among them. In spite of some initial success they could not achieve much due to the adamant and uncompromising attitude of the mill owners, who have succeeded in breaking the unity among the workers by planting and patronising a few black legs among them. In May 1920, when the workers of Savana Mill resorted to strike, by way of retaliation, the owners settled all their accounts and thrown all of them out of the mill. Then they started fresh recruitment and imposed several stringent conditions on the new workers. Since the former workers of the mill had no other alternative they joined the mill as fresh hands, accepting all the conditions imposed by the owners. The same tactics was followed by other mills also in suppressing the workers movement in their organisations and the working class itself was divided by the creation of workers who were more loyal to the owners than to the interest and welfare of fellow-workers.

The Civil Disobedience movement launched in 1930s opened the eyes of the French Indian Youth. This helped in awakening the political and social consciousness among the people, which resulted in the demand for social reforms and for the end of alien rule in India. 'Harijana Seva Sangam' was established by the French Indian Youth in Pondicherry in December 1933. Branches of the Sangam were also established in other French Indian Establishments like Karaikal.

In February 1935, 3000 workers of the Savana mill started an agitation demanding increase in wages and decrease in the working hours and succeeded in wresting an increase in daily wages from three to six annas and a reduction in the working hours from twelve or fourteen to ten hours. They also demanded that women should not be asked to work during night times and they should be given one month leave with half pay during confinement. There was also a demand for ban on employment of children below fourteen years of age.[34] With the active backing of the French Indian authorities, the mill owners resorted to dismiss the leaders and active participants of the working class movement. However, in the end, they had to revoke their earlier orders to appease the working class.

In June 1936, the mill workers resumed their movement clamouring for the right to form into labour unions, eight hours work, the right to collective bargaining, increase in wages and weekly holidays. The Governor initially accepted to promulgate all progressive labour legislations after due consultation with the French Government and requested the labour leaders to stop their agitation. But he failed to fulfil his promise by the end of the stipulated period and the labour leaders had to resort to their agitation. On July 30, 1936 French military was deployed to suppress the labour movement and in the firing incident of that day twelve workers had lost their life.

The labour leaders like Subbiah maintained contacts with Nehru, a trade union leader in his own right, who assisted them in gaining contacts with their comrades in France. This enabled the former in securing their helping hand in the on-going struggle for protecting labour rights and to get the liberal and progressive labour laws of France introduced and implemented in the French Indian settlements.[35]

Meanwhile, in June 1936, Popular Front, a joint forum of the French Communist and Socialist parties came to power in France. The French Communist Party members and labour leaders demanded for the extension of progressive labour laws of the French Republic to the Indian colonies as well. Justin Gaudart, a former minister in the French Government, came to Pondicherry as a special envoy of the President of the French Republic to study the problems of workers in the French Indian colonies.[36] On his recommendation the decree of April 5, 1937, hailed as Workers' Charter was passed in France and was promulgated in French India in May 1937.[37] Taking benefit of this Act, numerous trade unions came into existence in all the settlements of French India and they were brought together under one central federation called the French India Labour Federation. Most of them were affiliated to the French Federation of Labour in Paris individually or collectively, thus cementing the fraternal unity of working class of French India with those of France.

From Labour Movement to Political Movement

The success of the labour movement and the rights secured by the industrial workers encouraged the public and they came to realise the strength of united action. The struggle for economic rights transformed and developed into clamouring for political privileges and right for self-determination, in due course. This was followed by the establishment of Mahajana Party in 1937, by Subbaiah and other politically volatile elements like Marie Savary, Dorairaj and Purushotama Reddiar and they wanted to do away with the inordinate power enjoyed by the Governor of French India on the strength of the Ordonnance organique of 1840, to remove the existing anomaly of two-list voter system and to ensure the conduct of free and fair elections.[38]

Subsequently branches of Mahajana Party were established in the other French Indian Settlements as well.

In the municipal elections of May 2, 1937, Franco-Hindu party, which was supported by the French Indian authorities, with their police and administrative machinery and the Mahajana party contested. Although, the latter could gain the popular support, through sheer muscle power and governmental support, Franco-Hindu party was declared elected and Mahajana Party disputed the veracity of the results. The ruling party used police and its goonda elements to terrorise all remnants of opposition and the labour leaders. The mill workers had to fight pitched battles with them and in the end, the Government had to come to terms with the working class leaders. However, even in the elections for the Conseil General, which was held on October 10, 1937, Mahajana Party lost due to the political maneuvering of Crocicchia, the then Governor of French India.

Mahajana party and other democratic elements retaliated by launching a non-co-operation movement. They established Gram Panchayats, sealed the civil registries and government offices, disregarded the authority and orders of the police and judiciary and started running a parallel government.[39] As part of the no-tax campaign, the people refused to pay taxes to the Government. The French Indian administration came to a standstill. Moreover, the people demonstrated in front of the houses of the Municipal Councilors, who were declared elected by the Government and demanded their immediate resignation. As a result, few councilors resigned their office. The Government had to come to terms with the popular leaders and to agree to conduct free and fair elections within six months period.

About this time, the Popular Front Government in France was dissolved and the reactionary Radical Socialist Party came to power on April 16, 1938. As a fall out, the French Indian authorities threw their assurances to the wind. They resorted to the policy of repression against the workers. A French army battalion was brought from Indo-China to Pondicherry to suppress any political agitation. Several mass leaders were imprisoned. Gram Panchayats organized earlier were dissolved and village libraries were destroyed. Thousands of people had to leave Pondicherry and to take asylum in the surrounding Indian territories.

The use of force proved to be counter-productive and resulted in the eruption of political violence. There was an unsuccessful attempt on Joseph David, one of the leaders of the ruling Franco-Hindu party. Selvaradjulu Chettiar, another pro-French leader, who led the suppression of the working class elements, was assassinated by Ramaiah, a worker of Savana mill on December 16, 1938.[40] Later, he shot himself to death and joined the band of martyrs of the ilk of Bhagat Singh of Punjab and Vanchinatha Iyer of the Thirunelveli District of Tamil Nadu. Ramaiah's action aimed at warning the natives, who turned out to be more pro-French than the French themselves and traitors to the native cause, by joining hands with the colonial oppressors in suppressing the working class movement.

End of Separate Electorate

In 1944, Zivarattinam, the representative of French India in the Consultative Assembly in Paris, demanded a single list of voters and called for the abolition of the reserved seats or separate electorates for the Europeans and their descendants. On August 32, 1945, the separate electorates were abolished and a single list of voters came into force in the French colonies in India.

Negotiated Settlement to End French Colonial Rule

August 15, 1947, the day of India's deliverance from the yoke of the British slavery, was heartily welcomed by the French Indians and it spurred them into action. On August 3, people of Pondicherry surrounded the Government offices and demanded freedom from the French rule. The workers, students and the general public organized strikes and called for bandh. Kamal Prasad Ghosh, the mayor of Chandernagore, declared on August

4, 1947: "Chandernagore forms an integral part of Bengal and has every right to break its links with imperialist France". A general strike was called for and a hartal was announced but withdrawn after the release of about 100 persons who had been arrested earlier. On August 9, the French Indians took to direct action to achieve their goal. The public agitation brought the French Indian administration to a stand still at Chandernagore, the people sealed the government offices, forced the police to lay down their arms and driven away the French Administrator. It appears that they went to the extent of unilaterally declaring themselves free from the French colonial rule.

Gandhiji in his speech at the prayer meeting of August 12, 1947 condemned the action of the Indians who lived in the French and Portuguese possessions for declaring their freedom from France and Portugal, as thoughtless and a sign of arrogance. While agreeing that the Indians in these possessions were bound to merge with Independent India in good time, he warned them that they should not take the law in their own hands. He suggested that they had constitutional means open to them and assured that Nehru was not going to neglect his own kith and kin in the two possessions. He advised that they should act on the advice of Nehru.[41]

On August 25, the Governments of French Republic and the Indian Union released a Joint Communiqué expressing their resolve to settle the problems of French establishments in India, "with due regard to the interests and aspirations of the population of these territories, to the historical and cultural links of these people with France and to the evolution of India."[42] Moreover, as a measure of goodwill, the French had relinquished their sovereignty over their loges in India on September 1, 1947.[43]

However, the French had their plan for French India. They tried to convince the Indian Government to accept their pet formula of conducting of referendum, as it was a constitutional requirement, since any alienation of French territory or any change in its status could be effected only with the consent of the people concerned, as per Article 27 Paragraph

2 of their Constitution of 1946. However, they were for the conduct of referendum in no less than three years and no more than five years for obvious reasons.[44] On the other hand, India made it clear that the postponement of referendum even for a period of three years might cause considerable embarrassment to both the Governments and would give rise to serious popular feeling throughout India.

On June 8, 1948 the terms of the Indo-French Agreement, which aimed at settling the future status of the French Indian settlements to the satisfaction of all concerned were announced. The Indian Government agreed to the French Government's contention that the future status of the French Indian territories should be left to the decision of the people concerned and that their wishes would be ascertained by means of a referendum, the modalities of which were left to be finalized by the Municipal Councils of all the settlements.[45] In principle, both the Governments of France and India accepted the right to self-determination of the French Indians by the exchange of letters dated June 29, 1948.[46]

In spite of the popular resistance, referendum was held at Chandernagore on June 19, 1949, as scheduled and to their dismay the French found out that the locals rejected their claim for the continuation of their colonial rule over their tiny settlement. To the question, whether you accept to continue to be the part of the French Union, some 7,473 voters of Chandernagore replied in negative, while just 114 reacted positively, against heavy odds of the misuse of state power, terrorising tactics of the pro-French goonda elements and the carrot and stick policy followed by the authorities.[47] Thus, the people of Chandernagore set out a clear warning for the French on what was in store for them in the rest of India. Fearing such an eventuality, the French as well as the pro-French elements tried to postpone the conduct of referendum in other settlements, thus, creating an impression that France was not very serious about the constitutional requirement. This as well as the deteriorating politico-economic conditions of the French

Indian settlements forced the Indian Government to demand for the transfer of the settlements without any referendum.

The developments in March 1954, when even the staunch pro-French Socialist Party leaders, changed side and assumed pro-Indian posture, the French Government approached its Indian counterpart for negotiations. Accordingly, peace talks between the two parties took place from May 14 to June 4, 1954. However, the talks failed to bring any solution, as the French Government continued to insist on holing a referendum to ascertain the wishes of the colonised, while the Indian Government felt that the French Indian settlements must be handed over to them at the earliest, without the formality of referendum. To the French suggestion for introducing 'dual rule' in their Indian settlements, the Indian answer was a categorical 'no' The later insisted on handing over at least the departments of justice, police and finance to them and were ready to allow French to run the interim government with jurisdiction over other spheres. The Indian government believed that the problem could be solved amicably by conducting election in due course, as per the French constitutional obligation. As the French Government refused to surrender the police department, the talk ended in a fiasco.

This deadlock resulted in the resumption of popular movement to force the phase of events and to influence the French Government to fall in line with the order of the day. Most parts of French India, except Pondicherry city and Karaikal, extricated themselves from the colonial control. This development forced the French Government to invite the Indian Government on July 8, 1954 to resume the talks for settling the French India problem. The French offered that India should take over the administration of the "liberated areas" pending a formal agreement in regard to the transfer of the remaining territories. India had consistently taken the view that there should be an over-all and not a piecemeal settlement.[48]

On August 15, 1954, the National Assembly of Paris after a discussion on the French India question approved the merger of the French Indian colonies with the Indian Union.[49] On October 12, 1954 a Franco-Indian declaration announced a settlement regarding the French territories in India, which was to be placed before the members of the Municipal Councils and Representative Assembly for approval.[50] Kijéour Convention was held on October 18, 1954 in which 170 out of 178 representatives of the people voted for the merger of the French Indian Settlements with the Indian Union.[51] The agreement for the de facto transfer of the French colonies to the Indian Union was signed in New Delhi on October 21 and it came into effect on November 1, 1954, thus bringing almost two-centuries old French colonial dominance to an end.

Conclusion

The French dominated the political, socio-cultural and economic life of the people domiciling in their Indian colony. Dominance of the native elite was also permitted as they would be playing second fiddle to the colonial power. Awards and rewards were conferred on the elite so as to ensure their cooperation in the political and economic activities. Avenues were created for them to earn and thrive in trade, land revenue collection and other such fields. From the earlier stages, the general public resisted the colonial dominance whenever their tolerance level was tested. However, the popular movement was less violent as people resorted to mass exodus and constitutional methods rather than violent measures. Peaceful resolution of the colonial problem by adopting constitutional means make the case of French India something unique in the annals of decolonization. Transfer of French colonial possessions to the Indian Union through constitutionally approved means did credit both India and France as well as the people of French India.

References

1. H.I. Priestely, *French Overseas through the old Regime - A Study of European Expansion*, New York, 1939, pp.190-1.

2. Refer B. Krishnamurthy, *Jawaharlal Nehru and the Freedom Movement in French India*, Centre for Nehru Studies, Pondicherry University, Puducherry 2007, Chapter 2 for further details. Dupleix's plan for France in India was spelt out by him in his Memoir dated October 16, 1753 (*Bibliothèque Nationale Fond Nouvelles Acquisitions Françaises* (henceforth B.N.N.A.), 9355, ff.343-370). In this memoir addressed to the Directors of the Company, Dupleix confessed profusely the situations, which prompted his actions in India. He points out that "no commercial company whatsoever can subsist solely on the profits derived from its commerce, but that fixed and assured revenue is essential, especially when such a company maintains a large number of trading centers." Unfortunately, for the French Company and Dupleix, this memoir reached France too late to fetch him any substantial and meaningful support.
3. *Les establishments francais de L'Inde, Notes Documentaires et Etudes*, No.735, *serie France d'Outre-Mer* –XXVIII, Paris, September 30, 1947, p. 3.
4. *Bibliothèque Nationale Departement des Manuscrits Français* (henceforth B.N. Mss. Fr.) 6231, f. 55; Castonnet de Fosses, *L' Inde Française avant Dupleix,* Paris, 1887, p.157.
5. B.N.N.A. 9090, f. 160; *Memoires et Correspondence du Chevalier et du General de la Farelle*, published by E. Lennel de la Farelle, Paris, 1896, p.16.
6. Veera Naicker, *Diary of Veera Naicker II (1778-92)* (henceforth Naicker's Diary), (edited andpublished by Orsay M. Gopalakrishnan) Chennai, 1992, p. 258.
7. Francis Cyril Antony (ed.), *Gazetteer of India – Union Territory of Pondicherry* (henceforth *Gazetteer)*, Vol. 1, Pondicherry, 1982, p. 228.
8. *Ibid.*, p. 233.
9. *Ibid.*, p. 237.
10. William F.S. Miles, *Imperial Burdens – Counter Colonialism in Former French India,* Lynne Rienner Publishers, London, 1995, p. 8.

11. *B.N.N.A.* 9354, f.76. In the colonial townships developed under the jurisdiction of the European trading organizations, both in Madras and in Pondicherry, we can observe these white and black towns. While in the 'White town' Christianity alone was tolerated, the native customs and ways of life were allowed to be practiced in the other. In Pondicherry, a canal was dug and developed parallel to the sea to clearly demarcate the 'White' from the 'Black' settlement.
12. Ananda Ranga Pillai, *The Private Diary of Ananda Ranga Pillai 1736 – 1761* (henceforth Pillai's Diary), Trans. and published by J.F. Price and Dodwell, Madras, 1904-08, Vol. 9, pp. 25, 124, 328. Pillai was given permission to ride on horseback or in a palanquin in the fort area and to move around with all paraphernalia like white flag and umbrella, the right to wear slippers in the Governor's presence and to military honours like gun salute on ceremonial occasions, as at wedding or funeral.
13. Naicker's *Diary*, pp. 217-8.
14. Paul Olagnier, *Un grand colonial inconnu: le gouverneur Benoist Dumas, Société le l'histoire des colonies françaises,* Paris, 1936, pp. 43, 74 and 161.
15. Joseph Minattur, "*Tribunal de la Chaudrie* 1728-1827), *Revue Historique de Pondichéry* (henceforth *Revue...*), Vol.12, p.13.
16. *B.N.N.A.* 9090, f.160.
17. *B.N.N.A.* 9225, fls. 292-3; B.N.Maa.Fr. 6231, f. 55.
18. *Pillai's Diary*, Vol.V, p. 311.
19. *Proces-verbaux des deliberation du Conseil Supérieur de Pondichéry* (henceforth *Proces-verbaux*), tome 1, Pondicherry, 1911- 14 , tome 1, p. 93.
20. *Ibid.*, pp.147, 292.
21. B.Krishnamurthy, "The Revenue System of the French Administered Territories in India in the First Half of the Eighteenth Century", in *Revue...*, Vol. XVI, 1989-1990, Pondicherry, 1991, pp.1-18. Veera Naicker (pp.198-200) gives details about the fixation of tax collection in December 1789 for three years from January 1790 to December 1792 as follows:

For monopoly goods like betel leaf and tobacco	- Rs.12,210/-

For customs duties - Rs. 6,160/-
For goods moving through land route - Rs. 10,330/-
For liquor etc. - Rs. 3,200/-

22. *Proces-verbaux* , tome 1, pp. 24-25.
23. S.P. Sen, *The French in India 1763-1816*, Calcutta, 1958, p.107.
24. Naicker's *Diary*, p. 125.
25. *Gazetteer,* Vol.1, pp. 213-214.
26. Naicker's *Diary*, pp. 246-8.
27. Sen, n. 23, pp. 482-3.
28. Naicker's *Diary,* pp. 229-30.
29. William F.S. Miles, *Imperial Burdens – Counter Colonialism in Former French India,* Lynne Rienner Publishers, London, 1995, p.8.
30. Miles, n. 10, p. 8.
31. *Gazetteer*, Vol.1, p. 233.
32. V. Subbaiah, *Puthuvai Manila Desiya Iyakkam, Iymbathandu Sudandira Varalaru 1935-1985*, (Tamil) Pondicherry, 1985, pp. 10-11. Subbaiah was a well-known leader of the Communist Party of India and is being considered as the Father of the Freedom Movement in French India.
33. V. Subbaiah., *Saga of Freedom of French India (Testament of my life),* Madras, 1990, pp. 57-58. Subbaiah brings out the French duplicity very clearly and maintains: By Article 421 of the Treaty of Versailles of June 28, 1919, the French Government had agreed to apply ratified conventions of the International Labour Organisations to its colonies, protectorates and possessions, which are self-governing, except where owing to the local conditions, the provisions are inapplicable or local conditions require any modifications. The French Government took recourse to this exceptional clause and justified the non-enforcement of the conventions in French India on the ground that the provisions of the conventions were inapplicable owing to local conditions. Since the French Indian workers were denied of right to association, they were not in a position to take benefit of the provisions contained in Article 409 of part XIII (Labour) of the Treaty of Versailles of June 1919 to make necessary

representation to the International Labour Office directly. The nationalist and pro-labour newspapers like *Sudandiram* highly criticized the anti-labour policies of the French Indian Government and accused it for deliberately with-holding the promulgation of progressive labour laws of the French Republic in its Indian colonies.

34. *Ibid.*, p. 49.
35. S. Vijayalakshmi, "Jawaharlal Nehru's Visit to Pondicherry in 1936 and the Labour Movement in French India" in B. Krishnamurthy (ed.), *India and France – Past, Present and Future,* Centre for Nehru Studies, Pondicherry University, Pondicherry, 2006, pp. 41-48
36. Documents preserved in the collection of National Archives of India (NAI) 463-X/Secret/1936 and NAI.313-X/Secret/36, Government of India – Foreign and Political Department – External Branch, throws interesting light on the labour movement in French India and the response of the Government of France in this regard.
37. This French India Labour Code provided rights to industrial and agricultural labourers to organise themselves into Trade Unions. Even the Government employees including the policemen secured the right to collective bargaining under this code. The first article provided for the right to collective contract of labour. This was an unique feature which provided for a mutual discussion between the representatives of the trade union and employers and reach a settlement across the table. There were also provisions for conciliation and arbitration. The right to strike work was the most significant provision of the Code.

    Another important provision was the restriction of working hours to 9 hours till December 1937 and to 8 hours from January 1, 1938. For overtime work, an employee was entitled to one and a half times of his wages and for work during night times between 9 p.m. to 6 a.m. twice the wages. Industries were prohibited from employing women during night times. Moreover, maternity leave with half wages for 8 weeks was provided under this Code.

Again, 30 minutes per day were granted to mothers to feed their babies during the course of work. Compulsory weekly holidays on Sundays and a fair compensation against accidents too were provided. The most important provision of the Act was that the employers were subjected to severe punishment if they were found to have failed to enforce any of its provisions.

38. Subbiah, *Saga of Freedom of French India,* p.145.
39. *Gazetteer*, p. 245.
40. Subbaiah, *Puthuvai Manila Desiya Iyakkam*, pp. 16-17.
41. *The Collected Works of Mahatma Gandhi, LXXXIX (August 1, 1947-November 10, 1947*) Delhi, 1983, pp. 29-30.
42. S.L.Popali (ed.), *Selected Documents on Asian Affairs – India 1947-1950,* Vol. II, External Affairs, OUP, Bombay, 1959, p. 55.
43. K.J.S Chatrath, *India in the Debates of French Parliament*, Delhi: Indian Publishers Distributors, 1994, p. 36.
44. Ajit K. Neogy, *Decolonisation of French India- Liberation Movement and Indo-French Relations 1947-1954, Institut Française de Pondichéry,* Pondicherry, 1997, pp.83, 85. Neogy quotes Baron's telegram to the Overseas Ministry to the effect that he was against immediate holding of referendum because that would give rise to excitement and he believed "a reasonable delay" of three to five years would dampen the Indian enthusiasm and spirits and that would strengthen the French position in India.
45. *Gazetteer*, Vol. 1, p. 253.
46. N.V. Rajkumar, *The Problem of French India*, New Delhi, 1951, pp. 25-27.
47. *Ibid.*, pp. 60-69. The poster captioned 'Mama' and showed a woman in Indian dress representing Mother India stretching out her hands to a weeping child, Chandernagore, held by another woman dressed in the Western style to represent France captured and reflected the sentiments of the people of Chandernagore.
48. *The Hindu* (Chennai)., August 5, 1954.

49. *Puthuvai Murasu*, August 15, 1954. Some 317 Deputies voted for the merger of the French Indian colonies with India, while 215 voted against it and 33 remained neutral.
50. *Ibid.*, October 13, 1954.
51. *The Hindu*, October 19, 1954.

6

Contractual Work And Fragmented Social Security

M. Lakshmanan

While some studies on industrial labour in colonial India have highlighted the parasitic nature of mercantile capitalism which made use of pre-capitalistic features such as sardar in India for its own purpose,[1] others have argued that from employers down to the supervising staff at work place, pre-capitalistic relations have determined the nature of relations between employers and workers and therefore the bourgeois notion of 'contract' had not taken root in colonial India.[2] Hence understanding of system of jobbers or sardars as recruiters of labourers and controllers of labour in colonial period acquires significance. Therefore an attempt has been made to discuss what methods employers used to recruit workmen and how work was organized in various firms. Equally an attempt has also been made to study the response of the employers towards social security measures for the workers.

Recruitment Pattern: In spite of the fact that Madras had a few industrial units, there was a constant supply of labour from its neighbourhood, i.e. Chinglepet district. The few industrial units like Buckingham and Carnatic mills recruited their workmen directly. Though the mills experienced a shortage of skilled labour in the early years of their establishment, such shortage was made up by the recruitment of skilled personnel from Bombay and of technical and supervisory personnel from England. In fact, even in the second decade of the twentieth century a good number of managerial and technical positions were reserved for the Europeans and Anglo-Indians.[3] The system of jobber as well was used to recruit workmen in the beginning.[4]

The method of recruitment was done on modern lines: A notice was put up at the gate of the mills to the effect that so much labour was required. The factory manager or some other official from among those who presented themselves at the factory gate made selection. This method was found effective for securing unskilled workers or substitute workers.[5] Skilled workers, however, were recruited generally by inviting applications. In the mills run by the Europeans such method was to weed out corruption in recruitment of labourers through middlemen. Over a period of time, the mills started recruiting boys from the mills schools run by the management for the children of the factory men and found such arrangement as "the best source of supply" of labour.[6]

The workers in industrial establishments were chiefly recruited from among the Hindu castes. Muslims contributed between 6 and 8 percent and the Indian Christians contributed over 13 percent of the skilled and 9 percent of the unskilled workers. Though the Christians in the Madras Presidency were only half as numbered as the Muslims, their contribution to the labour force in industrial occupations was considerably higher. This was more probably due to the fact that they belonged to the same religion as the managers or owners, i.e. Christianity.[7]

Among the Hindus the principal castes undertaking industrial work were the Adi-Dravidas. The Parayan, Mala, Pallan, Madiga, Chakkiliyan, Cheraman and Holeya were the prinicpal castes within the category of the Adi-Dravidas or

Panchamas. Among these the most numerous were the Paraiyans, Malas and Pallans who were chiefly engaged in agricultural labour, while the Madigas and Chakkiliyans who were the largest constituted the leather workers of the Telugu and Tamil country respectively. The Vellalas who contributed over 15 percent of the skilled and over 11 percent of the unskilled were a comparatively well-to-do agricultural caste, more than half their number being workers and tenants of land.

Historians have argued that the jobbers were main sources of labour recruitment in textile and jute mill industries. They recruited men and women of their caste or community or those belonging to their villages. They provided them housing in their social neighbourhood till they found employment. These connections were extended to inside the factory where the jobbers exercised control over their men, paid wages and made deductions for poor quality of output. Some times they had the power to dismiss the workmen too. In short it has been argued that the jobbers were "the immediate employers of labour." But, in fact, the role and influence of the jobbers was not uniform throughout the country and varied from region to region and industry to industry.[8]

It has been argued that traditional loyalties based on caste or community were no hindrance to recruitment of labourers or trade union organization. But these ties of caste or community were not irrelevant in the early years of industrialization. Chitra Joshi's study of Kanpur workers made it clear that a sense of caste and community existed among the textile workers and loyalty to caste and community was reinforced by a sense of insecurity.[9] In Madras this sort of ties based on caste and community existed among the new migrants who lived among the members of their caste or community in their social neighbourhood.

Adi-Dravida workers lived in Puliyanthope Paracharries, haphazard clusters of homes without any adequate sanitary facilities. High caste Hindu workers like Mudaliars and Balijas lived in and around the mills and factories. But the segregation along the lines of caste or community was not so marked and acute in Madras as the members of one caste depended on the services of another caste.

That unlike other industrial centers of India, jobbers in Madras had very little control over the workmen is evident from the fact that when a weaving head jobber was dismissed by the management of the Carnatic mills with a month pay in lieu of notice, on the ground of neglect of duty and carelessness the workers did not come out in support of him. The workers in the mills were at first inclined to strike, but they recoiled from strike action fearing loss of their gratuity money. The Government report noted that the workers had "resolved to use every constitutional means of getting the man back to his job".[10]

A similar procedure of direct recruitment was followed in other European firms like the Western India Match Factory owned by a Swedish national. In the engineering units young men were selected and trained as mechanic men and molders. No wages were paid during the training period. Soon after the young men acquired some skill in about six months, some of them were put on daily wages and later were absorbed in the concerns themselves, but a large number of them had to go out for job elsewhere. In the engineering establishments in Madras generally unskilled workers were selected from among persons gathering at the gate or from among relatives or friends of existing workers. Skilled workers were recruited after interview and trade tests. In the public concerns, recruitment was done through the Employment Exchanges.[11]

The workers recruited by various methods in different firms were mostly drawn from villages or neighbouring areas of the Madras city. The study conducted in the early 1950's confirmed that the worker was pushed not pulled to the towns.[12] The Royal Commission on Labour as well noted this phenomenon. In Madras city the labour force was getting stabilised by the end of the 40's as it had a stake in the industry. As a considerable section of the workforce formed Adi-Dravidas, they had very little connection with ownership of land in the rural pockets and this section became stable in the city's working class population.[13]

The absence of jobbers and direct recruitment of labour by the managements was unique to Madras city. As their industrial units were small and catered mainly to local markets, they did away with the system of jobbers from the beginning. This fits into the thesis of one scholar that modern industrial units such as steel and engineering units recruited labour without the help of jobbers since these units had stable markets, while the jobbers were used as the main source for recruitment of labour in unstable industries such as jute and cotton industries where jobbers could exercise control over workman.[14] Of course, informal networks also served as conduit for recruitment.

The Government of Madras noted in 1929 that the employers seldom or never used public employment agencies for recruitment of labour since they found "it easier and more satisfactory" to recruit the labourers they required through the medium of their own "servants" or by picking it up at the factory gates where an ample supply of labour was generally found.[15] But neither the mills nor the modern engineering units employed a large number of women or children. The absence of women in engineering and printing presses was striking. Women in general were employed in the cotton mills in the mofussil areas and informal sectors.[16]

This was due to some economic reasons: the presence of a large number of male work force even for low wages obviated the need for employment of children and women; Factory Act of 1922 prohibited the employment of women in night shift, and of children less than 14 years of age in factories; certain kinds of jobs in predominantly European firms required certain amount of skill or apprenticeship; and the size of the firm and the market for their products demanded a higher level of productivity which was expected to be achieved by only the males in the engineering units. The economic logic, however, was not extended to informal sectors such as beedi-making, which employed a large number of children in Madras city alone.

The case of child employment in such sweated trades was for the paltry amount of wages the males and females earned and their debt which forced them to put their children in bondage to the beedimasters.[17] The children continued to be employed in the sweated trades, though the Government of Madras passed the Children Act (pledging of labour Act 11 of 1933), which declared void any bond pledging the labour of a person under 15 years if executed or on account of any consideration. It also made the employment of child under such bonds as offence for both the employer and the person pledging the labour.[18]

Contrary to the tradition in Bombay, Calcutta, or Kanpur where the jobbers had a control over the textile and jute mill hands, as recruiters and providers of various obligations, the jobbers in Madras had no influence over the workmen.[19] The absence of jobbers had a certain political significance. In times of conflict as there was no jobber, an "outsider" a euphemism for a trade union leader, played the role of a mediator between the worker and the employer. This direct contact of the worker with his leader weakened caste or communal feeling among the workers and led to the radicalization of labour struggles. The opposition to the union organization came not from the institutionalized network of jobber, whose influence, was dominant among his caste or village men, but from the homogeneous class of Europeans who were united by racial feelings and common economic interests. Apart from this political significance, the absence of jobbers had certain economic advantages for those who had skill and efficiency. The direct recruitment of labour by the Europeans enabled men of long and satisfactory service to be promoted to the position of foremen.

Of course merit was not the only consideration. There were cases that only those who helped the European managements in their partisan policies reached the position of foreman and supervisor. But they also came to wield the mantle of authority as their Europeans masters. The result was, as one report notes, "Indian supervisors or foremen commanded little respect from their foremen and co-workers in the rank and file". [20] In fact, some of the strikes in the Public Works Department workshops, the Tramways and other industrial units were against the Indian supervisors who exercised their authority arbitrarily, "victimizing" the trade unionists.[21]

Caste as well seemed to be a least important factor in recruiting workers.[22] Due to lack of evidence it may be stated that men of low caste background carried out certain categories of work like construction, loading and unloading in the Madras Port Trust. Tannery industry could have employed probably a large number of Adi-Dravida workers and Muslims.[23] In spite of the industrial backwardness, Madras city had a large proportion of the Muslims and Adi-Dravidas even in the beginning of the twentieth - century.[24] The high caste non-Brahmins such as the Vellalas and Balijas, Telugu speaking caste Hindus, predominated in the weaving section of the B and C mills that maintained caste discrimination against the Adi-Dravida workers.[25]

The B and C mills kept separate meal-sheds for Adi-Dravidas and caste Hindus.[26] In the Burma Oil Company separate sheds were erected for Muslims and Christians.[27] While the worker's demand for separate sheds was reflective of their traditional taboos, the employer's willingness to provide such accommodation in the factory premises was linked with the managerial ideology, which sought to underplay caste inside the factory to maintain production. At the same time the employers could also employ caste conscious workers as black - legs to break strikes. The strategy of the employers to play upon caste feelings, take advantage of the deprived economic conditions of workers for their own interests was more important than the demonstration of "primordial loyalties" by the workers in times of strikes. The factory environment did not weaken certain customs of the workmen but was built on them.[28]

Contract Labour : If the employers recruitment pattern reflected the rational policy of the employers to remove jobbers and eliminate corruption in the recruitment of the workers, the process of work organisation in the factories confirmed the exigencies of the firms in Madras city. Migration to Madras of the rural labourers without skill provided ample scope for employers who had drafted them for contract and subcontract work. In such conditions those migrants were "free" in the sense of there being dependent on the employers.[29] The contract work differed significantly from regular employment. The B and C mills had employed the majority of its workforce on regular basis, though they were differentiated on the basis of their skill. Such regular employment was due to the stability of the market for their goods and the long-term contract with the government of India for the supply of the khaki uniform for military personnel.[30] But in most of the firms, contract work was a rule.

Contract work was for a limited period of time and workers were under the control of the contractor who had taken orders for execution of work from a company or a government agency. Even if contract work lasted for a long period, the workers on such system were not entitled to any of the benefits such as gratuity scheme, bonus, etc. Moreover there existed a distinction between the private contractors and those under government control. This distinction was more relevant in case of accident to the workman. While workers under the private contractors were not eligible for compensation under the Workmen's Compensation Act of 1923, those under the government contractors were entitled to such compensation, even though the amount which could be paid first by the government would be recovered later from the contractors.[31] But workers employed under the Railway companies were not entitled to any compensation if they were engaged under the sub-contractors.

Abuses were glaring in the contract system, one feature of which was sub-letting. It created a new class of persons called middlemen, between the contractors and the workmen. The worst problems arose when the contractor supplied the material and the middlemen provided the labour for the execution of a contract. This pattern of labour deployment was common in Railways. Workers were not only paid low wages but were made to work for longer hours. The absence of basic facilities and high rate of accidents were also common in such employments. In the early 20s as a form of protest, this class of workers dubbed, as "gang men" was involved in the "sabotage" activities derailing the trains.[32]

As the employment of labour in Madras Port Trust was of seasonal nature depending upon the arrival and departure of ships, workers were put on contract basis. The Madras Government claimed that in the Port of Madras there was very little casual labour. It further said that labour employed by the Madras Port Trust to keep its shed cleaner and to tidy up the cargo was on a permanent basis. The Trust contractors, steamer Agents and steve-dores employed the major portion of the dock labour at the Port. The labourers were kept through times of slack season on a retaining fee.[33] Thus the employment of contract labour as employer strategy was to meet the fluctuations of the market.

There was no regularization of their services, nor was there even a register of those employed. The work organization was evolved in such a way that even a suggestion to introduce a regular register of the workers was frowned upon by the employers, one of whom was the management of the B and C mills. It was argued that any interference by the government in the "internal" organization of the Port Trust and in its relation with the workers would be likely to upset the present appropriate contentment of labourers".[34] But the *raison de tre* of such refusal was that introduction of regular register would lead to regularization of work at least for some groups of workers and standardization of wages as well.

The government's interference was considered curbing the employer's freedom of flexible labour deployment since the employers independent of the government support carried out the organization of a firm. Even in such a large engineering company like that of Messers. Massey and Company's engineering workshops in Royapuram, Madras, some workers were employed on contract basis. The European management discharged 30 workers on completion of contract.[35] The contract workers as well executed certain kinds of work in the Public Works Department Workshop. The transfer of workers from one department to another for execution of contract work provoked a strike in 1927 leading to violence.[36]

Workers in Informal Sector: The large class of workers was found in the informal sector of beedi-making. The members of Madras Youth League, a voluntary organization, conducted an enquiry into the condition of the beedi workers and the publication of the enquiry report brought prominently to the notice of the public the condition prevailing in such factories...[37] of course, one official in the Department of Industry and Labour disagreed with such kind of enquiry and noted his dissent. "It [the publication of the report] should surely not be necessary for unofficial organizations to bring such abuses to the attention of those specially charged with their prevention".[38]

The enquiry brought out startling facts about the hours of working of children in beedi factories. The committee noted 12 to 15 hours of working in unhygienic, ill-ventilated, dark places. But the Commissioner of Labour and the Factory Inspectors arrived at the conclusion of less hours of working on the impression that "most of the children employed seemed fairly bright and cheerful." The most astonishing fact was that of a boy of 7 who was chained by the leg to a log of wood in a beedi factory. The Commissioner of Labour had to admit the fact that "It is not unlikely that instances of cruelty of this character are, or at least were, until recently fairly common".[39]

The disclosure of such gruesome details about the young children who were put at a conservative figure of 814,000 besides 20,000 men and 1,000 women, by the national dailies,[40] was found, in the official view, sufficient to improve the conditions of the child workers. An amendment to the Factory Act which applied to only a group of 10 workers in a mechanized firm was regarded less practicable, for the employers, even if amended, were considered skillful at evasion. The only practical idea that sprung to mind was making education for children compulsory. But this idea was not put into practice. The Royal Commission on Labour itself commented, "The condition of child labour in these factories constitutes an evil which demands an immediate remedy".[41]

In the words of the Royal Commission: "there is reason to believe that corporal punishments and other disciplinary measures of a reprehensible kind are sometimes resorted to in the case of the smaller children. Workers as young as five years of age may be found in some of these places working without adequate meal intervals or weekly rest as low as 2 annas in the case of those of tender years. This recalls some of the worst features of child apprenticeship in England at the time of the agitation prior to the passage of the first Factory Act, particularly when it is realized that many of the parents of child workers are in debt to the employer. As a result, they are not in a position to enquire too closely into the treatment meted out to their children or to do other than return an absconding child".[42]

The worst part of the relations between the young children and the masters was that the former were subject to harsh treatment of which the enquiry pointed out; the parents themselves did not take care. The indifference of the parents to such situation was considered the outcome of their debt that they had incurred from their beedi factory owners. There was resistance to government's efforts to regulate employment of children because such intervention affected means of livelihood. Employment of children in beedi and cigar manufacture units was widespread in Trichinopoly town and other areas. The Government of Madras attempted to regulate employment of children in these units. By the last week of February 1938, Factory Inspector issued notice to some of the cigar and beedi manufactures asking them to show cause why they should not be prosecuted for employing children below the age of 12. This caused much annoyance among the employers of child labour and child labourers. All the beedi and cigar labourers of Trichinopoly town struck work on 8 July 1938 and ended their strike on 10th July 1938 only after they had submitted a Mahar to the Home Minister.[43]

Condition in the metal-based industries was also the same. "The workmen are completely under the clutches of the master-workmen and the merchants... The workmen have taken advances from the master-workmen who in their turn have received advances from the debtor... The debt is carried on from year to year. As in the case of weavers the debts of these men range from Rs. 50 to Rs. 200 or Rs. 300... Similarly the master workmen are under obligation to work for the dealers..."[44]

Reorganization during the depression: Individual units developed their own methods of reorganization of the firms to offset the depression. The worst affected were those, which depended on foreign trade such as the Madras Port Trust, which halved its workforce by 1933. Even the units, which had catered primarily to local markets, suffered heavily such as the Kerosene oil company and the Western India Match Factory. The less affected were modern industrial units such as the Aluminum Company and the East India Distillery and Sugar Factory at Nellikuppam and tannery units.[45] The B and C mills informed the Madras government that the prevailing depression had been aggravated by heavy importation of uneconomical pieces of cotton and silk piece goods from Japan, which resulted in the accumulation in all the main markets of India of heavy stocks of both Japanese and Indian piece goods. Since 1933, the situation became precariously worse and the letter continued:

> *"In spite of every inducement offered to buyers the full production of the mills under our control is not being absorbed, and while we hope that this will not result in the closure of any of our mills, should the situation not improve the prospect of our having to restrict production cannot be ignored, and any falling-off in the already small off-take would make this matter for immediate and serious consideration to avoid heavy trading losses, the alternative being a reduction in the standard basis of the wages".*[46]

Workers Response: In response to the employer's indiscriminate retrenchment policies, the unions of the Port Trust workers suggested a turn system, kind of job sharing, which would absorb some of the entrenched workers. But the standing committee of the Madras Port Trust noted that the abolition of the present contract system adopted for dock labour would not enable the Trust to use discharged engineering labour for the work, because the men would be unsuited to it.[47]

The government's labour policy was epitomized in the argument that the industrial units must economize in time of the Depression.[48] As workers on contract labour were the first to be re-trenched in the depression, the trade unions demanded the abolition of contract labour itself. But one official noted: "As the question of stopping contract labour is one which the Trust (Madras Port) must decide for itself, the Commissioner of Labour cannot reasonably interfere in the internal administration of the Trust". [49] But when such question arose in one of its own Departments the government failed to set an example: "It (contract labour) cannot be abolished merely on a resolution such as was passed at recent meeting of the union".[50]

This stand of the government only strengthened the worker's resolve to refuse to work under private contractors. Only in 1935 the Department superintendent agreed not to give work on contract basis and permitted the union to form 'gangs' to work on contract basis.[51]

Social Security. The evolution of social policy for the working classes in colonial India is one of the areas that remain unexplored. It is generally recognized that the evolution of social policy is directly related to the socio-economic development of the country. In so far as colonial India is concerned, historians have discussed the rise of Indian business classes, their social background, their political and economic ideas and their business strategies. But there is no systematic study of the attitudes of the Indian business classes to welfare legislation or of their influence on the evolution of social policy. Studies on history of labour have been written in terms of cultural exceptionalism, which in our context was caste or community. Surveying the recent trend in labour history, Sabyasachi Bhattacharya warned in a recent article "the explication of the history of labour or any other category in terms of popular or Indian culture may be no more than a variant of what Edward Said identified as orientalism". To avoid this pitfall, he suggests a comparative perspective, which avoids such dichotomies as rural/urban or industrial/pre-industrial categories.[52]

This comparative perspective brings into focus the nature of certain utilitarian legislations that the colonial state had transplanted in India. In so far as the working classes were concerned, the colonial state borrowed most of the legislative enactments from its metropolitan experience and even attempted to modify them according to Indian conditions. The study of the working of the Workmen's Compensation Act of 1923 partly confirms this approach.

The evolution of social security measures is directly related to the socio-economic development of the country. It has been argued that as industrialization proceeded in Western countries in the nineteenth century, employers in those countries came to view social welfare schemes for humanitarian, economic and social control reasons for some time in the 1880s.[53] The Bismarckian social insurance was only an extension of those practices.

The first cotton textiles industry was set up in 1853 in Bombay. The question of regulating the hours and conditions of factory work by legislation was raised only in 1872. But it was only in 1875 that the first commission to enquire the condition of the workers in the textile factories in Bombay and the necessity or otherwise for the passing of a factory Act was appointed by the Bombay Government. Two of the more progressive members of this commission recommended legislation on the following lines; adequate protection of machinery, prohibition of employment of children under eight, a twelve hour day for adults with one hour rest, a weekly holiday and the provision of drinking water.

It is said that these proposals seemed too radical for those days and failed to win the approval of the majority of members of the commission. S.S. Bengali, a member in the Bombay

Legislative Council took up the matter of factory legislation, but the Government of India in their anxiety to protect children and young persons employed in factories conceived the idea of all-India legislation. Lytton, then viceroy, decided to legislate and proposed a law prohibiting the employment of any person under fourteen for more than eight hours a day and requiring children to be kept away from dangerous machinery. This could hardly be deemed drastic or far-reaching. Nothing was said, for instance, about limitation of the working hours of women, compulsory holidays, sanitation, and ventilation, fencing of dangerous machinery or inspection to enforce the laws. Even so, when circulated for opinion to local governments, while Bombay, Assam, the Central Provinces and the Punjab favoured some such legislation; Madras, British, Burma and the Northwest provinces reported it as unnecessary. Above all Bengal decidedly disapproved.[54]

But after a great deal of discussion in the course of which a draft bill underwent considerable alteration, the Imperial Legislature passed Act XV of 1881, which came into force in July the same year. It applied to the whole of India. The factory was defined as any premises wherein was carried on for not less than four months in the year any process utilizing mechanical power and employing not less than a hundred persons. Indigo, tea and coffee plantations were excluded. No one under seven years of age was to be employed in a factory, the burden of proof of age urging on the employer. Children fewer than twelve were not to be employed for more than nine hours a day, or a dangerous work or in two factories on the same day. They should be granted at least an hour interval during the day and four holidays per month. Dangerous machinery was to be fenced. Provision was to be made by local governments for inspection of factories, and governments for infringement of the law could impose fines up to Rs. 200. But the sponsors of the Act were themselves dissatisfied with its extremely limited scope and doubted its adequacy. Viceroy Ripon himself felt that he had been wrong in giving way to the strong phalanx of conservative opinion opposed to this measure.[55]

Bipan Chandra has shown in his major work on economic nationalism that the manufacturing interests in India had objected to factory legislation because it would retard the growth of the rising cotton textile industry by raising its costs of production and thus reducing its competitive capacity vis-à-vis the mills of Lancashire. It has been argued by the Indian interests that the law confined to Indian interests was clearly a discriminatory one and should be applicable throughout British India. No doubt the motive behind the Act of 1881 was to yield to Lancashire interests.[56] But the protective clauses in the 1881 Act for children were not honoured. Once again Lancashire interests became vigorous in protesting against the unfair competition of India on account of the lack of effective factory Act. The public opinion in India was also in favour of further legislation. In 1890 the Government of India set up factories commission. Based largely on the recommendations of this commission, a new Act was passed in 1891. The Act now embraced all factories employing fifty hands and provided for a weekly holiday.[57] The employing age of child workers under nine to 14 years was increased from seven to nine and their working hours were fixed at seven hours a day. Women could be employed for eleven hours a day, but should not be employed during night.

Once again the evasions of the law in regard to women and children became too obvious. The Government of India was therefore compelled in 1906 to appoint the Textile Factories Labour Committee (the Freer-Smith Committee) to go into the question and consider, inter alias, the case for the limitation of the working hours of adult males and the minimum age and certification of children. After the publication of their Report in 1907, the Factory Labour Commission was appointed to investigate in respect of all factories the questions referred to the Freer-Smith Committee. They submitted their report in 1908, in which they admitted that if the industry employed worker for any length of time, they would almost certainly result in the physical deterioration of the operative.[58]

In Tamil districts workers were found to be working between seventeen to eighteen hours a day in the ginning factories, twenty to twenty two hours in the rice mills and twenty-two hours in the printing presses for seven consecutive days. Hours of work for children were normally between ten to fourteen hours a day. Workers in Engineering units worked for a fewer hours a day but the nature of work was more arduous and intensive. Not only were the hours of work spread over the whole day, but also even the statutory interval of an hour was not followed so that there was no time for the labourers to take food.

A distressing feature of factory employment in Madras was the employment of children in the textile mills and other unorganized units in mofussil areas like Coimbatore and Tuticorin. Children were made to work during the entire running hours of the mills. One official, W.G. Richard stated that it appeared to be the custom for owners to place boys on full-time employment irrespective of age. Half-time employment of children less than nine years of age was also widespread in Madras Presidency. The Factory Labour Commission recorded the evasions of law relating to holidays and recess time for children in Coimbatore. Holidays and Sundays were usually working days.[59]

The question of contractual relations between an employer and his workman was determined by the nature of work the workman was assigned to do. Recruited on piecework and contract work, the status of the workmen was made uncertain and ambiguous before the court of law. An injured worker encountered the colonial court, which at times was compassionate, and statute-bound, interpreting the Workmen's Compensation Act of 1923 rigidly. If the worker faced an uncertainty of employment in the workplace, his claim to compensation was also disputed in the courtrooms. The court followed the spirit of the Act.

Workmen's Compensation Act, 1923: This Act was one of the direct outcomes of the deliberations of International Labour Organisation that prompted the colonial government of India to introduce a social security measure.[60] This Act came into force in July 1924. But when the Workmen's Compensation

Bill was tabled in the Central Legislative Council, the Bill had reflected to some extent the alliance of landholders and industrialists. Though the exact social background of members who spoke for a more restricted Workmen's Compensation Act is not available, the absence of elected labour representatives in the Council where debate took place indicated that the views of the dominant industrial and landowning classes predominated. Sir Zulfiqar Ali Khan (East Punjab) was forced to remark in the Council of State: "the interests of the landholders and of the capitalists are sometimes considered to be identical especially which has created a bond of sympathy and created a kind of unholy alliance between those two people. Labour is not at present respected in this Chamber and when it does appear on the scene,... they will make the position of those who find themselves very strong in this Chamber very difficult".[61]

Debate in the Council of State saw a polarization of opinion between those in favour of a liberal Workmen's Compensation Act and those determined to oppose such a measure. Sir Arthur Froom of the Bombay Chamber of Commerce had an illogical view of the injured workers. His view is: "Labourers in this country are well known as being able exponents of malingering... He procures a small accident, he gives notice of this accident, goes away up-country and in due course he dies".[62] He sought an amendment of the sub-section (4) which he considered did not insist upon the production of a medical certificate before an injured workman left for his village. This wild allegation was based on the misreading of the clauses by the member and the Bill did not provide any room for such lapses.[63]

C.A. Inn (Commerce and Industries Member) stated that when the Bill left the Joint Committee it provided that a workman was required within three days to submit himself to medical examination, if the employer required him to do so. Clause 2 of the Bill then stated that if a workman refused to submit himself to such examination his right to receive compensation should be suspended during the continuance of such refusal unless in case of refusal he was prevented by any sufficient cause from so submitting himself. If such sufficient cause existed the Commissioner of Labour had the power to give compensation. In fact, though the first draft of the Bill sent to various Presidencies for elicitation of public opinion had liberally interpreted the clauses for workmen injured, there was a departure from that. Even those who were seriously injured or disabled were not covered under the Act if their injury was proved to be of their own willful act.[64] In practice, however, even before the Act came into existence the onus of proving the willful disobedience or negligence on the part of an injured worker fell on the employer.

Employer's response: Under sub-section 1 of section 22 a dependant who found no compensation had been deposited on behalf of a deceased workman must first approach the employer. This appeared to be illegal as in the case of fatal accidents, it was not possible for the parties to reach an agreement that could be final, Reality of deciding what compensation if any, should be given to each dependant rested solely with the Commissioner and an agreement between any dependent and an employer was effective only in so far as it was an agreement on the employer's side to deposit compensation. As all cases of fatal accidents came before the Commissioner of Labour and refusal to deposit compensation was equivalent to a denial of the claim, the Government of India held to the view that section 22 should be amended in such a manner as to enable a dependent who claimed compensation to approach the Commissioner for the settlement of his claim without first applying to the employer. This claim would not affect the right of the employer to a notice of the accident.[65]

The Madras Chamber of Commerce accepted the idea of payment of compensation in the form of recurring payments, at least in part whenever possible, but opposed enhancement of the scale of compensation. It also opposed the suggestion that the amount of compensation should vary with the number of dependents and the extent of their dependents on the deceased workmen.[65]

The Employer Federation of Southern India argued that the ultimate liability for compensation should lie with the Principal and it was to him to pass on the liability if desirable or possible in his agreement with his contractor and further to see that the liability was in turn again passed on to the sub-contractor by suitable agreement between the contractor and those to whom they sub-let their contract.[66]

The Board of Revenue in its response said that it saw no reason why the provisions of the Act should not be extended to the planting industry. The Board also recommended for the consideration of the Government the proposal of the collector of East Godawari and Madras to extend the Act to persons employed on board motor and steam launches that plied for hire on rivers and canals and to labourers in factories as defined in section 2, clause 3(a) and (b) of the Indian Factories Act, 1911, without any provision as to the number of persons employed in such factory.[67]

S.H. Slater, the Commissioner for Workmen Compensation agreed that the only limiting factor to the inclusion of all classes of workmen within the scope of the Act should be the possibility of fixing responsibility for payment of compensation. On that criterion workmen employed in factories which could be notified under section 2 (3) (b) of the Factories Act should be brought within the benefit of the Act, i.e. all the employees in plantations whether employed in the factory or outside, because deaths due to snake bite of the plantation workers occurred.[68]

In 1932 the Government of India brought in an amendment to fix liability on the employers even if the accident was caused by the deceased's misconduct. Quite often in case of death of a workman it was extremely difficult for dependents to rebut evidence that the accident was caused by the deceased in misconduct.[69]

The employers always argued that the workmen disobeyed a safety rule, e.g. a rule against cleaning the machinery in motion. Moreover the withholding of compensation for fatal accidents, which were covered by the exceptions, gave rise to great hardship to dependents and had not had any appreciable educative effects on other workmen. The amendment therefore sought to make the exceptions inapplicable in the case of fatal accidents. Other provisions of the amendment were (a) reduction of waiting period from 10 days to 7 days and applicability of the Act to plantation labourers who were not less than 50 in number. Amendment gave compensation to illegitimate children. As illegitimate unions were rather common among the working classes owing to the somewhat free association of families especially on estates, it was found desirable to give the offspring of such unions the right to compensation by being included in the definition of "dependents".[70]

An amendment gave effect to an increase in the amount of compensation. The new schedule also provided for compensation up to Rs. 200 a month, as against a limit of Rs. 80 under the old schedule, with a consequent extension of the scale of compensation in the case of death or total disablement. The major increases were applicable to the worst paid work people. The Madras Chamber of Commerce did not consider the revised scale to be not unduly onerous. The Employers Federation of Southern India accepted the revised scale of compensation. United Planters Association of Southern India qualified its support to the extension of the Act to plantations labourers provided the Act covered the plantations employing less than 50 workers every day.[71]

The amount of compensation for the same category varied from firm to firm. While the Choolai mills paid Rs. 457 as compensation to the dependents of a deceased worker, the Binny & Company paid a compensation of Rs. 1,650 to the dependants of a deceased worker. While variation in the amount of compensation was due to status of the deceased worker, his age and income, the prosperity of the firm was no less important in the payment of compensation. Deaths due to natural causes were not covered under the Act, but would fetch only a paltry amount as ex gratis.

Peon employed in printing press died due to natural causes, but he left behind two dependent families, they were paid Rs. 25 each.[72] But it suggested that the work of toddy tapping, coconut and pepper collecting was hazardous, but the Act was silent on the employment of the workers in these works. The Corporation of Madras suggested inclusion of salt renewal and well construction in the Act. Some judges accepted the Act prima facie on the ground that the bill was based on the recommendations of the Whitely Commission. South Indian Chamber of Commerce noted that maximal of 3,500 rupees to 4,500 rupees as against the proposed rate of 3,500 to 6,300 were desirable. Board of Revenue considered the amendment too generous and hence unnecessary. Chief Conservator of Forests suggested only a provision of medical treatment to injured workmen in timber falling, but not monetary compensation.[73]

The most striking feature of the Workmen's Compensation Act was the payment of allowances at half the wage rate for workman temporarily disabled, with provisions for compensation. In a country where industrial labour was drawn to a large extent from different areas the payment of lump sums involved much less administrative difficulty than the payment of pensions. There was no doubt that money received in the form of lump sums, particularly by ignorant workmen and their dependents was apt to be expended in an improvident manner and the payment of pensions if it could be smoothly effected, would result as a rule in the receipt of substantially greater benefit for an equivalent amount of expenditure.[74]

The dependents generally preferred payment in a lump sum of the compensation allotted to them. Their requests were complied with only in case where either the compensation amounts deposited were small or the enquiry officer reported that the parties were capable of taking care of the money. In other cases, i.e., in cases where the amounts deposited were big and the dependents were illiterate, the amounts were deposited and paid to them in installments. In a number of cases lands were purchased on behalf of the dependents through the Revenue Department.[75]

The Commissioner of Labour was invested with authority to administer the Workmen's compensation' Act and his powers were wider than those of "a judicial official". The majority of accidents occurred to workmen earning between Rs. 15 and Rs. 25 per month. In cases of fatal accidents, the government report stated, the deceased left on an average not less than four dependents and the maximum compensation administrable was not enough to maintain them even for a short period.[76]

Under the Workmen Compensation Act, a person who was injured temporarily was entitled to a fortnightly payment of half a month's wages exclusive of the waiting period of 10 days during which no allowance was permissible. This statutory rule hindered the immediate relief to the injured besides providing him with a paltry sum. The report on the working of the Workmen's Compensation Act mentioned: "The employers denied liability on the ground that the accidents were due to the carelessness and negligence of the workmen. Though the Act required evidence of the willful disobedience to orders, carelessness and "negligence" would not necessarily absolve the employers from liability under the Act."[77]

Furthermore, long delay in the disposal of cases caused an enormous hardship to the dependents. Particularly the report in 1932 pointed out the difficulties to which the workmen meeting with non-fatal accidents were exposed owing to the absence of early disposal of cases. Hence, the Commissioner of Labour wrote to Secretary, Public Works and Labour Department Government of Madras in the following terms: "It appears to me better in the interest of these ignorant workmen to empower the Commissioner (of Labour) to make enquiries not only in cases of fatal accidents but also in cases of accidents resulting in permanent disablement".[78]

In practice some of the employers had not complied with the provisions of the WCA and followed their own methods of paying compensation. Though this practice, the Commissioner of Labour complained, led to lack of maintenance of accounts, the employers boasted that they had paid their injured men more than what was due under the Act. For instance, a person employed in the Canara Public Conveyance was paid Rs. 22-1-10 as compensation for his disablement. His monthly pay was Rs.15 at the time of the accident and he was on leave for forty-two days on account of the accident. If the provisions of the Workmen's Compensation Act were followed, the company claimed injured man was entitled to a sum of Rs. 8 only as a compensation.[79]

This does not in any way reflect the benevolence of the employers and might be considered exceptional; accident was caused by the negligence of the injured workman. The Act was in general more advantageous to the employers than the workers. The government itself recognized, after administering the Act for about 6 years that "the English law is even less lenient to employers. Since under it even proof of willful behaviour on the part of an injured man does not exempt an employer from liability, when the accident results in death or serious permanent disablement".[80]

Furthermore the WCA was inadequate in coverage of the workers employed even in the same place or same kind of employment. Under item (V) of Schedule 11of the Act labourers employed in unloading, or loading any ship came under the Act. It's scope was extended to persons doing similar work in ships out lying in contact with the land, e.g., ships at moorings in the streams etc., but did not cover those working in harbour road stead, navigable river, etc., doing other kinds of work equally hazardous.[81]

The initiative and logic behind this Act, which proved to be more disadvantageous to the workers, was stated by one of the Government of India's members. C.A. Innes noted in his speech: "They (the Indian employers) see that it is very much better than that legislation should come by consent on the part of employers, by agreement between the employers, the workmen and the Government, rather than that this legislation should be forced upon employers by a long course of industrial. That was the way in which the legislation of this kind was brought about in England; it was the fruit of a long period of strife and stress, struggle between capital and labour, we in India are more fortunate".[82]

Other serious difficulties were encountered in the administration of the Act. The Act entailed the payment of process-fees and batta for claiming compensation. The workers, being poor, were unable to meet the charges of the compensation proceedings. This often led to an inordinate delay in the disposal of the claims for compensation and to the accumulation of arrears.[83] The solution lay in the appointment of more local officials. But that was not done due to stringent economic conditions in the depression years.

This was evident in the field of safety and health of the workers covered by the Factory Act of 1922. From 1907 to 1930 the aver-age rate of fatal accidents was 9.6 per cent; serious 16.54 per cent; and minor 65 per cent. Most of the serious accidents took place in ill-organized factories where workers were exposed to serious hazards and where factory rules were flouted.[84] Though carelessness of industrial workers contributed to 'minor' accidents such as loss of fingers, or partial loss of fingers, serious accidents were not due to the lack of "machine sense",[85] nor the "religious outlook" of the workers.[86] The causes of the serious and fatal accidents were due to the absence of proper safety provisions in the factory premises. The large number of minor and fatal accidents occurred in the Railway workshops owned and managed by the Europeans.[87]

Moreover, if we analyze the nature of the fatal accidents they were related to the unskilled nature of the employment: the majority of the accidents occurred to workmen earning wages between Rs. 15 and Rs. 25 per month. In cases of fatal accidents the deceased left on an average not less than four dependents. It means the low paid workmen took up the highly risky jobs. The amount of compensation was decided on the basis of his health at the time of his death and on that of his monthly wages; not more than three years were taken into account for fixing the amount of compensation. Other factors such as number of dependents were not considered.[88] It was strictly maintained that the relation of the worker to his employer was characterized by the 'market wage', not extra-economic considerations. In fact, if the price of labour-power was cheap, the cost of life of the deceased worker was much cheaper. The amount of compensation paid to the workmen injured or members of the de-ceased was so insignificant as to maintain the defendants for only a short period.

The Indian Fatal Accidents Act of 1855 before it was repealed by the Workmen's Compensation Act was applied to the injured workmen in restricted number of cases. The Workmen's Compensation Act overrode the doctrine of common employment by which the employer was not normally liable to pay damages to a workman, if it was of his own making.[89]

In a significant case of South Indian Industries Ltd. the defendants, and Alumalu Ammal–the plaintiff, Schwab of the Madras High Court invoked the maxim: *volenti non fit injuria*. By this maxim it was necessary for the defendants to prove that the person injured knew of the danger, appreciated it and voluntarily took the risks. That he had some knowledge of the danger was not sufficient. The judge further said: "A man cannot voluntarily undertake a risk the extent of which he does not appreciate".[90] Wallace of the Madras High Court agreeing with his peer, demanded evidence of "reasonable precaution" that was given to the deceased in a large number of cases such as one under consideration, falling weights and flying splinters caused accidents. No previous warning would be of any help.

In the case under consideration the defendant used a method of breaking up cast iron which consisted of dropping a heavy weight of pieces of iron resting on a bed of iron with the purpose that those pieces should be broken into smaller pieces. The weight was dropped from a height of 35 feet with the inevitable result that pieces of iron flew about to distances of four or five yards. But the employers did not bother to issue warnings to workmen at distance to go on working at the risk of being hit. Splinters flew and fell at a distance of 70 to 90 feet at which the deceased was standing at the time of the accident. Schwab did not accept the defendant's view that he had not predicted the accident of the type and expected him to have a scientific knowledge:

> *"Scientific knowledge has surely by this time reached the length of being able to tell with some accuracy what the effect of dropping a weight of a certain amount from a height of 35 feet upon pieces of iron will be and to what distances pieces of that iron will or may be sent."* [91.]

Discussion on accidents must focus on production process,[92] nature of accidents and the impact of a utilitarian legislation like the Workmen's Compensation Act.[93] The significance of the Act lies in the fact that it enabled certain categories of workmen to claim compensation, if they were injured in the course of employment.

Unfortunately the scope of the Workman's Compensation Act was very much restricted. Section 3(1) of the Act disqualified the workman employed in bridgework for compensation, when an injury did not result in death or total permanent disablement. This section was applied when the applications for compensation of a brick-layer employed in building work for the loss of his leg was made.[94] Similarly, a workman was denied the benefit of the Act for an injury to his eye, while he was working on a railway bridge.[95]

Labourers employed by contractors on railway work such as repairs to culverts were not covered by the Act. But if they were employed directly by the Railway administration, they came under the Act. While excavating earth for the laying of a new railway line, a workman employed by a contractor met with a fatal accident on account of landslips. The defendants of the deceased claimed compensation but their claim was rejected on the ground that the deceased was not a 'railway servant' as defined in the Indian Railways Act.[96] On the other hand, the workman under the government contractor were entitled to compensation which could be paid first by the government but which could be recovered later from him.[97] Even the blasting operations, which were hazardous, were not covered under the Act. A workman, while engaged in blasting a culvert with gunpowder lost the sight of both eyes, but was denied compensation. A person employed on daily wages, even if he was injured seriously, was not a "work-man", as defined in the Act.[98]

In one case one of the grounds for the appeal was that the deceased, who was a daily-paid worker, was not a workman within the meaning of section 2(1) II of the Act. The Madras High Court held that the words "monthly wages" occurring in that section as amended in 1933 applied only to those workmen who were employed and paid on monthly basis. Following this decision, the High Court dismissed the appeal in another case. The Commissioner of Labour was forced to comment that either a full bench decision of the High Court be sought on the issue or the government of India addressed for amendment of section 2 (1) II of the Act so as to make the intention of the legislature clear. In fact, the government of India introduced a bill in the Legislative Assembly providing the necessary amendments to the Act. The Bill was passed into the law in 1939.[99]

These were specific cases of workmen who were not covered under the Act. The denial of compensation to these classes of workmen reflected the limited scope of the utilitarian Act, which did not cover the diversity of occupations and unpredictable nature of accidents. In none of these accidents the pre-capitalist mentality of the workmen could be discerned. All of these were accidents beyond the control of the workmen. However, in lieu of compensation as defined in the Act, injured workers had been given 'ex gratia' payment, sometimes higher than the amount fixed by the Act was paid. But what was common among the employers was that they refused to employ any of the seriously injured workmen or even those whose limbs were lost. One official noted that though the Act was based on England's experience it did not provide any separate additional allowances for the children of the injured.[100] He was referring to a lack of comprehensive insurance policy in colonial India.

The shortcoming of the Act was that if the word "workman" was extended, there would be no limit to its extension since different types of employment without standardisation of work and pay were executed by the workers on contract, regular and daily wages. The decision of the Calcutta High Court made it apparent that no indemnification could be obtained under the Act from a sub-contractor in respect of compensation awarded against the principal for injuries sustained by a sub- contractor's workman. The principal would recover from the sub- contractor by whom he was directly employed. Thus sub-section (2) as it stood had the undesirable effect of enabling a workman to decide on which of the parties the ultimate authority should lie.[101]

The Madras High Court interpreted the word "workman" in such a restricted sense as to exclude the vast mass of the workers. The full bench of the Court constructed the meaning of "loading and unloading" in the Act literally to mean, "loading begins where unloading ends by the side of the ship".[102] A worker (Perumal) was employed in hoisting and lowering by means of a hydraulic crane certain goods. Some of which - casks of ghee - had been unloaded from a ship; others - bales of cotton - were about to be loaded on to another. Some bales of cotton, which were being lowered, fell on him and injured his right leg. The Commissioner of Labour who was in overall in charge of administring the Act held that under the Act the injured man was a "workman". However Walker of the Madras High Court disagreed with this construction noting," if it is to be held that the process of loading can begin at a warehouse at a distance. In this instance it is quarter of a mile".[103] The full bench consisting of Chief Justice Coutts-Trotter and Beasley besides Walker set aside the orders of the Commissioner of Labour. But Coutts - Trotter observed that he regretted their own verdict for the reason that;

> *"It presumably precludes an appeal to the Privy Council from whom we should have obtained further guidance if only because we are told that our decision affects over a million labourers in this country. The*

employers could and would appeal, had our decision been against them, but labour is as yet so little organised in this country, that there are no funds available, so far as I know to take up a test case... The employers are fighting the case on principle only and that this individual workman will be given a generous ex-gratia payment in any event."[104]

These *obiter dicta* reveal the strong organisation of the capitalist class vis-a-vis working classes. In fact, one of the stated objectives of the Employers Federation of Southern India, body of European interests, was the filing of a common suit in the interest of the employers. The courts in colonial India did not take into account some of the causes which today influence the award of compensation to workmen, such as the nature of work and stress and strain of the workman: "If you are working on piece-work, you cannot be expected to take quite so much care for your own safety as if you are not".[105] As the employers recruited and remunerated workmen on the basis of their skill and productivity, so the courts as well followed a method of itemizing the award of compensation into items for serious, minor and fatal cases; into items for certain classes of workers on the basis of their rates of wages at the time of accident.

The workmen in the conception of the employing class or in that of the judiciary were individual workmen, not a homogeneous class of workmen engaged in particular kind of employment. The concept of class, though shaped by workplace, was demonstrated and played out in the neighbourhood of the factory. The heterogeneity of workers based on different skills sustained by the managerial ideology was overshadowed by the collective action of the workers. But for the workers, the diversity of work practices hindered their right to compensation. One is reminded of Marx's statement that certain loophole in any welfare legislation for workman was always detected by the "lynx eye of capital" and turned against the workmen.[106]

The interstices of the Act and its legal constructions by the judiciary deprived the workmen of any compensation. The court's role was confined to interpreting the relation between the workman and his employer strictly in accordance with the Act. Its judgments exposed the loopholes in the Act, which needed to be rectified by amendments to the Act. Moreover, the court's judgments proved to be of intrinsic merit. Certain classes of workmen who had been excluded earlier were brought under the Act after the necessary amendments. Institutional interaction between the Executive organ of the government and the judiciary led to a closer supervision of the factories and a stricter implementation of factory rules in matters of health and safety and their rights, and more notably, forced them to clamour for more radical amendments to the Act.[107] A liberal workmen's compensation Act became one of the rallying demands of the trade unionists in the 1930s. The attitude of the employers to social security measures in colonial Madras cut across caste/community differences among the workers and was administered within the framework of the low level of industrial development.

References

1. Ranajit Das Gupta, "Structure of the Labour Market in Colonial India", in *Economic and Political Weekly* (hereafter, EPW), Special number, November, 1981. pp. 1803-6.
2. Dipesh Chakrabarty, *Rethinking Working Class History, Bengal 1890-1947* (Delhi, 1989).
3. *The Census of India*, 1921, Vol. XIII (part 2), Madras, pp. 291-98; *The Census of India,* 1911, Vol. XII, pp. 251-58.
4. Eamon Murphy, *Unions in conflict: A comparative study of four textile centers* (Delhi, 1987), pp. 29, 230.
5. N.N. Natarajan, "Industrial Labour in the city of Madras" (M.Litt thesis, Madras University, 1951), p. 39.
6. Carnatic Mill manager's oral evidence in *RCL*, p.171.
7. G.M. Broughton, Labour in Indian Industries (London, 1924), p. 932.

8. Rajnaryan Chadndavarkar, The Orgins of Industrial Capitalism in India.
9. Chitra Joshi's work is critique of this aspect of Morris David Morris' work, *The Emergence of the Industrial Labour force in India : A study of Bombay cotton mills 1854-1947 (*Berkely and Los Angeles), See "Kanpur Textile Labour : Some structural features of formative years", *EPW*, XVI, 44-6 Special no. Nov. 1981, pp. 1823-38.
10. G.O. 111, Home, Political, Deposit, 19 August 1920, NAI.
11. N.N. Natarajan, *op. cit*, pp. 34-35.
12. *Ibid*. p. 29.
13. Eamon Murphy, *Unions in Conflict: A Comparative study of four textile centers* (Delhi, 1982).
14. Morris David Morris, "Modern Business organisation and Labour Administration: Specific Adaptation to Indian conditions of risk and uncertainty, 1850-1947", *EPW,* October 6, 1979, pp. 1680-7.
15. G.O. 2684, L 20 September 1929, PW and L, TNA.
16. File no. 3001 (14) of 1933, Department of Industry and Labour, NAI. 27. File No. 241/32, Home department, Judicial, NAI.
17. *The Report of The Royal Commission on Labour* (Calcutta, 1931), p. 96.
18. G.O. 390, 10 March 1936, Development Department, TNA.
19. B. Shiva Rao, a leader of the Madras Labour Union, had to withdraw his statement on bribery in the mills for recruitment. See details in the *RCL, op. cit.*, pp. 222-3.
20. G.O. 2684, 20 September 1929, PW and L, TNA.
21. The Madras Tramway and Electricity Supply Worker's Association letter dated 11 March 1938 in G.O.1289, 19 May 1938, PW & L, and TNA.
22. Morris David Morris, *The Emergence of the Industrial Labour force in India: A study of Bombay cotton mills 1854-1947* (Berkely and Los Angeles).
23. Nos. 30-32, Home Judicial, March 1891, *Proceedings of the Factory Commission, 1890, NAI.*
24. *The Imperial Gazetteer of India*, p. 506.

25. E.D. Murphy, *op.cit.*
26. Eamon Murphy, "Class and Community in India: The Madras Labour Union, 1918-21", in the *Indian Economic and Social History Review*, (hereafter *IESHR*) Vol. XIV, no. 3, 1977, pp. 291-321.
27. Dispositions of the representatives of the Kerosene Oil workers Union *RCL*, oral evidence, *op. cit.*, p. 149.
28. Chitra Joshi, *op.cit.*
29. K.Marx, "Wage Labour and Capital", in K. Marx and Engles, *Selected Works in one volume* (Moscow).
30. No. 41, Home political Deposit, 24 January 1921, April 1921.
31. Municipal Council v.William Foster, in *All India Reporter* (hereafter *A.I.R.)* (1918) Madras, pp. 264-72.
32. File No. 59, Home, Political Deposit, December 1920, NAI.
33. G.O. 1547, L, 22 July 1933, P.W. & L, TNA.
34. G.O. 3536, L, 17 December 1930, PW and L, TNA.
35. G.O. 1668, L, 2 August 1927, PW and L.
36. G.O. 1532, L, 15 July 1927, PW and L, TNA.
37. Commissioner of Labour's report dated 7 May 1930 to the Secretary to Development Department, Madras Government, G.O. 1714, 10/9/30, Development, and TNA.
38. File No. 1758 (1) of 1921, Department of Industry and Labour, NAI.
39. The Commissioner of Labour's report, G.O. 1714, 10/9/30, Development.
40. *The Hindu*, 10 April 1930; *The Madras Mail,* 17 April 1930; *The Bengalee*, July 1930.
41. Files. No. 241/32, Judicial, Home Dept. Judicial NAI.
42. *Ibid.*
43. G.O. 1714, 10/9/30, Development, and TNA.
44. Nasir Tyabji, "State Aid to Industry: Madras1921-37", *EPW*, July 30, 1988.
45. C.S. Krishna, *Labour Movement in Tamil Nadu 1918-1933* (Calcutta, 1990)
46. G.O. 869, 12 July 1933 Development (Confidential) TNA.
47. G.O. 1620, L, 1 August 1932, PW and L, TNA.

48. G.O. 2437, L, 21 November 1932, PW and L, TNA.
49. G.O. 1620, L, 1 August 1932, PW and L, TNA.
50. File. No. 878, L Department of Industry and Labour, 1931 NAI.
51. G.O. 1620 L, 1 August 1932, P.W. and L, TNA; *Labour Gazette*; December 1935, p. 259.
52. Sabyasachi Bhattacharya "Recent trends in labour history". *Indian Journal of Labour Economics*, Vol. 46, No. 1, January-March 2003, p. 29.
53. John Hay, "The origins of social policy in Great Britain in the 1880s" in *Social History*, Vol. 3, 1979, pp. 211-212.
54. S. Gopal, *The Viceroyalty of Lord Rippon* (Oxford, 1956), p. 131.
55. *Ibid*.
56. Bipan Chandra, *Rise and Growth of Economic Nationalism in India* (New Delhi, 1977), p. 346.
57. P. Padmanatha Pillai, *The Indian Labour Problem* (Madras, 1933), p. 15.
58. *Report of this Indian Factory Labour Commission 1908* (Simla, 1908), Vol. I. Section VI, pp. 6-8.
59. *Ibid*.
60. File No. 835 (320), L, Department of Industry and Labour, 1930, National Archives of India (hereafter NAI).
61. *The Council of State Debates* (hereafter *CSD*), Vol. III, Part II, p. 840.
62. The *CSD*, Vol. III, Part II, 1923, p. 911. But in fact there was a general agreement on the need for compensation to the injured workmen. Sir Alexander Murray of the Bengal Chamber of Commerce stated: "We accept responsibility for all accidents of specific description with the exception of those particular accidents, namely injury to a workman resulting from an accident which is directly attributable to the influence of drink or drugs, willful devises".
63. *CSD*, Vol. III, Part II, p. 854.
64. This was pointed out by Raja Ali (of the United Provinces), *CSD*, Vol.111, part II, 9923, p. 849.
65. G.O. 1515, L, 19 July 1932, Public Works and Labour, Tamil Nadu State Archives.
66. *Ibid*.

67. *Ibid.*
68. *Ibid.*
69. *Ibid.*
70. File No. 1288, L, 1936 Department of Industry and Labour, NAI.
71. G.O. 1515, L, 19 July 1932, P.W &L.
72. G.O. 2039, L, 22 July 1929, P.W & L.
73. G.O.1311, L, 17 June1932, P.W&L. TNA.
74. G.O. 334, L, 10 February 1932, P. W. & L. TNA.
75. G.O. 2039. L. 22 July 1929, P.W.& L. TNA.
76. G.O. 2684. L. 20 September 1929, P.W. & L. TNA.
77. G.O. 1311. L. 17 June 1932, P.W. & L. TNA
78. G.O. 1515. L. 19 July 1932, P.W. & L. TNA.
79. G.O. 2949. L. 20 October 1930, P.W. & L. TNA.
80. G.O. 2684. L. 20 September 1929, P.W. & L. TNA.
81. G.O.1511. L. 13 June 1928, P.W. & L. TNA.
82. *CSD*, Vol. III, Part II, p. 841.
83. G.O. 334. L. 10/2/32, P.W. & L. TNA.
84. N.T. Abraham, "Conciliation and Arbitration in Labour Disputes with special reference to Madras" (M.Litt thesis, Madras University, 1945), p. 48. : See also G.O. 2741, 14 December 1934, PW and L, TNA.
85. Margaret Reed, *the Indian Peasant Uprooted* (London, 1931), pp. 26-27.
86. Dipesh Chakrabarty, *Rethinking Working Class History-Bengal, 1880-1955* (Delhi, 1987), p. 89.
87. G.O. 373, L, 14 February 1934, PW and L, TNA.
88. G.O.1511.L. 13 June 1928, P.W. & L. TNA.
89. K.D. Srivatsava, *Commentaries on the Workmen's Compensation Act*, 1923 (Lucknow, 1965), p. 2.
90. *All India Reporter* (A.I.R.), (1923), Madras, p. 565.
91. *Ibid*. p. 566.
92. *Labour Gazette*, December 1925.
93. Janaki Nayar, "Production regimes, Cultural processes: Industrial Labour in Mysore", *Indian Economic and Social History Review*, 30, 3 (1993), p. 271.

94. G.O. 1511, L, 13 June 1928, P.W & L, TNA.
95. *Ibid.*
96. *Ibid.*
97. *Ibid.*
98. *Ibid.*
99. G.O. 1509, 12 June 1939, Development Department, TNA.
100. G.O. 1511, l 13 June 1928, P.W & L, TNA.
101. G.O. 2949, L, 20 November 1930 PW & L.TNA.
102. *Ralli Bros V. Perumal*, in A.I.R (1929) Madras p. 702.
103. *Ibid.*
104. Ibid., p. 703.
105. Boothman V. British Northroop in (1972) 13 K.I.R. 112, cited by Ion Eagelson, "The Last Bastion of Fault? Contributory Negli-gence in Actions Or Employers Liability" in *Modern Law Review*, November 1979, p. 652.
106. Karl Marx, *The Poverty of Philosophy* (Moscow, not dated), p. 93.
107. G.O. 1398, 18 July 1937, Development Department TNA.

7

"Ending up Making a Monkey While Intending to Portray a Gentleman"†: Controversy in a Women's Organisation in Colonial Andhra– Story of the *Shri Vidyarthini Samajamu*, 1902-1947

S. Mahaboob Basha

Women's organisations have contributed in no small measure to women's development in India. Yet little scholarly work has so far been done to assess their contribution.

Aparna Basu & Bharati Ray

The above statement indicates the poignant state of research on one of the most important aspects of women's movement in colonial India. Research on the question of social reform in colonial India had mostly focused on the organisations founded by men and their activities and the study of women's organizations has by and large been neglected. Works on the issue of social reform in Andhra present no different picture as they make only passing references to a few women's organisations.[2] This suggests that there is a severe lacunae in the historical research on the concerns of women's movement.

Studying women's organisations is essential because it helps us understand the women's perspective, which has generally been marginalised in historical writing. The women's organisations tell us the story of how and why women came together, what their desires and aspirations were, what they discussed, how they perceived the world around them, the difficulties they had to face in establishing, running and attending the organisations, and how they managed to overcome the obstacles etc. They dispel the deep-rooted perceptions that women were only passive recipients and also help us identify them as active agents shaping their own future. Therefore a systematic study of women's organisations helps us construct the history of women's movement in their own perspective. In other words, it helps us represent the self-representation and agency of women in the struggle for equality.

It is in this context that this paper acquires significance. It makes a humble attempt at narrating the story of the *Shri Vidyarthini Samajamu*, also known as the *Kakinada Vidyarthini Samajamu* (hereafter *Samajamu*), which emerged at the very beginning of the twentieth century. The *Samajamu* is important not only because it was very vibrant and played a vital role in the contemporary women's movement in colonial Andhra, but also for several other reasons. It is remarkable for it continued to function for more than half-a-century; published the first women edited women's journal, the *Hindu Sundary*;[3] played key role in convening the state level women's conferences i.e. the Andhra Mahila Mahasabhas; maintained a library, the '*Rajyalakshmi Pustaka Bhandagaramu*', and established/ managed a girls' school, the '*Stri Samskruta Vidyalayamu*' (Women's Sanskrit School). Most of the intellectual activist women in colonial Andhra were associated with the *Samajamu*.

Apart from these distinguishing characteristics, the *Samajamu* is remarkable for it became a site of heated controversy among women over the issue of the admission of widows, who remarried, (*punarvivahitalu*) in to it, their being allowed to attend its programmes and conferences, and whether the *punarvivahitalu* could be accorded the status of *kulanganas*. It was the only women's organisation in colonial Andhra, which generated a pitched controversy involving not only the two contending groups of women but also several others, including men. The protracted controversy, which continued for more than a year, resulted in both the groups publishing fiery articles condemning each other, making claims and counter claims over the organisations, and publishing rejoinders and polemics in contemporary journals and newspapers. There was virtually an intense war of words. The controversy was so intense and prolonged that the proprietor of the *Hindu Sundary* had to intervene and appeal to women 'to end the debate' and 'work for the promotion of [women's] education [/development] in the way they deemed fit'. As a result of the controversy, the organisation got divided, and was finally taken over by the progressive section of women.

Controversy surrounding the widow question is not new. We already know that rival camps – pro- and anti-widow remarriage groups represented by Kandukuri Vireshalingam and Kokkonda Venkataratnam [4] and others - had bitterly fought over the issue. However, it was an all men affair.[5] Now that we shall witness women fighting over this issue, it would be more refreshing. A women's organisation getting divided on this is something very significant and also surprising. Hence, a study of the organisation is very interesting. In a nutshell, the history of the *Samajamu* represents, to a large extent, the ups and downs in and the nature of the women's movement in colonial Andhra, particularly in the first two decades of the last century.

This paper has six parts. The first part makes a general survey of various women's oganisations founded in different parts of colonial Andhra. The second part narrates the story of the early years of the *Samajamu* i.e. until the eruption of the controversy. The third part discusses the captivating controversy in detail. The fourth part provides a biographical sketch of Narasamamba, the nucleus of the controversy. The fifth part focuses on the functioning of the organisation after the end of the controversy. In the sixth part, nature and limitations of the *Samajamu* are discussed in brief.

I

The efforts of the male social reformers in the nineteenth century in various parts of colonial India resulted in creating consciousness among a section of women, who, by the close of the nineteenth century, increasingly became conscious of their dismal position and the gender based inequalities in society. This gradually motivated them towards action to upgrade their deplorable conditions. They increasingly felt the need for forging bonds with other women, which ultimately resulted in their coming together for the establishment of separate women's organisations. From the dawn of the twentieth century there emerged a large number of women's organisations in different parts of the country like Bengal, Maharashtra and the United Provinces.[6] Apart from the organisations which sprang up in different regions, there emerged three national level organisations viz., the Women's Indian Association (WIA)[7], the National Council of Women in India (NCWI)[8] and the All India Women's Conference (AIWC)[9] which furthered the women's movement.

Similarly, colonial Andhra witnessed the emergence of a large number of women's organisations since the dawn of the twentieth century. The 'Brundavanapura Stree Samajamu' ('Women's Association of Brundavan'), founded in November 1902 at Machilipatnam by Orugauti Sundari Ratnamba, M.A., was the first known important women's organisation.[10] The 'Aska Stree Samajamu' was established at Aska (Ganjam District, now in Orissa) on 18 September 1902. Burra Butchi Bangaramma (hereafter Bangaramma) was its founder Secretary. The organisation showed keen interest in the promotion of girls' education.[11] Bangaramma started another organisation, the 'Bharati Samajamu', in 1904 in Vishakhapatnam. Buddhavarapu Veeralakshmamma and Bulusu Sooramma were its President and Secretary respectively.[12] The 'Satyasamvardhani Samajamu' was established on 6 January 1911 at Vijayawada. P. Lakshmikantamma was unanimously elected its President: Gundala Subhadramma and P. Tripura Sundaramma were its Secretaries. The organisation listed a total number of fifteen subjects that women discussed there.[13]

There were a large number of other organisations such as the 'Stree Sanantana Dharma Mandali' (founded in 1904-1905 at Bapatla by Eka Venkataratnamma)[14], 'Helapura Zenana Prarthana Samajamu' (24 November 1910 at Eluru by Sattiraju Shyamalamba)[15], 'Saraswati Niketanamu' (31 October 1918 at Peddapuram by Bulusu Sooramamba)[16], 'Sharada Niketanamu' (1922 at Guntur by Unnava Lakshmibayamma)[17], 'Bharata Mahila Mandali'(1928 at Vijayawada by Dr. Komarraju Atchamamba)[18], 'Stree Hitaishini Mandali' (1931 at Bapatla by Velagapudi Saraswatamma)[19], 'Stree Vidyabhivardhani Samajamu' (1938 at Narasaraopeta by Unnava Lakshmibayamma and Rayasam Ratnamma)[20], and the 'Andhra Mahila Sabha'.[21]

While such individual organisations were being established at various places, which helped create consciousness among women[22], attempts were also made towards bringing all women of Andhra under an umbrella. Thus, the 'Andhra Mahila Mahasabha' ('All Andhra Women's Organisation') came into existence: the first conference was held on 2 June 1910 at Guntur. Pulugurta Lakshminarasamma presided over it.[23] The Mahasabha regularly conducted its conferences every year in different parts of colonial Andhra.[24] The 'Andhra Rashtra Mahila Sabha' (hereafter ARMS) came into existence in 1927 as an Andhra branch of the All India Women's Conference: it regularly conducted its annual conferences at various places.[25] Such conferences helped mobilise women in the women's movement.

II

The 'Shri Vidyarthini Samajamu' came into existence on 30 January 1903 at Kakinada, an important port town.[26] Pulugurta Lakshminarasamamba (hereafter Narasamamba)[27], the founder Secretary of the organisation, provided detailed information as to how the organisation came to be established. According to her, when the famous Bhandaru Atchamamba[28] (henceforth Atchamamba) arrived in the town, a few women were invited to assemble at the residence of Narasamamba 'to felicitate and listen to Atchamamba'. That was the day the organisation came into existence. Upon the suggestion of Atchamamba, the enthused women conducted two more meetings: one on 31 January, and the other on 1 February.[29] From then on about 30 women regularly assembled on Fridays at the residence of Narasamamba. Thus, by the end of the year 1903, sixty meetings were held.[30] Each meeting began and ended with prayers. A few women such as Narasamamba, Balantrapu Sheshamma and Devaguptapu Mahalakshmamma delivered lectures. Issues such as fidelity ('*paativratyamu*'), friendship [among women] ('*snehamu*'), patience ('*orpu*'), courage ('*dhyryasthyryamulu*'), creation of God ('*eshwarasrishti*'), reading journals and newspapers ('*patrika prashamsa*') etc. constituted the themes of discussions. Inculcation of moral values among women and their good conduct were emphasised. A few meetings ended only with the reading of 'good books' ('S*adgrandha kalakshepamulu*') and singing auspicious hymns ('*mangalamulu*'). It is interesting to note that 'notices' were sent inviting women to attend the meetings.

The first annual celebration of the *Samajamu* was held in (probably) February 1904: Balantrapu Sheshamma presided over it. Narasamamba was happy to observe that the organisation gradually attracted many women: even the elderly/old women, who, earlier, had held the view that attending such meetings was 'wrong', and hence objected to their daughters and daughters-in-law going there, gradually realised the significance of attending such organisations, and themselves started attending the meetings. This, Narasamamba felt, was a 'good sign, which indicated that the *Samajamu* would register progress in future'.[31]

The organisation seems to have functioned well for a few a years. But it became defunct later only to be revived on 8 April 1910 (i.e. on '*Soumyanama Samvatsara Phalguna Bahula Trayodashi Shukravaramu*') with Narasamamba as the president. Balantrapu Sheshamma and Damerla Sitamma became its secretaries. The latter discharged the functions of Treasurer also.[32] Weekly meetings were conducted at the residence of Attota Lakshinarasimham. 'Promoting education among all the Telugu [read Hindu] women', 'raising their moral standards', and thus, 'making them useful to society and country' were its chief objectives. To achieve this goal, a five fold strategy was designed. It was as under:[33]

1. Enrolling all respectable and caste Hindu women ('*Hindu Kulastreelanellara*') as members of the organisaton and conducting weekly meetings. The meetings were to be held between 1-4 p.m. every Friday.
2. Mobilising funds for the organisation by way of collecting donation [and thus strengthening it economically].
3. Maintaining a [good] library, procuring books and making it useful not only to the members of the organisation but also to all women of the town.
4. Mobilising funds from among the concerned for the establishment of a Girls' School where the widows ('*Vitantu Sodarimanulu*'), girls ('*Kanyamanulu*') and the *Zenana* women would be enrolled. Special attention would be paid to the widows, who would be instructed well in '*Vyragyamu*' (freedom from passion or worldly attachments). They would be trained in to becoming women with 'noble character'. The girls would be specially trained in music, painting and other fine arts, which were 'in extinction', but were 'most essential' for Hindu women.

5. Establishing girls' schools and women's organisations in the neighbouring towns and villages, and encouraging others in that direction.

Thus, the organisation's vision for future programme of action was crystal clear. Matters went on well for a year after its revival. The organisation conducted the second conference of the Andhra Mahila Mahasabha on 28, 29 April 1911 at Kakinada in combination with the annual function of the *Samajamu*, which was held on 30. It was here that the differences broke out between Narasamamba, the president of the *Samajamu*, and its secretaries - Balantrapu Sheshamma and Damerla Sitamma - leading to a protracted and fiery controversy, and the consequent division of the organisation. Each group, claiming legitimacy over the organisation, put forward its arguments that are very interesting. Many others joined the contending groups, which resulted in the proliferation of articles in the contemporary press. The pages of the various newspapers and journals virtually turned into battlefields, where a severe war of words was intensely waged.

III

Controversy raged on the issue of the presence of the remarried women ('*punarvivahitalu*') in the conference, and also on the question whether the *punarvivahitalu* could be invited there. It culminated into arguing whether they could be treated as '*kulanganas*' (respectable / chaste women). The group headed by Narasamamba maintained that widows, who remarried, could and should never be accorded the status of '*kulanganas*'. But the other group contradicted this. This difference of opinion resulted in the expulsion of the secretaries - Balantrapu Sheshamma and Damerla Sitamma - from the organisation. With this the debate got further intensified and each of the groups claimed legitimacy over the organisation. Each group had an interesting story to narrate to us. Let us listen to the conservative group first.

The charge levelled by the conservative group[34] against the secretaries was that the latter 'transgressed the rules and regulations of the organisation'. They complained that the secretaries 'dared' bring the '*punarvivahitalu*' to the meetings of the organisation, particularly to its annual celebrations, and the second conference of the Andhra Mahila Mahasabha, which was 'against the norms of the organisation': by doing so, the secretaries 'caused displeasure not only among the members of the organisation but also the women of the town'. It was further complained that the secretaries did not stop there: they 'continued to bring the remarried women even after the annual function of the organisation' was over. As a result, they said, 'many women stopped attending the regular meetings of the *Samajamu* leading to its deterioration'. The conservative group charged that the 'divisive activities' of the secretaries became a 'hindrance' in the progress of the organisation affecting the 'educational advancement of sisters [women]'. This, they argued, they 'could not tolerate', and hence, conducted a meeting on the afternoon of 2 July (1911) at the residence of Narasamamba in Jagannathapuram, where it was decided to 'remove those members, who violated the rules and regulations of the organisation'. Also it was decided to shift the venue of meetings and the library to the residence of Narasamamba. The conservatives appealed to concerned men and women to observe that Damerla Sitamma and Balantrapu Sheshamma were no longer the secretaries of the organisation. They notified the change in address and requested that all further correspondence be made in the name of Narasamamba until a new secretary was elected. They appealed to concerned people to send their contributions on the changed address.[35]

The other group of women, whom we call the 'progressive group', given their stand on the question of widows, headed by the 'expelled' secretaries, presented an altogether different story.[36] The 'expelled' secretaries wrote that the writings of Narasamamba and the 'newly nominated E.C. members' (whose note appeared in the 7 July 1911 issue of the *Krishna Patrika*,

p. 9) regarding the organisation were not only 'strange' but also 'very saddening'. They maintained that the charge that they had transgressed the rules and regulations of the organisation was a mere 'wild allegation'. 'Had it been so, the [other] members themselves would have removed us', they stated. They went further stating that in fact, 'the story was the other way round: Sri Narasamamba herself deserted the organisation; this indicated who was actually going against the norms of the organisation'. They complained that Narasamamba did not attend any meeting of the organisation after the conference of the Andhra Mahila Mahasabha despite being repeatedly requested by them [secretaries], and also a few other members of the organisation. 'This made it very clear as to how concerned she was about the development of the organisation', they remarked sarcastically. Complaining further they said that Narasamamba never discussed the matter of shifting the venue and the library with the members of the organisation. 'The president did not have any right to take a unilateral decision either to remove the secretaries or to change the venue of the organisation without the consent of the members', they stressed. Aghast at her act, they said that 'they could not understand as to who gave her the right to do what she did'.

According to the 'progressive' group of women, a letter, signed by 13 members, was sent to Narasamamba on 1 July, 1911 requesting her to convene the Executive Committee meeting. But she neither replied to the letter nor came there. Moreover, invitation cards printed in her name reached them at about 1 p.m. on 2 July: the cards contained the information that 'the venue of the organisation was shifted to Jagannathapuram' [i.e. Narasamamba's residence], on the ground that the meetings at the earlier venue were 'conducted in violation of the norms of the organisation'. Also it was mentioned that 'widows, who remarried, would not be admitted into the organisation' ('*punarvivahital indunjerchukonbadaru*'). 'With this', the progressives said, 'they came to a conclusion that she [Narasamamba] was not going to attend the proposed meeting'. Hence, they conducted a meeting on 2 July, which was presided over by Duggirala Ramanamma. Decision was taken to replace Narasamamba with Kallepalle Venkata Ramanamma[37] as the president. Damerla Sitamma and Balantrapu Sheshamma were elected secretaries for a period of one year. Five new members were inducted as decision was taken to increase the number of members to fifteen. Attota Sehshamma was assigned the responsibility of looking after the library. They appealed to concerned people, particularly donors in various ways, not to be misled by Narasamamba's words and send their donations, and books and journals on the original address (at the residence of Attota Lakshinarasimham) in the name of Balantrapu Sheshamma and Damerla Sitamma.

The above narrative makes it clear to us that women fought intensely claiming legitimacy over the organisation. But a pitched war of words was waged on the issue - the issue of widow remarriage - that sparked off the controversy. Now several people joined the debate. Though there were many who questioned Narasamamba, owing to constraints of space, we discuss only a few, who flayed Narasamamba. She, in turn, fell heavily upon them roaring like a lioness. However, the number of people who wrote in support of her was far less compared to the number of those who came in support of the 'progressive' group. In the foregoing pages we find Narasamamba fighting a losing battle – a battle fought so bravely exhibiting expertise at language, rhetoric, wit, scholarship, sarcasm, captivating logic etc. – all alone. We cannot but appreciate her courage of conviction to defend her, of course, conservative point.

The *Andhra Patrika*[38] commented that the naming of the state level women's conference – 'Andhra Mahila Mahasabha' - was not justified given Narasamamba's stand on the issue of widows, who remarried. It said that 'going by its name, one would assume that the Mahasabha was open to all Andhra women, where they could go and also deliver lectures'. But Narasamamba had objected to the coming of the remarried women, and also the Andhra Christian [and Muslim] women. Hence, its name should not have been as it was. Rather, the *Andhra Patrika* remarked sarcastically that it should have been named as '*Punarvivahitastree Nishedha Andhra Brahmana Stree Sabha*' ('An Andhra Brahmin Women's Conference, where the remarried women and women of other castes were unwelcome').[39] Many others raised objections regarding the phrase '*jaaturvarnyamulaloni kulanganalu*' ('the respectable women of the four *varnas*'), which appeared in the invitation letters of the Andhra Mahila Mahasabha:[40] it was mentioned in the invitation letters[41] that [only] all the 'Andhra *kulangana* women belonging to the four varnas' were welcome to attend the conference. Now the debate shifted to arguing as to who could be called 'kulanganas' ('respectable women'), and whether the *punarvivahita* women [widows, who remarried], could fall in that category. Narasamamba was of the view that the term 'kulangana' did not include the *punarvivahitas*. Let us see how Narasamamba built her case to defend her point.

The characteristic feature of Narasamamba's writings/ rejoinders was that she wrote very lengthy articles, which, sometimes, surprisingly ran into about nineteen pages![42] Her writings were captivating for they were studded with stunning logic and exhibited her scholarship of the various Shastras, full of wit and humour, embellished with proverbs adding special effect to the content, and were highly polemical. In a nutshell, they were simply assailing her. She boldly faced the arrows of criticism raining from all the four corners.

Bitterly attacking the editor of the *Andhra Patrika*, who found fault with the naming of the Mahasabha, she said that such a criticism only exposed the 'jealousy in the minds of our highly scholarly brothers'. She wondered that she could not understand how a conference that was attended by Brahmin, Vyshya and Shudra women could be called a 'Brahmin's Women's Conference'. Countering the charge that she did not invite Christian [and Muslim] women, she said that 'Andhras meant only the Hindus living in the Andhra/Telugu country and not the others like Christians [and Muslims]'. Directly attacking on the name of the *Andhra Patrika*, an irritated Narasamamba argued that if the name, Andhra Mahila Mahasabha, was not justified, the name '*Andhra Patrika*' also could not be justified. She built a stunning logic to justify her arguments.[43] Pouring sarcasm she remarked that, in fact, the '*Andhra Patrika*' deserved to be named as '*angleyabhashasamskara sankalita sanghasams karapriyam-rutanjanapatrika*' ('A beloved paper published with the profit of a pain balm, claiming to be mixed in nectar, and is striving for social reform having been influenced by English language and culture').[44]

She dwelt at length on the issue of '*kulanganas*'. It was her firm stand that widows, who remarried ('*punarvivahitalu*'), could not come under the category of '*kulanganalu*'. She said that the pro-widow remarriage reformers cited the example of Damayanti's second '*swayamvara'* to defend their point. Citing the same quotations, which the social reformers like Kandukuri Vireshalingam and others used for defending their point, she pointed out that 'even if the *shastras* did not ban widow remarriage, they certainly did not treat it without contempt'. It was also her argument that the *shastras* agreed to the remarriage only of the 'ordinary women', not the '*kulanganas*'. Citing a quotation from the *Manusmriti*, which, she said, the pro-widow remarriage people used for arguing their case, she remarked that it did not approve of the remarriage of a *saadhvi* (chaste woman/wife). According to her, 'different *shastras* expressed different views regarding the issue: they contained both good and bad things, and all the things present in them could not be treated as good'! Hence, 'even if the *shastras* sanctioned remarriage for widows, it could/should not be practised by the *kulanganas*'. She further said that a 'widow's duty was to observe celibacy': remarriage amounted to 'prostitution'. According to her, the *shastras* reverberated that 'a *kulangana* had only one husband, whether dead or alive: his status of being husband did not disappear with death'.[45]

Holding that widow remarriage would 'taint the purity and glory of the Hindu country, which rested on its unmatched source of fidelity' ('*nirupamana paativratyamu*'), she questioned why the same men who bitterly attacked her spared Bangaramma, who expressed similar views on the issue. Attacking the pro-widow remarriage people as 'experts in creating nuisance', she sarcastically said that 'if the *saadhvimanis* (jewels among chaste women) like Sita, Savitri, Damayanti, Chandramati, Shakuntala, Ahalyabai etc., who brought glory and purity to 'our Hindu *deshamu*', came to Kakinada, the pro-widow remarriage men would blame even them saying that the former beat their husbands on their backs: 'there was no doubt about it'. *They were definitely such scoundrels!* (emphasis mine).[46]

Vituperating those, who, according to her, 'alleged' that she did not tolerate the widows who remarried ('*punarvivahitalu*'), she said that it was their '*kallabollipaluku*' (a wild lie). She accepted it as true that she had invited only the *kulanganas*. Explaining her act she maintained that she objected to *punarvivahita* women coming to the conference keeping in view the 'educational advancement' of the members of the organisation. According to her, the '*sumangali*' (a woman with a living husband) women did not like the presence of the '*punarvivahitalu*' in their gatherings. 'If ever a widow, who remarried, chanced to come, the *sumangali* women were aghast, looked at each other's face, got agitated thinking that attempts were being made to defile them by joining them with the *punarvivahitas*; a few of them suddenly left the venue, thought that they should not have come there, and decided never to come again'. Further, Narasamamba referred to the fear prevailing among these women (Sumangalis) that 'women's organisations were established for conducting widow remarriages, and also mixing us [the '*sumangalis*'] with them [*punarvivahitalu*]...'[47] Thus, she justified her stand.

On the issues of the removal of the secretaries, she said that 'it was the norm of the organisation to remove those who went against the established traditions ('*sadacharamu*' and '*saddharmamu*'). Also she said that 'there was no use working for the organisation transgressing its very rules and regulations and the traditions of society: it was because of this belief that she invited only the *kulanganas*, and not because of her intolerance for the widows who remarried'.[48]

She was sad that 'though she had been wholeheartedly accepting that she sent invitations only to the *kulanganas,* a few men, who, in fact, themselves had secretly sent invitations to their people [*punarvivahitalu*], alleged that she had invited the *punarvivahitalu* but did not accept it'. According to her, 'this they [pro-widow remarriage people] did only to create false stories that she did not tolerate remarried women'. A frustrated Narasamamba questioned: 'what would happen with this? Can hot water burn a house?' She further wrote that the pro-widow remarriage people could manage to bring a *punarvivahita* to the conference 'with great difficulty'. But 'when she actually arrived there, they simply vanished without bothering about providing her hospitality'. She claimed that 'she was the one who looked after her'. 'This indicated', she remarked sarcastically, 'as to who really could not tolerate the widows, who remarried'. Justifying whatever she wrote, she said that it was not her intention 'to degrade the *punarvivahita* sisters'. She emphasised that 'she did not have either any liking or disliking for the widows, [who remarried]. When we wanted to work for the welfare of the country and the betterment of society, we needed to follow/observe its customs and traditions, and should not transgress them'. Thus, she concluded by making a humble appeal to 'her brothers and sisters' not to indulge in nefarious writings and malign her image.[49]

The above writing generated further controversy. Bangaramma, writing in the 25 August 1911 issue of the *Krishna Patrika* (p. 4)[50], responded that 'one could not be called a *kulata* (an adulteress/fallen woman) how many ever times one married'. Bangaramma further wrote that 'it was undesirable to have contempt for a woman, who did not have only one husband'. Narasamamba was aghast to learn such views. She lamented that 'bad times had fallen on the virtuous land, the Aryavarta'. For her, 'it was a matter of great sorrow for women themselves held such strange views ('*viparita dharmamulu*'), which were bound to uproot the *pativratya dharma* of fellow women'. Narasamamba further observed that 'if we went by the words of Bangaramma, even the prostitutes would have to be treated as *kulanganas*'.[51] An angry Narasamamba warned the pro-widow remarriage people saying:

> O pro-widow remarriage brothers and sisters! Do not try to cheat the world for the purpose of establishing your prodigious *Dharma*s. Do not bring ill-fame to the word reform by drowning those, who do not agree with your views, in the mire of blame, and by pouring your rebuking scholarship on them! ...Blaming is not the way of doing any good. Following ones duties and also allowing the others to follow their duties alone would bring good to the world...[52].

Narasamamba attracted the sharpest and bitterest criticism from Kotikalapudi Sitamma (hereafter Sitamma)[53], who virtually bashed her. Sitamma, in her five-page length article, reviled Narasamamba.[54] Sitamma complained that 'though she [Narasamamba] established herself as a scholar, she failed to recognise the changes taking place in society, and struggled hard to perpetuate the blindly practised traditional evils'. Sitamma observed that with her practice Narasamamba made it clear to her that 'there was no connection between mere scholarship and general / practical knowledge of the world'. She sarcastically remarked that Narasamamba 'ended up making a monkey, while intending to portray a gentleman' i.e. her efforts resulted in creating just the opposite of what she had actually intended. Narasamamba's orthodox views and authoritarian attitude were held responsible for such a situation. They fetched her [Narasamamba] 'so much of condemnation' from various quarters. Suggesting Narasamamba, Sitamma said that 'it was not befitting a woman to blame and [irrationally] fight the editors [reform-oriented men], who stood by women, with bitter and unpleasant words and abominable examples'. Sitamma charged that 'she [Narasamamba] tried to hide her own faults: her behaviour brought ill fame to the entire woman folk for which one was to be ashamed off.'

She criticised that 'Narasamamba committed every mistake in conducting the Andhra Mahila Mahasabha right from the printing of the invitation cards'. She [Narasamamba] 'imposed several restrictions, pressurised the women, who attended the conference, to dance to her tunes, and did not allow them to express their views freely and frankly'. Sitamma further said that if people understood that the term *'kulangana'* did not include the *punarvivahita*s, it was justified given Narasamamba's views on the issue of widow remarriage. To substantiate her stand, Sitamma reminded Narasamamba of her speech delivered at Bandar (Machilipatnam), where the latter had opposed widow remarriage. Brushing aside Narasamamba's claims that she had not invited the *punarvivahita*s, and that a few pro-widow remarriage people secretly sent invitations to them in her name, Sitamma questioned 'why she had not taken proper care to avoid any such alleged misuse of the invitation cards printed in her name'. Condemning that 'there were several liars like her [Narasamamba] in the world', Sitamma ridiculed that 'there was no consistency in what she [Narasamamba] said and did', and 'she had many faults piled up in her'. Sitamma even rebuked her to be a 'woman of blemished character' (*'kalankavartanamu'*). She wondered as to how a learned lady of Narasamamba's stature 'behaved just like an ordinary woman', and there was 'so much contradiction in her'. Also Sitamma said that the examples that Narasamamba provided opposing widow remarriage were 'extremely ridiculous' and 'caused wild laughter'. Narasamamba's 'arrogant' writings only proved her to be a 'foolish woman' (*'alpagna'*) and 'did and could not have any adverse effect', on the widow remarriage movement'. She reminded Narasamamba that 'it was the responsibility of the wise to distinguish the good from bad, and uphold the former: to do that there was no need to read many *shastra*s; mere common sense was enough'. She suggested Narasamamba 'not to indulge in giving futile replies anymore' and 'behave wisely'.

There were several others, who criticised Narasamamba. The editor of the journal, *Deshamata*,[55] Sattiraju Shyamalamba,[56] Bangaramma,[57] Madabhooshi Choodamma were a few among them. While Narasamamba was being attacked from all sides, a certain 'Hitavadi' (pseudonym, meaning 'well-wisher') argued on her side. Madabhooshi Choodamma exposed the hollowness in the arguments and allegations of 'Hitavadi'.[58] As the debate seemed to continue further, Sattiraju Sitaramaiah, the proprietor [patrikaadhipati] of *Hindu Sundary*, intervened and suggested to women to 'end the debate and work for the improvement of women's education in the way each group deemed fit'.[59]

The controversy attests the deeply divided opinion among women on one of the crucial issues of social reform i.e. widow remarriage. It indicates that not all educated women were in favour of it: a few of them, as we have seen, were bitterly opposed to it. Also it informs us that the remarriage, though removed a few of the difficulties of widows immediately, lowered their social status. They were treated contemptuously and were largely unwelcome. Their very association, let alone close company, was treated as blemishing. They were blamed as the ones, who tarnished the pure image of a Hindu woman. Also they were condemned as characterless women and denied any respect. Widows, who remarried, had to suffer from the want of social acceptability/respectability. In a nutshell, this indicates the widespread prejudice against a *punarvivahita*. However, the ignominious defeat of the 'conservative' group in the hands of the progressive section of women, who were supported by many, indicates that the wind was blowing in favour of reform.

It is important to learn that all this happened when Vireshalingam was alive i.e. towards the end of his life (he passed away in 1919). But it appears that he did not respond to this. Given the fact that he had encountered Narasamamba about five years before the eruption of the present controversy (we shall see this in the following section) his silence is really a great puzzle.

IVs

Now let us know a few more details of Narasamamba, who generated such a heated controversy. Narasamamba, who lived for about 80 years, was born in 1878 in a family of scholars. Chintalapudi Nilachalam and Aggamamba were her parents. She was the disciple and follower of Kashibhatta Brahmaiah Shastry[60], a conservative per excellence, and an arch rival of Vireshalingam in reform matters. Though she did not receive any formal education, she acquired amazing scholarship: her family's scholastic pedigree helped her in this. A prolific writer, she was hardly fifteen years old when she authored a tract on women's education, the *Mahilakalabodhini*, in *Kavya* style. A polyglot, she had good command of Hindi and Bangla: she translated a few works from those languages into Telugu. She has a large number of works to her credit. They include *Yogeeshwari* (two volumes), *Vaamana Puranamu*, *Mangalaharatula Shatakamu*, *Subhadra*, *Kamalaakumari*, *Lokabandhavi*, *Kaamamanjari*, *Stree Nitigitamulu*, *Sati Dharmamulu*, *Niti Padamulu* etc. Apart from these books she published extensively in the contemporary journals such as the *Telugu Zenana* and *Hindu Sundary*. She was not only a scholar but also an activist. She started the 'Shri Vidyarthini Samajamu' at Kakinada. As we have already seen she was instrumental in convening the first all Andhra women's conference in 1910, which she also presided over. She commanded enormous respect from her contemporaries.[61]

More importantly, she edited one of the earliest women's journals, the *Savitri*.[62] Narasamamba used it as a platform for accommodating, advocating and propagating conservative ideology, and fighting social reform. Narasamamba wanted to cast women in the mould of traditional *pativrata*s. Hence, writings on this theme, mostly in verse form, inundated the *Savitri*. '*Niti Padamulu*'[63] ('Verses on Mortality'), '*Sati*

Dharmamulu'[64] ('Duties of a Virtuous Woman/Wife'), '*Stree Niti Dipika*'[65] ('A Guide to Women's Morality'), '*Stree Niti Ratnavali*'[66] ('A String of Gems on Women's Morality'), and '*Stree Niti Gitamulu*'[67] ('Hymns on Women's Morality') etc. were published. A few essays such as '*Sadvartanamu*'[68] ('Good Conduct') and '*Pativratyamu*'[69], which emphasised morality and chastity, appeared in prose form also. All these writings had a single point agenda of casting women in the mould of the *pativrata*s by inculcating in them morality, good conduct, devotion to husband, humility, submission and self-sacrifice. *Pativratyamu* was propagated as 'the paragon quality of a woman', which ensured her 'wellbeing in life here and hereafter'[70], and good conduct 'the invaluable ornament'.[71] They stressed that 'all wishes of a woman who observed *pativratyam* would be fulfilled'. But how did one prove to be a *pativrata*? This was possible only through ensuring complete submission to husband! They offered certain do's and don'ts in that noble journey! Women were threatened that their life without a husband was 'like a steamer boat without a languor'.[72] *Sadvartanamu* ('Good Conduct/Proper Behaviour'), which brought 'reputation' and made a person live [even after death] 'until the universe lasted', was seen as the 'most invaluable embellishment' to the character of a woman, and was held to be more 'essential' for women than men.[73] Women's education was sought for it was held to be a potential instrument that ensured all the qualities of a *Pativrata* among women.[74]

Narasamamba was a staunch advocate of child marriages, and a bitter critic of the very idea of widow remarriages. Though she recognised that the practice of child marriage was against the *Dharmashastras*, she still held it to be a 'noble' practice, which 'saved the noble virtue of *Pativratyam*, the source of India's ('*Hindu Deshsmu*') honour and reputation': child marriages contained and nipped women's evil thoughts in the bud, lest they flowed in 'wrong directions' causing damage to women's chastity. She quoted from several English works, which praised such marriages. According to her, it was good to marry off girls 'before [the evil idea of] love sprouted in them'. Hence, she angrily remarked that the modern social reformers, 'who were hell-bent on spoiling the world acclaimed *Hindu Dharma*', should note that fact and 'stop creating nuisance'.[75] She did not even hesitate to endorse the practice of *Sati*.[76]

Such was the magnitude of conservatism in Narasamamba. This, not unnaturally, dragged her in to repeated controversies. The controversy that we have discussed so far is only her second innings: she started playing her first innings by taking cudgels with Kandukuri Vireshalingam, with whom she was involved in a virtually protracted intellectual battle for more than a year.

Manyam Subbamma, a Vyshya woman, published the '*Sati Dharma Prakashika*' ('Illuminator of the *Sati Dharma*s'), in the August 1904 issue of *Savtri*, in which, she hailed the *Manusmriti*, and justified the servile position of women. To substantiate her stand she extensively quoted from the *Manusmriti*, the *Veda*s, several *Shloka*s, and also a few English works.[77] The amazing scholarship that she exhibited in it stunned Vireshalingam: he could not believe that a woman, particularly a Vysya woman, could write so incredibly well. His doubts hardened and he became convinced that in fact a Brahmin man ['*Bramhigadu*'; a derogatory expression meaning 'a Bramhin fellow'] wrote it with the name of Manyam Subbamma. What alarmed Vireshalingam more was not the incredible scholarship exhibited in it, but the pernicious content it contained: he thought that it would have 'disastrous effects on women's development'. Hence, he published a burlesque, the 'Savitri Satyavati Sambhashanamu - Stree Vidya', in the October 1904 issue of the *Telugu Zenana*, in which, he ridiculed and reviled Manyam Subbama by adding the suffix - '*Shastri*' - to her name.[78] The dialogue contained many derisive remarks.[79]

Deeply disturbed by this, Narasamamba paid him in the same coin by publishing a rejoinder, the 'Kamala Vimala Samvadamu – Stree Vidya' ('Dialogue between Kamala and Vimala on Women's Education'), in which, she mounted a piercing attack on Vireshalingam. Of the two characters - Kamala and Vimala – the former voiced the views of Narasamamba. Kamala charged that 'out of sheer jealousy', the 'self styled favourites of women's education', in fact, 'worked against it'. To Vimala's question as to 'why they were jealous of women', Kamala replied that 'they [the male reformers, particularly Vireshalingam] were jealous because women did not hold the same views as theirs, did not praise them, did not follow their guidelines and were going in their own way by using their own brains'; they discouraged women by 'unleashing vile criticism' on women's writings. Also she said that as women moved forward, these 'jealous' men 'cruelly ridiculed and humiliated' them. Further, she did not spare Venkata Shivudu (though his name is not directly mentioned) for publishing Vireshalingam's article in his journal [i.e. *Telugu Zenana*]. Addressing Venkata Shivudu, she sarcastically remarked: 'how great is your love for women's education! Good! Good'.[80]

Manyam Subbamma, whose piece was the root of the controversy, also published a rejoinder. In her perforating piece, 'Oka Prakatanamu - Oka Manavi' ('An Announcement and an Appeal'), she expressed her anger in devastating terms and sharp tone. Abusing Vireshalingam in the severest possible terms, she challenged that 'she was ready to face any test to establish her scholarship.'[81] Enraged at this, Vireshalingam mentioned that he 'thought it to be below his dignity to react to such rebukes of the unwise', and ignored it. But his 'opponents took it to be his incompetence' and ridiculed him in the *Aryamatabodhini*. This provoked him to publish a reply.[82] Reacting to the criticism of Narasamamba, he wrote that 'he began working for the cause of women even before she had been born'. Condemning her, he remarked that 'she was a damn conservative who was averse to any progress.' Accepting the challenge of Manyam Subbamma, who became ready 'to face any test', he asked the editor of *Savitri* [i.e. Narasamamba] to arrange for it. He announced that 'he would go there wherever the test was conducted, and if she [Manyam Subbamma] proved her scholarship, he would change his views and tender a public apology through an announcement in the journal'. He urged that 'a meeting for the test be conducted sooner'.[83] But we do not know whether any such test was conducted.[84]

Whatever may have happened, the foregoing discussion establishes Narasamamba as a conservative per excellence, who, with her conservative conviction to counter social reform, boldly confronted a giant figure of Vireshalingam's stature. When the tides of social reform had been rising, through her writings, and particularly her mouthpiece, *Savitri*, which provided a platform to the anti-reform voices, Narasamamba courageously chose to check them in vain.

V

Now let see what happened after the controversy came to a halt. After the controversy ended, the *Samajamu* came to be owned with the 'progressive' group of women. It was registered in their name on 27 September 1911 with clearly laid down rules and regulations regarding the conduct of the organisation.[85] Kallepalle Venkata Ramanamma was elected president; Burra Venkata Subbamma, Balantrapu Sheshamma and Damerla Sitamma were elected Vice-president and Secretaries respectively. There were 11 other members.[86] Kallepalle Venkata Ramanamma served in the capacity of president till 1916:[87] Nalam Raghavamma became president later.[88] During the 1940s and after Koka Krishnavenamma and Vemuganti Papayamma looked after the *Samajamu*. It appears that the number of its donor members did not exceed 50 till 1920.[89] Members contributed *Anna*s Eight to Re. 1 per month.[90] That the *Samajamu* managed to erect its own building attests that it enjoyed considerable financial strength. The *Samajamu* appears to have continued well beyond the 1950s.

The organisation was remarkable for publishing one of the most important women's journals, the *Hindu Sundary,* which was the first women's journal to be edited by women. Started by a man, Sattiraju Sitaramaiah, in April 1902, it continued to be published till about 1960 i.e. for more than half-a-century.[91] Since March 1913, the *Samajamu* managed the journal.[92] Since June 1913 responsible women of the *Samajamu* i.e. Madabhooshi Choodamma and Kallepalle Venkata Ramanamma, became its editors, and Balantrapu Sheshamma, its Manager, and the journal came to be published from Kakinada.[93] During the 1940s Balantrapu Sheshamma became its editor: Vemuganti Papayamma became the honorary secretary. *Hindu Sundary* could be said to be the mouthpiece of the *Samajamu*.

The journal was an eloquent advocate of the women's cause: it regularly published articles on the need for women's education, evil effects of child marriages and the miserable plight of widows. The distinguishing feature of the journal was that it exhibited voluminous sensitivity towards the poignant situation of widows. Almost every issue contained articles on widows. Forcible tonsuring of widows was seen as the most brutal crime perpetrated on the widows: article after article condemned it in unequivocal terms. Terming it as a 'horrendous barbaric practice', Mosalikanti Ramabayamma, its first woman editor, launched a signature campaign against it.[94] *Hindu Sundary* published a large number of articles, which advocated widow remarriages.[95] It undertook a sustained campaign against child marriages[96], and paid greater attention to the promotion of women's education.[97] Apart from these, it published with prominence detailed accounts of various women's organisations, and full-length speeches of women delivered there.[98] Since these organisations were a living testimony to women's activism, such details are of immense help to us to construct the history of women's movement in colonial Andhra. Thus, it provides vast information, which helps us understand women's views on various issues. Transforming women into accomplished writers was another outstanding contribution of the journal.[99]

Though the journal suffered from a few limitations,[100] its contribution to the women's movement in colonial Andhra was significant. At a time when the avenues for women's public self-expression were so extremely limited, it provided a platform for women to express themselves freely. That it was entirely managed by women and sustained for more than half a century, despite pressing difficulties, speaks volumes of the enthusiasm and commitment of women associated with the *Samajamu* to maintain and sustain their movement. Thus, the journal contributed in its way for the creation of a 'new woman' in colonial Andhra.

The *Samajamu* took initiative and lead in convening the state-level women's conferences (Andhra Mahila Mahasabhas), which provided a wider platform for women of the entire Andhra region: women assembled here, shared their views, discussed and debated, delivered lectures and passed resolutions on various issues that concerned them.[101] The organisation's involvement in the state level conferences appeared so monopolising to others that they questioned its hegemony.[102] The organisation was so active and thoroughly engaged in furthering the cause of women that a few criticised the women associated with it as being 'too independent', and alleged that they were 'rejecting their husbands'.[103]

According to its stated objectives, the *Samajamu* started a women's/girls' school, the 'Shri Mahila Vidyalayamu',[104] and a library, the 'Rajyalakshmi Pustaka Bhandagaramu'.[105] The library was immensely useful not only to the members of the organisation but also to the women of the town.

VI

Now let us assess the nature, the extent of success, and the limitations of the *Samajamu*. It was the first most important women's organisation founded in colonial Andhra, the second being the 'Andhra Mahila Sabha' of Durgabai Deshmukh. It was also the first organisation, which undertook multiple activities such as publishing a journal, convening the state-level women's conferences and running a school. Inspired, founded and successfully managed exclusively by women, the organisation continued to function well beyond the 1950s: this distinguishes it from all other women's organisations[106] except the 'Andhra Mahila Sabha'. It was with the establishment of the *Samajamu* that the women's organisations in colonial Andhra began to acquire a definite shape.

As an ardent advocate of women's cause it undertook a sustained campaign in favour of women's education, and against child marriages and enforced widowhood. Given the context it was fairly progressive: while many women's organisations were hesitant to discuss the issue of widow remarriages, it boldly advocated the same. The *Samajamu* undertook a rigorous campaign in favour of widow remarriage through its mouthpiece, the *Hindu Sundary*.

The organisation created a public space for women, however limited it was. It served as a training ground for women into becoming public speakers and organisers, who boldly advocated their cause: at least a few of them got transformed into awesome orators. By taking initiative in conducting the All Andhra Women's Conferences, it brought all women of Andhra on a single platform.

The organisation was overtly upper-caste in character. The very first rule of the organisation, even after it was taken over by the 'progressives', barred women of the lowered castes such as the 'Mala' and 'Madiga' – the 'untouchable' castes of Andhra Pradesh - not only from becoming its members but also attending its meetings.[107] The various issues that it advocated established its middle class and upper caste orientation. Hence, the sisterhood that it envisioned inevitably became a fractured sisterhood. This was certainly a serious limitation of the organisation.

In a context when the avenues for women's public self-expression were so extremely limited, the organisation opened up the same for them. By bringing women together it helped them forge the bond of sisterhood, though a fractured sisterhood, and ventilate their collective aspirations. Rather than limiting itself to the mere convening of meetings and anniversaries, as was the case with several other contemporary women's organisations, it took certain concrete steps like publishing a journal, running a school, maintaining a library etc. It means to say that it did not reduce itself to be a mere rhetorical sisters' group. It successfully sensitised women on their issues and raised their level of consciousness. It was this consciousness that helped women to assess their actual condition in society and propelled them towards upgrading themselves. This also helped women in positively responding to the call of the freedom movement of the country. However, with its sustained campaign on the women's issues, the organisation did not allow the freedom movement to dominate and dilute the women's movement. This is a remarkable aspect of the organisation. Thus, the organisation rendered great service to women's movement in colonial Andhra. Given the context in which the *Samajamu* operated, the achievements that it registered blur its demerits and limitations.

References

* I express my deep sense of gratitude to my supervisors, Dr. Indivar Kamtekar and Dr. R. Mahalakshmi, who have shaped my academic career. I specially thank Shri Kopparthi Venkata Ramanamoorthy for his invaluable observations and suggestions on an earlier draft of this paper, and my friends Dr. G.S.S. Reddy, Dr. B.R. Prasad Reddy and Mr. S.P. Gafar for their comments.

† This is an English translation of the Telugu proverb "*Ayyavarlanu Jeyaboyina Kotiyayyenannattu*". It means getting exactly the opposite of what one actually intended to do. Kotikalapudi Sitamma, who condemned the regressive views of Pulugurta Lakshminarasamamba, the central figure in the controversy we are going to see, used it. The proverb is full of sarcasm, extremely humiliating and summarises the whole arguments of the progressive group of women involved in the controversy. See Kotikalapudi Sitamma, 'Andhra Mahila Mahasabha Karyadarshinigaragu, Srimati Pulugurta Lakshmi narasamambagarikoka Vinnapamu' ('An Appeal to Smt.

Pulugurta Lakshminarasamamba, the Secretary of the Andhra Mahila Mahasabha'), *Hindu Sundary*, August 1911, p. 2.

1. Aparna Basu and Bharati Ray, *Women's Struggle: A History of the All India Women's Conference 1927-2002* (Second Edition), Manohar, New Delhi, 2003, p.15.
2. The nature and scope of such works is a reason for this. For example, see V. Ramakrishna, *Social Reform in Andhra (1848-1919)*, Vikas Publications, New Delhi, 1983; S. Inna Reddy, 'Social Reform Movements in Andhra (1920-1947)', Ph.D. Thesis submitted to the University of Hyderabad, 1998. One possible exception is the work of Malladi Subbamma, which focused on the contribution of women's organisations to the women's movement in Andhra. However, this being not a very systematic study does not allow us to have a comprehensive understanding of the nature and functioning of the organisations. Given the vast canvas of time on which her painting of the organisations was done, one cannot expect much. See Malladi Subbamma, *Women's Movement and Organisations: Regional Perspective (1860-1993)*, Booklinks Corporation, Hyderabad, 1994. This book, translated by M.V. Ramamurty, was originally published in Telugu, and was titled *Andhra Pradeshlo Mahilodyamam: Mahila Sanghalu (1860-1983)*, Prajaswamya Prachuranalu, Hyderbad, 1985.
3. For details of the journal, turn to part-V in this paper.
4. A distinguished scholar in Telugu and Sanskrit, Venkataratnam (1842-1915) was a lecturer in Telugu in the Presidency College, Madras. A conservative per excellence, he was the leader of the orthodox sections which opposed reforms in both Telugu language and society. A one time friend, and later an arch rival of Vireshalingam. He published the *Andhra Bhasha Sanjivani*, a monthly (started in 1871), through which he opposed reform. There was a virtual war between Vireshalingam's journal, *Vivekavardhani* (started in 1874), and the *Andhra Bhasha Sanjivani*. To ridicule the writings of Vireshalingam, Venkataratnam started another journal, the *Hasyavardhani*, and appended it to his *Andhra Bhasha Sanjivani*. To counter

the conservative propaganda of Venkataratnam, Vireshalingam started the *Hasyasanjivani*, and appended to his *Vivekavardhani*. They condemned each other through the columns of their respective journals. Opposing women's education Venkataratnam published extensively. One such piece, published in his *Hasyavardhani*, had the title, 'Women do not Deserve Education'. Venkataratnam founded the 'Andhra Bhashabhivardhani Samajam'. The British honoured him with the title *Mahamahopadhyaya*. For a brief note on Venkataratnam, see V. Ramakrishna, *Social Reform in Andhra*, op.cit., p. 215.

5. Vedam Venkataraya Shastry (1853-1929), Dasu Sriramulu (1846-1908), Kashibhatta Brahmaiah Shastry (1863-1940) were a few among the many remarkable personalities, who opposed widow remarriages. For details, see *ibid*., pp. 116-118.

6. For women's organisations in Bengal, see Bharati Ray, 'The Freedom Movement and Feminist Consciousness in Bengal, 1905-1929' in Bharati Ray ed., *From the Seams of History: Essays on Indian Women*, Oxford University Press, New Delhi, 1995, pp. 204-205. For women's organisation in Maharashtra, see Vir Bharat Talwar, 'Feminist Consciousness in Women's Journals in Hindi, 1910-20' in Kumkum Sangari, Sudesh Vaid eds., *Recasting Women : Essays in Colonial History*, Kali for Women, New Delhi, 1999 (first published 1989), p.206. For the United Provinces, see *ibid*.; see also Suruchi Thapar-Bjorkert, *Women in the Indian National Movement: Unseen Faces and Unheard Voices, 1930-42*, Sage Publications, New Delhi, 2006, pp.218-222.

7. The Women's Indian Association was formed in 1917 in Madras with the efforts of Margaret Cousins and Dorothy Jinarajadasa. Annie Besant was its first President. The most important function of the WIA was educational. Also it had been active politically since its inception: it sent a delegation to meet with the Secretary of State, Montague, in 1917, to request franchise for women. It published a monthly journal, the *Stree Dharma*. For details see Geraldine Forbes, *Women in Modern India*,

Cambridge University Press, South Asian Paperback edition, pp. 72-75.

8. The National Council of Women in India was established as a national branch of the International Council of Women. For details see ibid. pp. 75-78.

9. The All India Women's Conference was the 'most truly Indian' of the three national women's organisations. For more details see *ibid.* pp.78-83. For an in-depth study of the AIWC, see Aparna Basu, Bharati Ray, *Women's Struggle: A History of the All India Women's Conference, 1927-2002,* op.cit.

10. For more details, see Dronamraju Durgamma, 'Brundavanapura Stree Samajamu', *Hindu Sundary*, December 1906, pp. 7-10; 'Brundavanapura Stree Samajamu – Gata Samvatsara Charitramu – Secretary Riportu' ('The Women's Organisation of Brundavan – Last Year's History – Secretary's Report'), Hindu *Sundary*, December 1906, pp. 10-17; 'Brundavana Stree Samajamu', *Hindu Sundary*, May 1905, pp. 41-46.

11. For details, see Burra Butchi Bangaramma, 'Aska Hindu Stree Samajamu Prathama Samvatsarika Reportu' ('The First Annual Report of the Aska Hindu Women's Association'), *Hindu Sundary*, December 1903, p. 18. See also *Hindu Sundary*, May 1904, pp. 73-75.

12. For details, see *Vivekavati*, July 1912, pp. 301-302. *Vivekavati* was a women's monthly journal.

13. The first anniversary of the organisation was held on 6 January 1912. On the basis of this it can be said that the organisation was established in 1911. See 'Satya Samvardhani Samajamuyokka Dwiteeya Samvatsara Reportu' ('Second Annual Report of the Satya Samvardhani Samajamu'), *Hindu Sundary*, January-February 1913, pp. 9-15.

14. As its Silver Jubilee was celebrated in 1930, the year of its establishment could be taken as 1904-1905. See 'Subhashitamu', *Grihalakshmi*, (?) November 1930, pp. 820-826.

15. For more details, see Sattiraju Shyamalamba, 'Helapura Prarthana Samajamu', *Hindu Sundary*, April 1912, pp. 28-31.

16. For details, see 'Saraswati Niketana Samaja Kaarya Nivedanamu' ('A Report of the Saraswati Niketanamu'), *Anasuya*, November 1918, pp.7-8. For details on its first anniversary celebrations, see 'Muchchatalu' ('Tidings'), *Anasuya*, November-December 1919, pp. 28-30. *Anasuya* was a women's monthly.

17. It was inspired by D.K. Karve's Women's Educational Institution in Maharashtra, and the Hitakarini Samajam of Kandukuri Vireshalingam at Rajahmundry. For details, see V. Kotishwaramma, *Bharata Swatantrya Samaram–Andhra Mahilala Mahojvala Paatra*, (Telugu) (*India's Freedom Struggle - The Fantastic Role of Andhra Women*), Author, Vijayawada, January 2001, pp. 158-159. Unnava Lakshmibayamma played a significant role in the women's movement in Andhra. She was married to Unnava Lakshminarayana, one of the leading figures in the social reform as well as the freedom movement. She propagated in favour of widow remarriages and took personal care in the wellbeing of the widows: in this she reminds us of Kandukuri Rajyalakshmamma, wife of Vireshalingam. Apart from actively participating in the social reform movement, she played a crucial role in the freedom movement. During the Non-Cooperation Movement she toured all over Andhra, and inspired several ladies through her speeches towards taking part in the freedom struggle. Also she took part in the Salt Satyagraha Movement and courted six months' imprisonment: she was imprisoned in the Vellore Jail from 9-6-1930 to 8-12-1930. Again she was imprisoned in the same jail for three months for taking part in the Individual Satyagraha Movement. For more details on her, see Kanuparti Varalakshmamma, *Unnava Dampatulu* (Telugu) (*Unnava couple*), Shri Goda Granthamala, Vijayawada, 1963; V. Kotishwaramma, *Bharata Swatantrya Samaram*, op.cit., pp.157-162; Sarojini Regani ed., *Who's Who of Freedom Struggle in Andhra Pradesh*, Volume One (Three Volumes), The State Committee for the compilation of the History of the Freedom Struggle in Andhra Pradesh, Ministry of Education and Cultural Affairs, Government of Andhra Pradesh, Hyderabad, 1978, p. 244.

18. See 'Bharata Mahila Mandali, Bezawada', *Grihalakshmi,* May 1940, p. 193; Malladi Subbamma, *Andhra Pradeshlo Mahilodyamam*, *op.cit.* p. 176; for the Presidential Address of Kanuparti Varalakshmamma delivered at the thirteenth anniversary celebration of the *Mandali,* see *Grihalakshmi*, May 1941, pp. 155-158.
19. 1931 is assumed as the year of its establishment on the basis of its fourth anniversary celebrations held on 13, 14 July 1935. See 'Sabhalu-Nivedikalu: Stree Hitaishini Mandali, Bapatla', *Grihalakshmi*, September 1935, pp. 569-572. For more details see Kanuparti Varalakshmamma, 'Streela Vesangi Pathashala, Bapatla', *Grihalakshmi*, September 1941, pp. 427-428. See also Malladi Subbamma ed., *Stree Swechcha,* Mahilbhyyudaya Samstha, Hyderabad, August 2001, p. 50. For details on Malladi Subbamma's association with the organisation, and her reform activities, see *ibid.* pp. 47-76.
20. See *Andhra Mahila*, February 1946, p. 43.
21. Started under the able leadership of Gummadidala Durgabayamma, later famous as Durgabai Deshmukh, in June 1938, it has been functioning successfully till date with several branches in Andhra Pradesh and Tamil Nadu (Chennai). It had its genesis in a small children's club, 'The Little Ladies of Brindavan'. In October 1939, it was attached to the 'Andhra Mahasabha', Chennapuri, as a women's wing. The organisation with the present name came into existence as an independent women's organisation on 4 February 1942. Its proclaimed objective was to 'work for the success of the women's movement'. Women's education was given supreme importance: fine arts were emphasised. It had an industrial training wing, where women were provided training in managing the cottage industries. By starting a debating club, it encouraged women to debate on several issues, particularly those that concerned them. It started a women's monthly, the *Andhra Mahila*, which later became a fortnightly. The journal provided space for a large number of women to express themselves: compared to all other women's journal, the *Andhra Mahila* was radical. Today the organisation runs several hospitals, schools and

professional colleges, homes for the aged, the Legal Aid Centre for Women (Hyderabad), the Institute for Training and Rehabilitaticn for Rural Women (Ibrahimpatnam), Durgabai Deshmukh Vocational Training Centre, the Rehabilitation Centre for the Handicapped (Hyderabad), and the Literacy House. For a detailed account of its early history, see 'Andhra Mahila Sabha Sankshipta Charitra' ('Brief History of Andhra Mahila Sabha'), *Andhra Mahila,* February 1944, pp. 9-16. For its present activities, see *Profile of Andhra Mahila Sabha*, other details N.A. (collected from the Andhra Mahila Sabha Office, Hyderabad).

22. For a detailed discussion on the women's organisations in colonial Andhra, see S. Mahaboob Basha, 'Spreading the Fragrance of Sisterhood: Women's Organisations and Consciousness in colonial Andhra, 1902-1947', Proceedings of the Thirty Second Session of the Andhra Pradesh History Congress, Warangal, 2008, pp. 143-156.

23. The conference was held under the aegis of the 'Stree Sanatana Dharma Mandali'. See 'Andhra Mahila Mahasabha, Kakinada', *Savitri*, March 1911, p. 6.

24. The second conference was held on 28, 29 April 1911 at Kakinada. For details see 'Andhra Mahila Mahasabha, Kakinada', *Savitri*, March 1911, pp.1-8. The lectures delivered by women are published in a book form. See *Upanyasa Manjari*, Shri Savitri Mudrakshara Shala, Kakinada, 1912. This is preserved in the Gautami Library, Rajahmundry. The third conference was held on 23, 24 May 1912 at Nidudavolu. Burra Butchi Bangaramma presided over it. For more details see 'Andhra Mahila Sabha, Nidudavolu', *Hindu Sundary*, April 1912, pp. 22-25. The fourth conference was held on 23, 24 March 1913 at Bandar (Machilipatnam). Other details such as who presided over the conference, how many women attended etc. are not available. See 'Andhra Mahila Sabha', *Hindu Sundary*, January-February 1913, pp. 22-24. The fifth conference was held on 11, 12 May 1914 at Vijayawada. Kotikalapudi Sitamma presided over it. For details see 'Aidava Andhra Mahila Mahajana

Sabha', *Hindu Sundary*, May 1914, pp. 13-14. The sixth conference was held in 1915 at Vishakhapattanam. See 'Saptama Andhra Mahila Mahasabha', *Hindu Sundary*, April, 1916, p. 48. The seventh conference was held in May 1916 at Kakinada. Nadupalli Butchi Venkata- subbamma and Manuri Sitamaa acted as Secretary and Joint Secretary respectively. See *ibid*. p. 48. The eighth conference was held on 1, 2 June 1917 at Vikramapuri (Nellore) with Kashinathuni Ramabayamma acting as the General President. See 'Enimidava Andhra Mahila Sabha', *Hindu Sundary*, June 1917, pp. 2, 6. Papers presented by women were published in full in *Hindu Sundary*. For these articles see 'Ashtama Andhra Mahila Mahasabha Swagatopanyasamu' ('Welcome Address'), *Hindu Sundary*, July 1917, pp. 6-16; 'Aahvana Sanghadhyakshurali Swagatopanyasamu' ('Welcome Address by the President of the Reception Committee'), *Hindu Sundary*, June 1917, pp. 13-16; *Hindu Sundary*, August 1917, pp. 9-19.

25. Its first conference was held in 1927 at Kakinada. But the details are not available. We came to know about it from a remark made by Begum Amiruddin, who presided over the fourteenth ARMS. See *Grihalakshmi*, January 1940, p. 754. Malladi Subbamma mistook the third conference for the first. She wrote that 'the first Andhra Provincial Women's Conference was held in 1929'. This is not true. See Malladi Subbamma, *Women's Movement and Associations*, *op.cit*. p. 51. Details of the second conference are not available to us. The third conference was held in 1929 at Vijayawada. Turlapati Rajeshwaramma was the President of the reception committee. Muthulakshmi Reddy presided over it. For details see 'Andhra Mahila Sabha – Bejawada', *Grihalakshmi*, December 1929, pp. 901-908. The fourth conference was held in 1930 at Bandar (Machilipatnam). No direct reference to it is available. We get to know about this from the remarks of Kanuparti Varalakshmamma regarding the proceedings of the fifth conference. See Kanuparti Varalakshmamma, 'Gunturu Mahilasabha Visheshamulu', *Grihalakshmi*, February 1932, p. 1054. The fifth conference

was held on 21, 22 November 1931 at Gunturu. Adipudi Vasundhara Devi M.A., B.Sc., presided over it. Dr. Danamma, a Christian lady, was the President of the reception committee. Rayasam Ratnamma took initiative in getting the conference held at Gunturu. Kanuparti Varalakshmamma vividly portrayed the proceedings of the Conference. See *ibid*. pp. 1049-1055. The sixth conference was held in November 1932 at Rajamundry. Achanta Laksmidevi presided over it. See Malladi Subbamma, *Women's Movement and Associations*, op.cit. p. 52. The seventh conference was held on 4, 5 November 1933 at Eluru, West Godavari District. Muthulakshmi Reddy presided over it. Chunduri Ratnamma was the head of the reception committee. For details see 'Mahila Sabhalu', *Grihalakshmi,* December 1933, pp. 832-837. The eighth conference was held on 18 November 1934 at Madanapalli. Gummadidala Durgabayamma, later famous as Durgabai Deshmukh, presided over it. See 'Sampaadakiyamulu: Andhra Mahila Sabha', *Grihalakshmi,* December 1934, p. 767. For the resolutions discussed at this conference see 'Vaartalu – Visheshamulu: Andhra Desha Mahila Sabha Tirmanamulu', *ibid*. pp. 754-755. The fourteenth conference was held on 16, 17 December 1939 at Kadapa. Begum Amiruddin presided over it. For details see 'Grihalakshmi Pratyeka Pratinidhi', 'Kadapalo Jarigina Andhra Rashtra Mahila Mahasabhalo Mahilamanula Gambhiroktulu', *Grihalakshmi,* January 1940, pp. 750-763. The fifteenth conference was held on 24 November 1940 at Nandyala. Kameshwaramma presided over it. See 'Sampadakiyamulu', *Grihalakshmi,* December 1940, pp. 666-667.

26. The year of its establishment was given as 1904 in several issues of the *Hindu Sundary* whenever the history of the Samajamu was published. For example, see the issues of August 1913, p. 10; June 1916, p. 5. The June 1914 issue gives it as 1914, which might be a printing error, p. 2. However, while detailing the origin of the Samajamu, Narasamamba, the founder, gave it as 30 January 1903: this is the correct date. See Pulugurta Lakshminarasamamba, 'Shri Kakinada

Vidyarthini Sanghamuyokka Praprathamavatsara Vishayagna panamu' ('The First Annual Report of the Kakinada Vidyarthini Samajamu'), *Savitri*, March 1904, p. 4. Madabhooshi Choodamma, while discussing the controversy, endorsed the date given by Narasamamba. See Madabhooshi Choodamma, 'Vidyarthini Samajamu', *Hindu Sundary*, October-November 1911, p. 34. But it is very surprising why most of the issues of the *Hindu Sundary* (while giving the biography of the Samajamu) gave the year of establishment as 1904.

27. Her original name was Lakshminarasamma. However, she was generally referred to as Narasamamba with a prefix, 'amba', added to her name. This denotes respect. We use her name as her contemporaries addressed her. Her biographical details are given in the fourth part of this paper.

28. Bhandaru Atchamamba (1874-1905), a scholar-activist, significantly contributed to the women's movement in colonial Andhra. She was the first Andhra woman, who authored a book on the history of women at the very beginning of the last century. The book - *Abala Sachcharitra Ratnamala* (*Lives of Noble Women*) - was written to prove the self-worth of women by dispelling the various deep-rooted prejudices against them. As an ardent advocate of the women's cause, she traveled extensively in the whole of India, and encouraged several women to start women's organisations. The organisation under discussion owes its origin to the inspiration provided by her. She is also credited with being the first short story writer in Telugu. She widely published in the contemporary women's journals such as the *Hindu Sundary*, and emphasised women's education. For example, see her piece, 'Bharya Bhartala Samvadamu - Stree Vidya' ('Dialogue between Husband and Wife on Women's Education'), *Hindu Sundary,* December 1902, pp.1-10, written in the form of a dialogue between a husband and wife, emphasising women's education. Contemporary women paid glowing tributes to the services she rendered to women's movement. For example, when she passed away, the December 1904-January 1905 issue of the *Hindu Sundary*

published an article appreciating her efforts. When she passed away, Kandukuri Vireshalingam, the pioneer of social reform in Andhra, published an article in the *Telugu Zenana*. In this, Vireshalingam appraised her contribution to the women's movement in Andhra. See 'Srimati Bandaru Atchamambagaru' ('The Late Mrs. B. Atchamamba'), *Telugu Zenana Patrika & Sati Hita Bodhini*, February 1905, pp. 225-229. However, Viresalingam's name did not appear in the journal as its author. But Venkata Sivudu, the editor of *Telugu Zenana*, mentioned Viresalingam as its author in his autobiography. See Rayasam Venkata Sivudu, *Atma Charitramu*, Andhra Patrika Press, Madras, 1933, p. 455. Atchamamba's photograph decorated the cover page of the June 1914 issue of the *Hindu Sundary*. She served as a role model to contemporary women in Andhra.

29. The first meeting was held at the residence of Smt. Duggirala Ramanamma, where Atchamamba delivered a lecture on the issue of 'morality'. The second meeting was held at the Girls' School: Atchamamba delivered another lecture on 'The Demerits of Girls' Schools and their Remedies'. It was followed by the lecture of Ayyagari Ghantalamma, who spoke on 'The ways Women could acquire and Improve Knowledge'. The meeting ended with a cultural performance. For details see Pulugurta Lakshminarasamamba, 'Shri Kakinada Vidyarthini Sanghamuyokka Praprathamavatsara Vishayagna panamu' ('the First Annual Report of the Kakinada Vidyarthini Samajamu'), *Savitri*, March 1904.

30. Keeping in view the distance of Narasamamba's residence, and also to attract women from various parts of the town, three other venues were arranged. Since August 1903 meetings were held on Tuesdays at the residence of Duggirala Ramanamma. Women of Ramaraopeta Street met at the residence of Balantrapu Sheshamma on Tuesdays. Women of Jagannathapuram Street met on Sundays at the residence of Kashibhatla Sooramma. *Ibid*.

31. *Savitri*, March 1904, pp. 1-7.

32. 'Sri Vidyarthini Samajamu, Kakinada', *Savitri*, March 1911, pp. 17-21.

33. *Ibid.*
34. Narasamamba led the group. The other members were Bhavaraju Mahalakshmamma, Kashibhatla Sooramma, Uppuluri Sundaramma, Chintalapudi Sitadevamma, and Manyam Venkata Subbamma. See 'Sri Vidyarthini Samajamu', *Savitri*, July 1911, pp. 3-5. Manyam Venkata Subbamma deserves to be specially mentioned for one of her writings had created a fascinating controversy about five years before the eruption of the present controversy. Kandukuri Vireshalingam was involved in this. Narasamamba supported Subbamma, and bitterly attacked Vireshalingam. We shall see the fascinating details in the fourth part of this paper.
35. *Ibid.*
36. 'Sri Vidyarthini Samajamu, Kakinada', *Hindu Sundary*, July 1911, pp. 4-8. The group had more than 10 members. They were: Madabhooshi Choodamma, Duggirala Ramanamma, Pemmaraju Lakshmidevamma, Mamidanna Kameshwaramma, Attota Sheshamma, Attili Subbamma, Burra Venkata Subbamma, Malladi Lakshmidevamma, Maddali Rajyalakshmamma, Goteti Lakshmikantamma and Kallepalle Venkata Ramanamma apart from Balantrapu Sheshamma and Damerla Sitamma, the 'expelled' secretaries. *Ibid.*, p. 6.
37. Venkata Ramanamma was an intellectual activist who played a prominent role in the contemporary women's movement in colonial Andhra. She was one among those who saved and successfully ran the Shri Vidyarthini Samajamu serving as its president for six consecutive years, during 1911-1916. In that capacity, she took a leading role in convening the conferences of the Andhra Mahila Mahasabha. She was instrumental in the revival of the prominent women's journal, the *Hindu Sundary*: she edited it for some time. A prolific writer, she published widely on women's issues in the contemporary journals. More remarkably, she published and edited a women's monthly, the *Andhra Lakshmi*. Started to be published from Barampuram (Berhampore), Ganjam District (now in Orissa), the northernmost Telugu-speaking district of the erstwhile Madras

Presidency, in December 1921 the journal lasted probably till the end of 1924. Stating the reasons for starting the journal Venkata Ramanamma observed that women's journals like the *Zenana*, *Hindu Sundary* and *Anasuya* had stopped publication. Hence, she thought of 'filling a gap by publishing a journal that would be useful to women'. In terms of its name the *Andhra Lakshmi* was different from a few other women's journals: while a few journals like *Savitri* and *Anasuya* invoked the memory of the Hindu *Pativratas*, a few others like the *Hindu Sundary* and *Hindu Yuvati* stressed religious identity, *Andhra Lakshmi* emphasised regional identity.

38. It began to be published since 9 September 1908 from Bombay [Mumbai]. Initially it was a weekly; later a daily was also started with the same name. Kashinathuni Nageshwara Rao was the founder. Since 1 April 1914 it shifted the place of publication to Madras. The paper was started with the profit that Nageshwara Rao made by selling the famous pain balm, *Amrutanjan*. The *Andhra Patrika* supported the cause of social reform as well as the freedom movement. For an in-depth study of the *Andhra Patrika*, see C.V. Raja Gopala Rao, *Andhra Patrika Charitra* (Telugu) (*History of the Andhra Patrika*), Press Academy of Andhra Pradesh, Hyderabad, 2004. For a discussion on the contribution of the *Andhra Patrika* to social reform see Chapter-6 'Support for Social Reform' in K. Subramanyam, *The Press and the National Movement in South India,* Andhra, *1905-1932*, New Era Publications, Madras, 1984, pp. 123-147. Kashinathuni Nageshwara Rao (1867-1938) was a prominent leader in the Indian National Congress and rose to positions of eminence. He was one of the front leaders in the separate Andhra movement. He was hailed as *Deshodhdharaka* for the service that he rendered to the nation.

39. Pulugurta Lakshmi Narasamba, 'Andhra Mahila Mahasabha', *Savitri*, June 1911, pp. 3-4.

40. Ibid., pp.5-6.

41. Narasamamba notified the proposed Mahila Mahasabha in the *Savitri*, extending a warm welcome to 'the dear *kulagana* sisters belonging to the four varnas'. Also it was notified that

'special arrangements would be made according to caste and subcaste considerations and preferences, if the same was informed to her before hand'. A total number of 21 issues - divided into three heads as Education, Society and Domestic - were listed out for discussion. Essays authored by women on these issues were requested to be sent by 1 April [1911]. For details in the invitation letters see 'Andhra Mahila Mahasabha-Kakinada', *Savitri*, March 1911, pp. 1-8; 'Andhra Mahila Mahasabha-Ahvaana Patrika', *Savitri*, April 1911, pp. 1-2.

42. For example, see her essay 'Andhra Mahila Mahasabha', *Savitri*, June 1911, pp. 2-20, which runs into nineteen pages. See also 'Kulanganalu', *Savitri*, October 1911, pp. 1-9; 'Paativratyamu' ('Fidelity'), *Savitri*, July 1911, pp. 1-9; 'Paativratyamu' ('Fidelity'), *Hindu Sundary*, August 1903, pp. 11-22.

43. Attacking the editor of the *Andhra Patrika* she showered the arrows of questions. 'How does the paper deserve the name? Is it because it is published in the Andhra region? Is it because it is published by the Andhras? Is it because it is published in Andhra [Telugu] language? Or is it because it is published for the Andhras?' Answering these questions she tried to prove that the name – *Andhra Patrika* - was mismatched. She said that since the *Patrika* was published from Bombay i.e. outside Andhra region, the name did not match. A Brahmin published the *Patrika*. The Brahmins, according to her, were not Andhras. The Shudras were the real Andhras. Brahmins were foreigners who came to the Andhra region from north India. Since a Brahmin published the *Patrika*, the name did not match. Since three fourth of the vocabulary the *Patrika* employed was Sanskrit, and that it had a large number of Urdu and English words, the name did not suit. Since the *Patrika* was not exclusively meant for the Andhras, its name was not justified. See 'Andhra Mahila Mahasabha', *Savitri*, June 1911, p. 5.

44. Pulugurta Lakshmi Narasamba, 'Andhra Mahila Mahasabha', *Savitri*, June 1911, pp. 3-5.

45. *Ibid.*, pp. 5-11.

46. *Ibid.*, p. 12.

47. *Ibid.*, pp.18-19.
48. *Ibid.*, p.19.
49. *Ibid.*, pp.19-20.
50. Cited in Pulugurta Lakshmi Narasamba, 'Kulanganalu' ('Respectable Women'), *Savitri*, October 1911, p. 1. Uppuluri Nagaratnamma quoted Bangaramma's piece in her essay 'Stree Punarvivahamulu' ('Widow Remarriages'), *Hindu Sundary*, October-November 1911, pp. 30-31. Replying to Narasamamba, Bangaramma said that even if a few Shastras opposed widow remarriages, one needed to ignore that. According to her, such Dharma Shastras were framed keeping in view the needs of society. The traditions useful for a society in the past need not be followed now. Society should change according to times, and the laws should change accordingly. Since the Government has passed a law legalising widow remarriages, they should be performed. Given the need for marriage, a *punarvivahita*, according to Bangaramma, was definitely a *kulangana*. *Ibid.*, p. 31.
51. Pulugurta Lakshminarasamba, 'Kulanganalu', *op. cit.*, pp. 1-2.
52. *Ibid.*, p. 9.
53. Sitamma (1872-1934) was raised by Kandukuri Rajyalakshmamma, wife of Vireshalingam. Naturally, influenced by the latter's ideas, she developed interest in social reform, particularly, women's development. She assisted him in all his reform activities concerning women and worked as an honorary teacher in the Zenana School and was also one of the organisers of the women's wing of Rajahmundry Prarthana Samaj. A prolific writer, she published extensively in contemporary journals apart from having several books to her credit. Her writings include *Saadhurakshaka Shatakamu*, *Ahalyabai*, *Padya Bhagavadgita*, *Bhakti Maargamulu*. The most remarkable among her works was a biography of Vireshalingam written in verse form, *Sri Kandukuri Vireshalingam Charitramu*, which merited recognition in the literary circles. She presided over the ladies' section of the first Andhra Conference held at Bapatla in 1913. Her lectures delivered at various conferences

were published as *Upanyasasumamalika*. *Unnata Stree Vidya* was another book. Her father was Abburi Subbarao Pantulu of Jevudupadu in Tenali taluq. Kotikalapudi Rama Rao was her husband. V. Ramakrishna, *Social Reform in Andhra*, op.cit., p. 101. See also Utukuri Lakshmikanthamma, *Andhra Kavayitrulu*, (*Women Poets of Andhra*) (Telugu), other details N.A., pp.101-105.

54. Kotikalapudi Sitamma, 'Andhra Mahila Mahasabha Karyadarshinigaragu, Srimati Pulugurta Lakshmi Narasamambagarikoka Vinnapamu' ('An Appeal to Smt. Pulugurta Lakshminarasamamba, the Secretary of the Andhra Mahila Mahasabha'), *Hindu Sundary*, August 1911, pp. 1-6. Also Sitamma wrote on the issue in the September 1911 issue of the *Deshamata;* cited by Pulugurta Lakshmi Narasamba, 'Kulanganalu', *op. cit.*, p. 9.
55. It appeared in the 09.09.1911 issue. Cited in *ibid.*, pp. 3-7. Narasamamba reproduced excerpts.
56. Her views were published in the September 1911 issue of the *Krishna Patrika.* Cited in *ibid.*, p. 9.
57. Bangaramma published an article titled "Kulanganale varu?" ("Who are the Kulanganas?") in the 25 August 1911 (p. 4) issue of the *Krishna Patrika.* Cited in *ibid.*, pp. 1-2. Excerpts were reproduced by Uppuluri Nagaratnamma in her essay 'Stree Punarvivahamulu' ('Widow Remarriages'), *Hindu Sundary*, October-November 1911, pp. 30-31. With the pseudonym 'Kulangana', somebody published an article in the 8 September 1911 issue of the *Krishna Patrika*. Cited in Pulugurta Lakshmi Narasamba's 'Kulanganalu', *op. cit.*, p. 9.
58. An article appeared in the name of 'Hitavadi' in the 16.8.1911 issue of the *Andhra Prakashika* (p. 6). Madabhooshi Choodamma refuted the claims of 'Hitavadi'. See her article, 'Sri Vidyarthini Samajamu', *Hindu Sundary*, October-November 1911, pp. 31-38. In this she provided many interesting details regarding the *Samajamu*.
59. See *Hindu Sundary*, October-November 1911, p. 38.
60. An erudite scholar in Telugu and Sanskrit, Brahmaiah Shastry (1863-1940) proved to be the most formidable opponent of not

only the widow remarriage movement but also the reform movements as a whole. He started an association, *Aryananda Brindayini Sabha*, at Kakinada to spread the ideals of Hindu religion and simultaneously attack the reform activities initiated by Vireshalingam and others. He was very much opposed to Brahmo Samaj and its ideals. He edited and published the journal *Aryamatabodhini* from Kakinada. Through its columns he launched a severe attack against the reform movements. Vireshalingam in his autobiography conceded the adverse effects of the writings in the *Aryamatabodhini* on the minds of people, and to counteract its influence he started *Satyavadini*. For more details see V. Ramakrishna, *Social Reform in Andhra, op.cit.*, p. 117-118.

61. See Utukuri Lakshmikanthamma, *Andhra Kavayitrulu*, other details N.A., pp. 141-143.

62. A monthly, it was the second women's journal to be edited by and for women. It began publication since January 1904 from Cocanada (Kakinada), and appears to have continued till the end of 1912. Narasamamba felt the necessity of starting a women's journal that would be completely managed by women for certain valid reasons. She recognised that the educated women, despite being capable of writing essays and other things, had certain 'inhibitions' in communicating and corresponding with the heads of the contemporary journals, who were generally men. So as to 'encourage women' to write freely and exchange their views with other women, she thought it to be her 'due responsibility' to start a journal, and thus work for the 'development' of women. Hence, she started the journal. Narasamamba remarked that she 'dared to shoulder the burden of maintaining the journal'. See 'Vignapanamu' ('An Appeal'), *Savitri*, December 1904, p.1. Each issue of *Savitri* had 35 to 40 pages. The annual subscription rate, inclusive of postage, was Rupees One; price of a single copy was 2 *paisa*. It appears that *Savitri* had more than a thousand subscribers. It enjoyed a fairly good circulation and reached to such far off places like Bellary, Kadapa, Dharmavaram, Chandragiri, Rayachoti,

Vayalpadu (in the 'Ceded Districts'), Kanigiri, Nellore, Bangalore, Bombay, Madras and Hyderabad. *Savitri* lived up to its stated objective of 'promoting women's writings': most of the writings in it were by and on women. Essays, burlesques, verses etc. by women were regularly published. Narasamamba, the editor, Balantrapu Sheshamma, Damerla Sundaramma, Burra Butchi Bangaramma, Gundu Achchamamba, Manyam Venkata Subbamma, Damerla Sitamma, Uppala Narasamamba, Atmuri Annapoornamma, K. Kanakamma and Kallepalle Venkata Ramanamma were a few among the women contributors. Narasamamba, the editor was the most frequent contributor: most of her works were serialised in the *Savitri*. The *Savitri* was an extremely conservative journal, which unsuccessfully tried to check the rising tides of reform. Unlike the other women's journals, the language in the *Savitri*, being hard *Grandhika*, complemented its conservatism. For a detailed discussion on the *Savitri* see S. Mahaboob Basha, 'Against the Tides of Reform: Conservative Women's Journals in Colonial Andhra – The Story of *Savitri*, 1904 – 1912', Proceedings of the Indian History Congress, New Delhi, 2008, pp. 1001-1020.

63. See the January, March and April 1904 issues of *Savitri*.
64. It was serialised. See the January, February and April 1904 issues of *Savitri*.
65. It was written by Kolagnati Kotaiah and was serialised in the *Savitri*. It had several parts like 'Gurujana Priti' ('How to Make the Elders Happy'), 'Pativratya Padhadhati' ('Methods of Maintaining Fidelity'), 'Griha Karya Nirvahakata' ('Domestic Management'), 'Shishu Poshana' ('Child Rearing') etc. See *Savitri*, August 1904.
66. It was authored by Sunkara Rangaiah and was serialised in the *Savitri* since October 1904.
67. Pulugurta Lakshmi Narasamamba wrote these verses. See the February, March and April 1912 issues of *Savitri*.
68. The essay was written by Damerla Sundaramma. See *Savitri*, October 1904.
69. The lengthy essay running into seventeen pages was authored by Pulugurta Lakshmi Narasamamba, the editor. See *Savitri*,

July 1911, pp. 2-17. Since it had been her favourite theme, she published on this issue elsewhere also. See 'Pativratyamu', *Hindu Sundary*, August 1903, pp. 11-22.

70. Pulugurta Lakshmi Narasamamba, 'Pativratyamu' ('Fidelity'), *Savitri*, July 1911, p. 2. This is one of the few articles which best attests the dreadful dance of conservatism in Narasamamaba. Holding *Pativratya Dharma* as the quintessence/hallmark of Indian womanhood, she mounted a scathing attack on the social reformers who, according to her, had been tarnishing the 'world famous' *Pativratya Dharma* with their 'pernicious agenda of social reform'. She vituperated them for their alleged aping of 'western values'. For her, criticising the practice of child marriage and enforced widowhood was nothing but a clumsy crusade against the 'highly acclaimed' Hindu *Dharma*. The magnitude of her conservation and obsession with *Pativratyam* was such that she even endorsed the practice of *Sati*. However, one cannot but wonder at, and also appreciate the logic she built to substantiate her regressive views. Also worth mentioning is her dazzling scholarship; she extensively quoted from the *Veda*s, the *Purana*s, the *Smriti*s, the *Dharmashastra*s, Vivekananda's works, and the works of a few Western Scholars to corroborate her conservative stand. The irony and wit that she employed is simply superb!

71. Damerla Sundaramma, 'Sadvartanamu' ('Good Conduct'), *Savitri*, October 1904, p. 5.

72. 'Niti Padamulu', *Savitri*, January 1904. A verse said: 'She [a woman] should serve her husband like a *Dasi* (servant); assist him like his counselor, feed him sumptuously, provide him comforts, abstain from giving pain to him, and bear the burden of family like *Panchali* [i.e. Draupadi, the polyandrous wife of the Pandavas, heroes of the epic, the *Mahabharata*]'. 'Sati Dharmamulu', *Savitri*, January 1904. Another verse instructed: 'attend to the problems of your husband first; do not believe the words of even your nearest ones, if they informed you about your husband's sexual promiscuity; do not question him; do not blame him; do not curse him even in your heart, if you get angry with

him.' 'Sati Dharmamulu', *Savitri*, February 1904. 'God will bless and reward you in the proportion of your devotion and submission to your husband; treat it to be ignoble to trouble your husband for jewelry; treat him like God, however worst he is', instructed another verse. 'Stree Dharmamulu', *Savitri*, April 1904. Yet another verse stated that 'salvation was possible only through devotion and absolute subordination to husband': the self-effacing women would be the first to attain salvation! It suggested: 'do not reveal your problems to your husband when he returned home tired; [first] give him water [preferably hot water, if it is winter season] to clean his feet, allow him to rest and press his feet; thus, provide him comfort; do not question husband even if he scolds [and brutally beats] you. Only those women attain *mukti* (Salvation), who have [unquestioned] *bhakti* (devotion) towards their husbands; [hence] always pray to him wholeheartedly'. 'Stree Niti Ratnavali', *Savitri*, October 1904. Another verse emphasised that 'it was the duty of women to serve men [like a slave].' 'Stree Niti Deepika', *Savitri*, August 1904.

73. It was because 'bad conduct of a woman caused more harm than a man for the latter brought ill fame to his parents only: but the former tarnished the reputation of both parents and parents-in-law'. So as to ensure that it did not happen, *Savitri* provided certain guidelines to women about how they should conduct themselves both within and outside the home; guidelines were provided regarding how to conduct with parents-in-law, brothers and sisters-in-law, neighbours, relatives etc. *Ibid.*, See also 'Stree Niti Ratnavali', *op. cit.*, But curiously enough, it was very rarely that men were asked to be virtuous!

74. Narasamamba wrote that though the quality of *pativrata*s did not completely disappear from Hindu women, they certainly declined during the *Kali* age. Hence, women needed to be educated to 'regain' the considerably lost qualities. For more information see Pulugurta Lakshmi Narasamamba, 'Pativratyamu', *Hindu Sundary*, August 1903, p.13. Several other writings published in the *Savitri* held such views. For example, the '*Stree Niti Dipika*'

explained the various advantages of women's education. One among them was that it enhanced women's skills in domestic management. Since a woman's duty was to serve her husband like a *Dasi*, an educated woman could provide her husband enlightened company and better service. Also it inculcated good conduct, kept her involved/busy, and saved her from indulging in unnecessary and cheap gossip. 'Stree Niti Deepika', *op. cit.*

75. Pulugurta Lakshmi Narasamamba, 'Pativratyamu' ('Fidelity'), *Savitri*, July 1911, pp. 5-12.

76. *Ibid.*, pp. 13-14.

77. Manyam Subbamma, 'Sati Dharma Prakashika' ('Iluminator of the Sati Dharmas'), *Savitri*, August 1904.

78. He called her 'Manyam Subbamma Shastri'. 'Shastri' is used only for men: Viresalingam added this suffix to Subbamma's name to ridicule her.

79. Kandukuri Vireshalingam, 'Savitri Satyavati Sambhashanamu - Stree Vidya', *Telugu Zenana*, October 1904, pp.121-126.

80. See *Savitri*, November 1904, pp. 1-8. Narasamamba continued to take on Vireshalingam. Addressing women in the December 1904 issue, she alleged that the self styled social reformers were impeding women's progress. She appealed to them not to get discouraged by such vile criticisms, which were 'far from truth'. See 'Vignapanamu', *Savitri,* December 1904, pp. 1-6.

81. An infuriated Subbamma said that she considered it to be 'ignoble to react to such vile criticism' [of Vireshalingam], whose sole aim was 'defaming' her. A few of her friends suggested her to 'ignore' such a 'mean criticism as one ignored a monkey, which ridiculed others being ignorant of its own beauty, and a dog ('*Grama Simhamu*'), which simply barked at those who were going on a royal path.' But a few others suggested her 'to do something about it to expose the meanness' in the writer [i.e. Vireshalingam]: hence, she became ready to publish the rejoinder. Brushing aside the charges of Vireshalingam as 'baseless allegations' she warned that such writings 'humiliated not only her, but also all the educated women, who had been writing in the journals'. She stated that believing in such 'self styled favourites of women's education/development' was like

'swimming the Godavari (the famous river flowing in Andhra Pradesh) by holding the tail of a dog'. Finally she appealed to women 'to treat it as an issue concerning all of them, react and reflect upon promptly'. See Manyam Subbamma, 'Oka Prakatanamu - Oka Manavi', *Savitri*, December 1904, pp. 1-9.

82. He wrote that 'the rejoinder written in the name of Manyam Subbamma' had 'no substance other than rebukes and allegations', and was befitting 'the stories narrated by a buffoon in street plays'. He claimed that he knew the person, based in Kakinada, who was 'notorious' for such things [writing with women's names], and said that 'he did not want to desecrate his journal [i.e. the *Telugu Zenana*', which he was jointly editing with Venkata Shivudu at the time] by mentioning that sinner's name'. He confidently stated that he came to know about that 'fellow' through a few gentlemen in Kakinada, to whom Pulugurta Venkataratnam, husband of Narasamamba, informed about that. Quoting from Subbamma's 'Oka Prakatanamu - Oka Manavi', he tried to prove that she *did not* author that. His contention was that no self-respecting woman could write in such a 'nasty way'. Also he claimed that 'he knew several men who had been writing with the names of women'. See 'Zeena Patrika - Savitri', *Telugu Zenana*, April and May 1905, pp. 322-329.

83. *Ibid.*, pp. 327-329.

84. The contemporary women's journals, particularly either the *Savitri* or the *Telugu Zenana*, did not mention any such test: had it been conducted, certainly they would have published it with prominence. Given the absence of the matter in them, it may be safely assumed that such a test had not taken place. What is more surprising is that even Vireshalingam did not mention it in his autobiography despite the fact that he mentioned even very minor things, particularly the obstacles in the way of reform, that he had witnessed.

85. 'Sri Vidyarthini Samajamu, Kakinada', *Hindu Sundary*, October 1914, pp. 1-6.

86. *Ibid.*, p. 2.
87. 'Sri Vidyarthini Samajamu, Kakinada', *Hindu Sundary*, June 1916, p. 5.
88. 'Sri Vidyarthini Samajamu, Kakinada', *Hindu Sundary*, June 1917, p.17.
89. By 30 March 1912 it had 32 donor members; by August 1913 the number rose to 40. See *Hindu Sundary*, August 1913, p. 12. But by June 1914 it decreased to 31. See *Hindu Sundary*, June 1914, p. 4.
90. Apart from this, many philanthropists made liberal donations. The *Samajamu* regularly published the names of the donors and the sum they contributed in its journal, the *Hindu Sundary*, and profusely thanked them for the same. For example, the August 1913 issue published the names of 38 donors: the total sum it received was Rs.591 (pp. 17-19); see also June 1914 issue (p. 8). Many generously contributed on festival occasions like the Diwali. In the year 1945 Rs. 355 was collected. See *Hindu Sundary*, April 1945, p. 3. Apart from these occasional donors, it had a few chief patrons and patrons who made regular contributions. Kashinathuni Ramabayamma (Rs. 25), Rampu Annapoornamma (Rs. 25), Mantripragada Narasimham Pantulu (Rs. 25), Raja Vishwasundara Rao Zamindar, Vikramadeva Verma, N. Rukminamma, Patruni Yagnamma were a few among them. See *Hindu Sundary*, April 1945, pp. 2-3. Numbers in brackets are the sum contributed per annum. It regularly published its annual income and expenditure sheet (balance sheet). For instance see August 1913, pp. 24-25; June 1914, pp. 10-11 and April 1945, pp. 7-8 issues of *Hindu Sundary*. During the year 1944-45 the organisation had a capital of Rs. 2013.
91. As no woman came forward to edit the journal, initially it was edited by the founder himself, and was published from Kanteru. From mid 1903 onward Mosalikanti Ramabayamma and Vempali Shantabayamma became its editors. Its publication had stopped for about two year i.e. probably from the end of 1907 to May 1909. Later, with the encouragement provided by

Balantrapu Sheshamma and Madabhooshi Choodamma, Sitaramayya restarted it in June 1909. See Sattiraju Sitaramayya, 'Swa Vishayamu' ('Ourselves'), *Hindu Sundary*, June 1909, pp. 1-6. See also Tumu Venkata Narasaiahamma, 'Vignapanau' ('An Appeal'), June 1909, pp. 33-35.

92. 'Swa Vishayamu' ('Ourselves'), March 1913, pp. 1-4. Sitaramayya made an announcement regarding the transfer of the journal to the *Samajamu*. See 'Prakatana' ('An Announcement'), *ibid*., p. 4. While handing the journal over to the organisation, he hoped that, being a women's journal, it would 'prosper' under the management exclusively of women without any male association.

93. 'Swa Vishayamu' ('Ourselves'), June 1913, pp. 1-3.

94. She prepared a seven page length petition to be sent to the British Government. She urged the Government to make a law banning 'enforced tonsuring': this was to be appended to the Widow Remarriage Act of 1856. She first notified about the proposed petition in the May 1904 issue (p. 75). For the full text of the petition see Mosaliganti Ramabai, 'Vitantu Shiromundanamunu- goorchina Mahajaru' ('Petition Regarding the Tonsuring of Widows'), *Hindu Sundary*, July 1904, pp. 146-153. See also 'Hindu Vitantuvula Shiromundanamu' ('Tonsuring of Hindu Widows'), *Hindu Sundary*, October-November 1905, pp. 198-2001.

95. The characteristic feature of all these writings was that they vividly described the poignant conditions of and the multiple disabilities inflicted on widows. For example, see Varanasi Kameshwari, 'Mana Hindu Vitantuvula Dusthiti' ('The Miserable Plight of Our Hindu Widows'), *Hindu Sundary*, April 1905, pp. 1-5. See also 'Krupa' (pseudonym), 'Vitantuvula Durgati' ('Plight of Widows'), *Hindu Sundary*, May 1905, pp. 53-56. They mounted a scathing attack on the 'merciless' parents for selling away their daughters to 'old vampires'. See Aitaraju Jeedikanti Rama Rao, 'Haindava Yuvati Duravastha' ('Miserable Condition of Hindu Women'), *Hindu Sundary*, March 1912, pp. 8-16. The articles strongly suggested that widows

should be remarried and emphasised that the *Dharmashastras* approved of such marriages. While many of them cited the *Shastras* to defend their point, women like Uppuluri Nagaratnamma felt that since an Act (The Widow Remarriage Act, 1856) was passed in favour of widow remarriages, one did not have to bother about the sanction or ban of the *Shastras*. Given the time this was a fairly radical idea. Paying attention to the sexual needs of widows, which made her remarkable, she wrote that 'the only *mantra* that annihilated the vampire [of enforced widowhood] was the '*Parinaya mantra*'. See Uppuluri Nagaratnamma, 'Stree Punarvivahamulu' ('Widow Remarriages'), October-November 1911, pp. 26-30. Most of the articles supported their stand with statistical evidences.

96. A large number of articles were published highlighting the evil effects of child marriages. They were held responsible for the high incidence of widows and were treated as a major obstacle in the way of women's education. Hence, they advocated post-puberty marriages. For example, see Kalagara Pitchchamma, 'Balya Vivahamulavalana Kalugu Nashtamulu' ('The Evil Effects of Child Marriages'), *Hindu Sundary*, April 1912, p. 8; Kallepalle Venkata Ramanamma, 'Stree Vidyaku Bhangakaramulagu Vaivahika Dharmamulu: Vanini Tolaginchu Upayamulu' ('The Present Marriage System Harmful to Women's Education: Remedies'), *Hindu Sundary*, May 1912, pp. 19-22; Mosalikanti Ramabayamma, 'Rajaswalanantara Vivahamulu' ('Post-Puberty Marriages'), *Hindu Sundary*, March 1912, p. 30.

97. Articles published in the *Hindu Sundary* dispelled the various deep-rooted prejudices against women's education: it was held by the conservatives that women, if educated, would become immoral, turn disobedient etc. The dominant view expressed was that education would make women 'good housewives' and 'nurturing mothers', though there were also such views that education was necessary for women to earn a living and thus become independent. A few others felt that women 'definitely needed English education'. See Bhandaru Atchchamamba,

'Bharya Bhartala Samvadamu-Stree Vidya' ('A Dialogue between Husband and Wife on Women's Education'), December 1902, pp. 1-10; Unnava Lakshmibayamma, 'Stree Vidyanugoorchi Sambhashana' ('Dialogue on Women's Education'), March 1904, pp. 4-16; Gundala Subhadramma, 'Stree Vidya' ('Women's Education'), December 1903, pp. 23-24; Mangamma, 'Streelu Nerchukovalasina Vidya Ettidi?' ('What kind of Education Should Women Receive?'), October 1909, pp. 14-22; Unnava Lakshmibayamma, 'Stree Vidya' ('Women's Education'), November 1903, pp. 14-16; Uppuluri Nagaratnamma, 'Stree Vidya' ('Women's Education'), April 1912, pp. 19-22; 'Oka Stree', 'Stree Vidyabhyudayametulanagu' ('How can Women's Education Progress'), May 1912, pp. 11-16; Damerla Sitamma, 'Stree Vidya Vishayamu' ('The Issue of Women's Education'), January 1912, pp. 1-4; Achanta Rukminamma, 'Stree Vidya, Vivahamunaku Tagina Vayassu' ('Suitable Age for Women's Education and Marriage'), February 1912, pp. 20-25; Subhadra, 'Streelaku Englishu Vidya Avasarama?' ('Do Women Need English Education?'), February 1912, pp. 5-7.

98. For example, the December 1903 issue published the annual report of the '*Aska Hindu Stree Samajamu*'. The December 1906 issue published the full details of the '*Brundavanapura Stree Samajamu*' (pp. 7-16). The February, March and December issues of 1912 published the reports of the *Stree Vidyabhivardhani Samajamu* at Kurnool. As the *Samajamu* published it, not surprisingly, its details, reports, history, programmes and everything related to it was regularly published. The May 1905 issue published the speech of a girl by name Kanakavalli Krishnavenamma delivered at the Seventh Krishna District Social Reform Conference held on 11.6.1905. The August 1905 issue published the speech of Motupalli Rajabayamma delivered in the anniversary celebrations of the '*Brundavanapura Stree Samajamu*' (pp. 153-157). The February-March 1910 issue published the speech of Balantrapu Sheshamma delivered on 8 January 1910 at the Girls' School in

Kakinada (pp. 1-6). The same issue published the speech of Madabhooshi Choodamma delivered at the same place (pp. 10-14). Apart from these it published all most all the Presidential Addresses and the speeches of important women delivered at the All Andhra Women's Conferences.

99. This was duly acknowledged by contemporary women such as Balantrapu Sheshamma who wrote in the January 1910 issue that 'though it was not a full fledged journal, it published everything that women wrote' to encourage them. 'As they [women] kept on writing', they became well versed with the art of writing. She further said that 'she, along with a few others, became habituated to writing' and gradually got transformed into good writers. See Balantrapu Sheshamma, 'Aikamatyamu' ('Unity among Women'), *Hindu Sundary*, January 1910, pp.13-17. It is heartening to note that from 1903 onward the number of women who contributed to it steadily increased to around one hundred. Sattiraju Sitaramaiah mentioned the names of 84 women who contributed to *Hindu Sundary* by June 1909. By the end of the second year of its publication there were 43 women writers. The number increased to 63, 76 and 84 by the end of the third, fourth and sixth year respectively. Sitaramaiah hoped to publish their photographs and brief accounts in the year to come for 'they were the first among women in Andhara *desha* to dare to write to journals'. See Sattiraju Sitaramaiah, 'Swa Vihayamu' ('Ourselves'), *Hindu Sundary*, June 1909, pp. 1-6.

100. It mirrored the aspiration of upper caste and middle class women only.

101. As the conferences were conducted regularly in several parts of Andhra, the mission and message of women's movement reached different parts. The conferences provided an expanded public space for women and opened up new opportunities: women enthusiastically participated, often travelling long distances all alone. Another significant feature of these conferences was that women attended them in large numbers: the number sometimes surprisingly exceeded 1000.

102. Sattiraju Shyamalamba, Kalagara Pitchchamma, 'Kakinada Stree Vidyarthini Sanghamuvarikoka Vinnapamu' ('An Appeal

to the People cf Stree Vidyarthini Samajamu, Kakinada'), *Hindu Sundary*, April 1912, pp. 31-33. However, this complaint only attests the keen interest the *Samajamu* took in forging the bond of sisterhood among women of Andhra, and its unwavering commitment to accelerating the women's movement.

103. Somebody, with the pseudonym 'Andhra Vanitaratnamu', published an article in the 12 June 1916 issue of the *Andhra Patrika.* She leveled several allegations on the *Samajamu*, and particularly abused Achanta Rukminamma. The editor of *Hindu Sundary* devoted an editorial essay to condemn the 'prejudiced writing'. See 'Sampadakiyamu' ('Editorial'), *Hindu Sundary,* August 1916, pp.1-5. This charge was nothing but the stomach burning of the conservatives, who could not tolerate women's functioning independently, and who did not like women crossing the patriarchal *Lakshmanarekhas.* All these only establish the intense activism of the organisation.

104. Primarily a Sanskrit School, it was started in September 1913 as a Primary School and was later on upgraded to an 'Advanced School'. Its aim was to spread education among girls/women, particularly the widows. Subjects like Telugu, Sanskrit, Hindi, Mathematics, History, Stitching, and Music constituted the curriculum. By 1943 there were forty students including a few child widows. *Hindu Sundary*, August 1943, p. 1. A note on the date of its establishment: Its date of establishment was given differently in different issues of the *Hindu Sundary.* The April 1945 issue gave it as September 1923. See p. 3. The June 1943 issue, in its editorial, stated that the school was established 'about 30 years ago'. p. 1. If we go by the latter, the date of establishment should be 1913, and this must be the correct date. The year 1923 given in the April 1945 issue must be a printing error. Hence, we may safely conclude that the year of its establishment was 1913.

105. Inspired by the Gautami Library at Rajahmundry, the organisation started a library in the year 1910. See *Hindu Sundary,* August 1913, p. 15. From 1916 onward it was named after Kandukuri Rajyalakshmamma, wife of Vireshalingam.

See *Hindu Sundary,* April 1945, p. 5. By August 1913 the library housed 400 books. See *Hindu Sundary,* August 1913, p. 12. The same issue published the titles of a few of the books and the names of donors. See pp. 20-23. By June 1914 it had 450 books. See *Hindu Sundary,* June 1914, p. 5. For the titles of a few of the books and their donors, see pp. 8-9. By April 1945 the number rose to 1068. See *Hindu Sundary,* April 1945, p. 5.

106. Many of the contemporary women's organisations could not survive for more than a decade, and a few disappeared in just two to three years. They were highly local in nature and suffered from the want of human resource to manage them. A few of the organisations, particularly during the 1930s, seem to have degenerated into mere 'recreation clubs'. Kanuparti Varalakshmamma, a leading intellectual activist of her times, in her play-let, 'Ladies Clubbu' ('Ladies Club'), a burlesque, ridiculed such organisations. See *Grihalakshmi,* April 1942, pp. 87-95. Though organisations such as the 'Stri Sanatana Dharmamandali' survived for more than thirty years, they did not register any success. All these make the *Samajamu* stand out remarkably.

107. The rule stated that all 'respectable and family women' could become its members excepting the women of 'inferior castes' like the *Malas* and the *Madigas*. See *Hindu Sundary,* October 1914, p. 2. However, others rightly questioned this upper caste bias. Sattiraju Shyamalamba, Kalagara Pitchchamma, 'Kakinada Stree Vidyarthini Sanghamuvarikoka Vinnapamu' ('An Appeal to the People of Stree Vidyarthini Samajamu, Kakinada'), *Hindu Sundary*, April 1912, pp. 31-33. Though this criticism was in connection with the proposed third Andhra Mahila Mahasabha, where the coming of the untouchable women was banned, it would suit here also. They questioned as to what would happen if the untouchable women came there. Condemning the conservative stand of the organisation, they reflected on the contribution, the untouchables made to the society. Also they emphasised that the 'uplift' of the untouchables was a must, if the country had to make any progress.

8

Non-Brahmin Movement in Colonial *Rayalaseema*, 1916-1937

G. Samba Siva Reddy

The emergence of Non-Brahmin movement in colonial south India was one of the remarkable aspects of the social history of 20th century India. It was one epoch making movement, which had transformed the socio-political scenario of south India in particular and India in general. It was started vigorously in south India and spread to the entire country and influenced both social and political systems. Though there were several works on this aspect, their focus was more on south India as a whole thus neglecting the social processes at provincial, regional and local level. This paper therefore makes an attempt to address this lacunae, i.e., the exploration of Non-Brahmin Movement in the present *Rayalaseema* region or erstwhile Ceded Districts.

About the name '*Rayalaseema*', 'Ceded Districts' and Boundaries

Present *Rayalaseema* had its own antiquity or hoary past. The culture and civilization of Telugu people were started in this region. The early and rare Telugu inscriptions that were located at Kalamalla and Erragudipadu near Erraguntla in Kamalapuram taluk of Kadapa (hitherto spelt as Cuddapah) District of the region will testify this.[1] In the past, the region, '*Rayalaseema*' was known, variously, as Hiranyarashtra or Maharajaranadu or Maharajanadu or Marjavadinadu or Renadu.[2] The terms "Rayalavariseema" and "*Rayalaseema*" were in vogue to refer to some of the areas of present *Rayalaseema*.[3] Later, during 16th and 17th centuries parts of the region were ruled by the local Matli dynasty. Apart from these, the name *Rayalaseema* was mentioned in a Telugu literary treatise known as Abhishiktaraghavamu, which was written during their rule.[4] But these names did not cover the entire present *Rayalaseema* region.

Subsequently, during the colonial era (1800-1928), the '*Rayalaseema*' region was known as Ceded Districts comprising the districts of Kadapa, Bellary and Anantapur and parts of Kurnool and Chittoor districts. The then Nizam of Hyderabad, Nizam Ali Khan, ceded these areas to the East India Company in allegiance to the Subsidiary Alliance Treaty concluded on 24 October 1800. The Company Government named this area as "Ceded Districts".[5] Later, when the people of the region were under the grip of the nationalist consciousness, the Telugu people had started a sub-national movement for separate Andhra State. At this juncture, a great scholar and man of literary excellence or genius, Chilukuri Narayana Rao, came to Anantapur from Rajahmundry on his service transfer. By that time, the people of *Rayalaseema* were fed up with the word 'ceded' as it purports to signify 'slavery'. Chilukuri also felt ugly of the term, 'ceded'. He sung a beautiful song and highlighted the importance of *Rayalaseema* on the one side and on the other down played the word 'ceded' in satirical terms. At that time, the people of the region were agitating for their just rights, needs and aspirations and making strenuous efforts to unite each other. Similarly, prominent leader of the region, Gooty Kesava Pillai or P. Kesava Pillai, of Gooty in Anantapur district questioned the validity or benefit accrued for *Rayalaseema* in the event of Separate Andhra State. There was hue and cry, every where, for the development of *Rayalaseema* region.[6]

Under these circumstances, the intellectuals of *Rayalaseema* participated in one of the meetings of the *Andhra Maha Sabha* held on 17 and 18 November, 1928 at Nandyal in Kurnool district. At the same time, on 8 November, the Conference of the First Ceded Districts was held under the leadership of Kadapa Koti Reddi of Kadapa District. Chilukuri Narayana Rao had participated in the meeting. A heated debate was held on the naming of *Rayalaseema* area. Finally, Narayana Rao coined the name '*Rayalaseema*' for the region. Chilukuri influenced Pappuri Ramacharyulu of Anantapur district to pass a resolution in favour of it. All members of the meeting supported this resolution. The name spread like a wild fire within a short span of time. Further more, on 3 January, 1946 Chilukuri Narayana Rao gave a Radio talk on 'Our *Rayalaseema* Literary Treasure' and said 'that he was proud of having been instrumental in giving the name '*Rayalaseema*' for the region and it was uncontested.' Apart from it, *Naa Vangmaya Mitrulu* (My Literary Friends) (Telugu) written by T. Kameswara Rao and a Weekly newspaper, *Mahodaya* of 1943 had also corroborated it. From these details, suffice it to say that Chilukuri Narayana Rao gave the name '*Rayalaseema*' to the region in memory of the Rayas of Vijayanagar, Krishnadevaraya in particular, who ruled the entire area for three centuries from the middle of 14th century to the middle of 17th century.[7] The present *Rayalaseema* region is consisting of Kadapa, Kurnool, Chittoor and Anantapur districts, the south-western part of Andhra Pradesh. The region is bounded by Karnataka State on the west, Mahaboobnagar, Prakasam and Nellore districts of Andhra Pradesh on the north, northeast and east respectively, and Tamil Nadu State on the south.

Regional Identity

Regional history has great value and rich potential as it makes possible to study the details usually ignored in large scale and conventional studies. It also enables us to test the macro-level theories and generalisations and their deployment. For instance, the writing of 'subaltern history or history from below' more accurately reveals the life and struggles for identity of the common people and regions who were, and are, neglected in conventional historical studies.[8] Regional history should be studied in relation to the larger milieu or national perspective.[9] In this connection, the views of Mahatma Gandhi[10] are noteworthy. Romila Thapar,[11] Sumit Sarkar,[12] Bipan Chandra[13] and Sabyasachi Bhattacharya[14] have expressed similar views. So, regional studies have gained importance and momentum in historical writings.

Until recently, in majority works on India's past, we see that scant or no attention of the historians of modern India is given to South India.[15] Reasons for this may vary. But now there has been a sea-change among scholars and yet literature on the hinterland regions like *Rayalaseema* is minimum or meagre as the scholars have been working more on the Madras Presidency and Coastal Andhra than on the regions like *Rayalaseema*. It is in this context that this paper attempts to study a fascinating subject and one of the unexplored areas, i.e., Non-Brahmin Movement in the region. The main chief objective of this paper is to integrate the information with all-India literature, so that the nation as a whole will come to know about the regions like *Rayalaseema* and its reaction and response to various movements and activities like the Non-Brahmin Movement or the Justice Party.

Genesis of the Non-Brahmin Movement /Justice Party

One of the developments of the national movement in peninsular India in general and Madras Presidency in particular in the 1920s and 1930s was the rise of the Non-Brahmin Movement or Justice Party[16] against the domination of Brahmanism. The impact of egalitarian ideas and the ideals of social equality and justice had echoed on the non-Brahmin castes viz, Kshatriyas, Araya-Vaisyas, Kammas, Reddis/Kapus, Balijas,

Velamas (offshoot of Kapus) and Other Backward Classes including Muslims, Christians, Scheduled Castes and Tribes and significantly contributed to the emergence of the non-Brahman movement against the hegemony of the Brahminical ideology.[17] It was better known as "Dravidian Movement" in Tamil Nadu and the term *"Brahmanetharodhyamamu"* (movement by other than Brahmins) gained currency or momentum in Telugu areas. M.N. Srinivas and Irschick termed this movement as 'part of the backward classes movement'.[18] The prominent non-Brahmin intellectuals of Madras like Pitti Thyagaraya Chetty (1852-1925), Dr. T.M. Nair (1868-1919), and others started the South Indian People's Association on 20 November 1916 and later the South Indian Liberal Federation, its political counterpart, in 1917. They started daily newspapers, the *Justice* (26 February 1917) in English and *Andhra Prakasikc* (1885) in Telugu. Then they named their party as Justice Party, the pro-British, to enter into politics and to achieve their objectives in order to cater to the needs of non-Brahmins. They issued a Non-Brahmin Manifesto by incorporating various socio-economic-political issues and urged the colonial state to implement them.[19] The milieu of castes, caste associations and their conferences on the one side and the growth of consciousness and its articulation among non-Brahmins on the other side played an effective role to raise the movement.

Castes, Caste Associations or Movements and Consciousness

Castes

It is not easy to define the term, 'Caste'. However the word was, 'a unit of social action', 'a steel frame of Hinduism', 'a social institution', lasted or continued many centuries and became an integral part of Hindu Society. Castes are small and complete social worlds in themselves and marked off definitely from one another, though subsisting within the larger society.[20] Development of western education and egalitarian ideas, modern communications, social relations, print culture, and spread of education and literacy had strengthened caste and politicized it further in order to play a major role in the political system.[21] From the population of the castes in the early years of twentieth century, we can visualise the relative position of the non-Brahmin and Brahmin castes that are given below:[22]

1.	Brahmins	4,36,094
2.	Vysyas	4,47,347
3.	Kshatriyas or Rajus	1,06,846
4.	Kammas	9,73,723
5.	Kapus and Reddis	25,76,448
6.	Telagas	3,82,677
7.	Velamas	4,36,327
8.	Kamsala (Viswabrahmans)	2,71,583
9.	Balijas	10,08,036
10.	Golla	8,55,221
11.	Mala, Madiga and Adi-Andhras	21,60,343

From these details, the former were more than the latter. But Brahmins dominated non-Brahmins in all fields, especially education and employment, due to their access to western education and economic prosperity. Census Reports of the period under review were corroborated and confirmed this.[23] As far as the competition for the posts was concerned, majority of the posts were conferred upon one section of the community i.e., Brahmins. The Government's recruitment policy and competition tests or general tests were also more advantageous to Brahmins than non-Brahmins. The minority Brahmin section had appropriated all the government jobs. For instance, out of the total 41 $\frac{1}{2}$ million population of the Madras Presidency 40 millions were non-Brahmins. Similarly in 1912, the Brahmins, who were 3.2 per cent of the total population, had secured 55 per cent of the Deputy Collectors, 83.5 per cent of the Sub-Judges, and 72.6 per cent of the District Munsifs, while the non-Brahmin Hindus, who were 85.6 per cent of the population had got a paltry 21.5 per cent appointments.[24] Further, Brahmins had curtailed, prohibited and downplayed non-Brahmins in domestic rituals, ceremonies and social and political domains.[25]

Even in the Indian National Congress the Brahminical influence and domination can be noticed.[26]

In Andhra area, in which the *Rayalaseema* region was, and is, a part, Kshatriyas, Arya-Vaisyas, Kammas, Reddis/Kapus, Balijas, Velamas (offshoot of Kapus) and Other Backward Classes including Muslims, Christians, Scheduled Castes and Tribes were, and are, the non-Brahmin castes. Among them, Reddis, Kammas, Balijas and Velamas were land-owners where as Arya-Vaisyas or Vaisyas or Komatis were traders. They were upper non-Brahmin castes while the remaining were lower non-Brahmin castes. The upper non-Brahmin castes had dominated

Table I : Distribution of Castes in Rayalaseema Districts of the Madras Presidency, 1921.

Caste	*Kadapa*	*Kurnool*	*Anantapur*	*Chittoor*
Balija	13.2	10.3	10.4	19.0
Boya/Besta	4.5	4.5	6.0	4.3
Chakali	3.0	3.2	2.6	3.3
Golla	4.9	5.2	4.2	5.6
Kummari	4.7	5.9	3.7	5.9
Mangali	4.8	5.7	5.7	5.7
Mutrasi	1.8	0.7	1.7	4.7
Sal	3.0	1.7	1.7	2.2
Telaga	—	0.3	—	—
Uppara	7.6	10.5	11.4	1.9
Velama	0.3	—	—	1.9
Mala	3.3	2.7	1.3	8.7
Madiga	4.1	4.7	8.0	3.6
Brahmin	1.9	2.1	1.8	1.9
Kamma	2.3	0.9	4.5	10.7
Kapu/Reddi	7.1	4.1	4.6	6.4
Komati	4.9	7.6	4.3	4.1
Kshatriya	3.5	0.8	1.2	10.7

*The data pertaining to Bellary district was not available in the source consulted.

the political field. They aspired for Kshatriya status as well. Reddis, Kammas, Komatis and Balijas were, and still are, dominant castes in the *Rayalaseema* region.[27]

The distribution of Castes in the region in 1921 in Table 1 demonstrates the status or strength of the Brahmins and non-Brahmins[28].

From this Table 1, it is amply clear that Brahmins constituted a very thin minority where as the non-Brahmins were in majority in each district of the *Rayalaseema* region. All these factors influenced the non-Brahmins to raise, argue, question and resist the Brahmin superiority or supremacy in all respects. In this context Sumit Sarkar's observation:

> "...The old assumption of an absolutely rigid and unchanging hierarchy of castes has also been rejected, and numerous instances are being discovered, in the recent and not-so-recent past, of what M.N. Srinivas called 'Sanskritising' tendencies-*jatis* asserting a higher status for themselves through borrowing customs, manners and taboos from groups traditionally superior to them..."[29]

On account of their precarious position, the non-Brahmin castes of the region initiated their upward mobility akin or parallel to Brahmins. For instance, according to Susan Bayly:

> "...even before the British conquest, there were men of modest birth, who had advanced themselves by becoming commercial agents (*dubashes*) to the East India Company...they too began to involve themselves with Brahmin ritualists, investing above all in the rites of *shraddha* (funerary purification),...which mark successive stages in the life of the conformist twice-born 'cast Hindu'. Similar specialists in the South took up new forms of ritualised devotion at the expanding sacred sites of the Tamil and Telugu country, particularly the great pilgrimage complex at Tirupati,"[30] (in Chittoor district) of the region.

Some of these non-Brahmin castes have appropriated and re-deployed the past for their upward mobility and ritually higher status or position on par with Brahmins. Though not for Brahminical status, they fought for certain rituals and rites like birth and death ceremonies denied to them by Brahmins. This cultural struggle was revealed through a study of literature placed before the Chittoor District Court in an early 19th Century case involving claims to free cultural and ritual access to Vedic and Puranic traditions by the Vishva Brahmins. For instance, the text *Chittoor Jilla Adalatu Kortu Teerpu* ('Judgement of Chittoor District Court') compiled and written by Panduru Kuppacharyulu, reprinted in Tenali in 1984 in Telugu, is a compilation of seminal judgment upholding the right of Vishva Brahmins to perform marriage and other ritual rites, which were disputed by orthodox Brahmins. This text gives an insight into the way the Vishva Brahmin caste marshaled the Puranic and Itihasa traditions in their favour. Colonial judicial mediation seldom accentuated conflicts around ritual and cultural space and contests for social hegemony. There were a series of judgments delivered by the colonial courts during 19th and first half of 20th centuries which boosted the ritual and cultural struggles of the Vishva Brahmins often in the name of 'valid history'.[31]

The organization of caste associations and the articulation of caste consciousness among non-Brahmins by various castes of the region led the non-Brahmin movement to consolidate or strengthen its position further.

Caste Associations (*Kula Sabhas*) and Consciousness

Several intellectuals known as 'organic intellectuals'[32], "the thinking and organising elements" and 'mature sociologists'[33], "for whom the task is to maximize the welfare of its members" of the non-Brahmin castes were started caste associations (traditional *Kula Sabhas*), organized meetings and raised caste movements to ventilate their grievances and develop consciousness.[34] The 'intellectuals' or 'sociologists' were leaders or elites and activists of the caste associations.[35] As a result, each and every caste of the non-Brahmin castes formed its association. For instance, The *Arya Vaisya Mahasabha*, The *Kamma Mahajana Sangam* and The *Reddi Mahajana Sangam* or *Sabha* were founded in 1907, 1910, 1914 and 1920 respectively.[36] In the *Rayalaseema* region Vaisyas, Reddis, Kammas, Telagas, Padmasalis, were in forefront to conduct their respective caste associations.

Arya-Vaisya Mahasabha

Arya-Vaisyas had *Dwajahood* (twice born) like Brahmins.[37] The *Arya-Vaisya Mahasabha* had conducted its meetings in different parts of Andhra, Madras Presidency and South India. The *Rayalaseema* region, along with other regions of South India, participated in these conferences and the region had got its identity. For instance, when the Fourth Conference was held at Eluru in 1910 and was attended by 1000 delegates from South India, Bellary was selected as headquarters for the people of the region. Apart from it, Arya-Vaisyas started a hostel at Bellary with a donation of Rs.28000 given by Mrs.Subbalakshmamma.[38] Further, *Arya-Vaisya Mahasabha* conducted some of its Sessions in the region. For instance, the Seventeenth *Arya-Vaisya Mahajana Sabha* was held at Mahanandi in Kurnool district. Noted Telugu poet Nalam Krishna Rao was Presided over the meeting. He pleaded for unity between the *Rayalaseema* and Coastal Andhra people. Several resolutions were passed for the upliftment of the Arya-Vaisya caste people.[39]

Telaga Mahajana Sabha

Telagas were termed themselves as Kapus. By profession they were agriculturists.[40] The first *Telaga Mahajana Sabha* was met at Railway Kodur in Kadapa district in September 1920. The president of the association, Nanjappa, spoke on the local issues like the *Telaga* caste development, unity among *Telaga* people, national education, women education, removal of child marriages and dowry system, political awareness and the achievements of Europe and America in general and Japan in particular.[41] The later *Telaga* Conferences were held mostly in the coastal Andhra areas than in the *Rayalaseema* region, since the population of *Telagas* was more in the former than in the latter. But some of the leaders of the region were participated in these conferences as they had good rapport with the prominent coastal Andhra leaders like Kurma Venkata Reddi Naidu, who seldom visited the region.[42]

Padmasali Mahajana Sabha

Similarly, *Padmasalis* (cloth producers and merchants) were spread over the region in large number. They conducted meetings to awaken their caste people. For instance, they decided to organize the *Padmasali Mahajana Sabha* at Pullampet. They elected a prominent leader of the area, Nukala Venkatasubbaiah, as the Chairman of the Reception Committee. Later, Nukala Venkatasubbaiah, called upon the people of the caste to participate in large scale in the ensuing meeting to be held at *Sri Bahuttama Vidyadhana Sabha* Free School, Pullampet village in Kadapa district on June 22-23, 1921. He assured the people about their transport by bus and rail, hospitality or boarding and free meals on the occasion.[43] In 1921 under the aegis of Kondamachupalli Padmasali village Panchayat in Siddhavattam taluk of Kadapa district the *Padmasali* Caste Association was met in a grand way. The meeting gave importance to the prohibition of liquor and all the participants took pledge to implement the prohibition. Apart from it, they took keen interest in free education available through night school system. This change and awareness among the *Padmasali* people astonished the upper caste people of the region.[44] In the first week of January 1934 the Executive Committee of the *Padmasali Mahajana Sabha* met at Proddatur in Kadapa district of the region and resolved to conduct the seventh *Padmasali Mahajana Sabha* in Madras on the eve of Easter. The committee took several decisions for the success of the coming meeting and closed its session to meet on February 26 to take further steps. On this occasion one of the activists of the association appealed to philanthropists of the region to come forward to donate funds liberally for the success of the meeting in order to organise the eighth *Padmasali Mahajana Sabha*.[45]

Reddi Mahajana Sabha

In the same way, *Reddi Mahajana Sangam* was active in the region. As M.N. Srinivas and Rajani Kothari pointed out, this caste was one of the dominant upper non-Brahmin castes in the region in particular and other regions in general. They spread all over south India. This caste had its own hoary past. The credit for this socio-economic-linguistic genesis and development of the Reddi community, in all respects, goes to Savai Raja Rameshwar Rao Bhairi Balavanthu Maha Bhoopal of the Wanaparthy *Samasthanam* who lived between 1820 and 1869 and, later, his family. They started the Reddi Hostel in 1918 with donations. In the same year the first Reddi hostel meeting was held at Hyderabad. Under its impact, the *Reddi Jana Sangha* was formed in 1902 (1920?) by the Raja of Munagala Nayani Venkata Ranga Rao and Dr. C.R. Reddi. It was Dr. C.R. Reddi who presided over the two Provincial Reddi Conferences held in 1917 and 1920 at Nellore and started the *Reddi Jana Sangha* at Madras.[46]

The *Reddi Jana Sangha* had organized ten *Reddi Mahajana Sabhas* in different parts of south India to cater to the needs of the Reddi community during the period under review. The First *Reddi Mahajana Sabha* was held in Cuddalore in Tamil Nadu in 1913 under the Chairmanship of Raj Bahadur Agram Subbarayulu Reddiar, who later became the Chief Minister of the Madras State. It was first started as a District Conference, but was attended by the members of the Reddi community from other areas as well.[47] The Second *Reddi Mahajana Sabha* was met in November 1916 under the Chairmanship of Kadapa Koti Reddi. Kusam Bapi Reddi acted as the Chairman of the Reception Committee. Prominent leaders, Nambur-Devagiri Subba Reddi, Nellore-Kalam Reddi, Kurnool-Narayana Reddi and Mysura

Reddi were participated in the meeting. The next conference was held in June 1917 at Nellore under the Chairmanship of the Raja of Munagala, Raja Nayani Venkata Ranga Reddi Bahadur. The then Zamindar of Buchireddipalem, Dodla Venkata Rama Reddi was honoured with the Chairman of the Reception Committee. The Raja of Munagala, in his presidential address, raised the idea of having a permanent society for the welfare of the Reddi community. It was also decided to collect grants and donations from the philanthropists of the Reddi community and give scholarships to the poor students of Reddi caste. Thus, this meeting had laid a foundation for the uplift of the Reddi community. The Fourth *Reddi Mahajana Sabha* was held in 1920 under the Chairmanship of Dr. C.R. Reddi, a distinguished scholar and educationist of Chittoor in the region. Rao Bahadur A.Subba Reddi, a retired Deputy Superintendent of Police, was the Chairman of the Reception Committee. It was in this meeting that Dr. C.R. Reddi gave impetus to the Sabha to be consolidated and strengthened further. It was in this conference that Dr. C.R. Reddi gave an extempore, stirring and thought-provoking speech on the socio-economic-political conditions of the country and called upon the people to develop awareness to understand their position and achieve their goals.[48]

The Fifth *Reddi Mahajana Sabha* was organized in the same year at Anaparthi in East Godavari District. It was held under the Chairmanship of Kadapa Koti Reddi. Chairman of the Reception Committee was Dwarampudi Rama Reddi. Among the prominent leaders who attended the meeting was the editor of *Reddi Rani*, Mallidi Sathi Reddi. Later, the Sixth Conference of the *Reddi Mahajana Sabha* was held in December 1920 at Madanapalli in Chittoor district of the region. Dr. C.R. Reddi and T.N. Narayana Reddi were acted as President and Chairman of the Reception Committee respectively. The next Session, Seventh, of the Sabha was held at Kurnool in 1922. The Raja of Wanaparthy, Krishna Deva Rao, acted as President and C.V. Ranga Reddi worked as Chairman of the Reception Committee. It was in this meeting that the Raja of Wanaparthy donated

Rs. 50000, and the interest accrued on that should be earmarked for the distribution of scholarship to the poor Reddi students. Mrs. Annapoornamma, daughter of Subba Reddi of Nellore, who was the first woman graduate (B.A.), was honoured with a gold medal. Later, she was encouraged by the Sabha to pursue her M.A. degree and she became the first woman post-graduate from the Reddi community.[49] The secretary of the association, Kadapa Koti Reddi, informed the people about the amount of Rs. 4500 which was earmarked for the scholarships to be distributed to the poor students of the caste for the year 1926-27. He further said that due to the shortage of amount many applications were rejected. The amount was donated by the Zamindars, Vellivedu Narasimha Reddi, Wanaparthy Maharaja, Munagala Raja, Suddapalli Ramachandra Reddi and the Association itself.[50]

The Eighth *Reddi Mahajana Sabha* was inaugurated by Dr. C.R. Reddi in 1925 at Madras. V.C. Narasimha Reddi acted as Chairman. Prominent leaders and people from Madras, Mysore and the Nizam's State of Hyderabad were participated in these conferences. Later, for want of funds and followers the *Reddi Mahajana Sabha* went into oblivion for four years. But in 1929 the Ninth *Reddi Mahajana Sabha* was held at Kadapa under the Presidentship of Bahadur Sathi Venkata Reddi and Kadapa Koti Reddi as the Chairman of the Reception Committee. Noted intellectuals like Dr. C.R. Reddi and B.Ramachandra Reddi were present in the meeting. In 1931, on June 20th and 21st, the Tenth *Reddi Mahajana Sabha* was held at Anantapur. It was to be held under the Chairmanship of the Speaker of the Madras Legislative Assembly, Bejawada Ramachandra Reddi, but due to his illness, Minister of Education of the Madras State, Kumara Swamy Reddi had presided over the Session. Bejawada Ramachandra Reddi's speech, which was read inabsentia, lamented that Rs. 10 lakhs which was proposed to be collected a decade back as a permanent fund for the Sabha was yet to be materialized. He appealed to all members of the community to come forward and donate generously to educate the poor and deserving youth of the Reddi community. Gooty Lakshma Reddi, the then President of the Anantapur District Board, was the Chairman of the Reception Committee. In his speech, Lakshma Reddi had appealed to the Reddi community:

> "It is insulting to note that we have not many qualified members in our community, after all it was we who had given to life to many arts in the past. It is important that we contribute generously to the building of the infrastructure needed to educate our students. Our women have no education and it is a serious and shameful mistake which has to be set right. We, not only should organize *Reddi Mahajana Sabhas* at the State level, but, we must also have an exclusive Reddi Education Fund to help the needy Reddi students. We also must establish hostels, exclusively for Reddis' wherein the poor students are given free boarding which will help in the publicity of education in the community at a vast pace".[51]

Kshatriya Mahajana Sabha

The Kshatriya community was sub-divided into Agnikula Kshatriyas and Arya Kshatriyas. Even though, initially they were aloof from politics later they had entered into politics to ameliorate the grievances of their community. They had attended the Sessions. In this context, the Fourth *Arya Kshatriya Mahajana Sabha* was held at Chitradurga in the erstwhile Mysore State and the present Karnataka State. About 1000 people from different parts of South India like Madras, Bangalore, Mysore, Kolar and Hindupuram in Anantapur district of the region had participated in the meeting.[52] A prominent leader of both Kadapa and Kurnool districts of the region, Gadicharla Harisarvothama Rao addressed a huge gathering in 1908 in the *Andhra Kshatriya Sabha*. He laid impetus to women's education and the eradication of child marriages in order to develop the community.[53]

Kamma Mahajana Sabha

Kammas, along with others, had organized a number of meetings in several parts of south India. The First *Kamma*

Mahajana Sabha was held in November 1910 at Kowtavaram in Krishna district under the Presidentship of Kantamaneni Venkatarangaiah. The *Indian Patriot*, which was published from Madras, gave wide coverage on this meeting in its issue of 27th November 1910. Noted leaders, Kumara Raja of Challapalli and Mr.Ankivedu Prasad Bahadur had played a crucial role in this meeting. Both of them, according to the paper, invited the attention of the Kammas to take-up some of the burning issues like education, early marriages, dowry system, agriculture, cattle breeding, and pasture lands for the development of their caste. Noted intellectuals of the *Rayalaseema* region participated in this meeting.[54] Later, the *Kamma Mahajana Sabha* had conducted its conferences in different parts of Andhra and south India. The Seventh *Kamma Mahajana Sabha* held at Nidubrolu in Guntur district on 21 and 22 June 1919. Under the influence of Garapati Anjaneya Choudari of Ellore in West Godavari district, Ratakonda Vinkataswami Naidu of Madanapalle in Chittoor district had presided over the conference. He gave thought-provoking speech on various issues: Indians' Loyalty towards King George V and his wife and Queen Mary of England, historical background of Kamma Caste, present position of the Kammas, Education and Women Education, Hostels for Students, Removal of Early and Child Marriages, Encouragement of Widow Marriages, Development of Agriculture and Animal Husbandry, Co-Operative Societies, Local and Societal Funds, Promotion of *Swadeshi* Industries with special emphasis on Weaving, Encouragement of Telugu Language, Special Representation to Indians in the Assemblies, Neatness, Removal of *Purdah* System, and Spirituality.[55] Subsequently, on 15 June 1929, the Tenth *Kamma Mahajana Sabha* was held at Angaluru in Krishna district. Bollini Muniswami Naidu of Chittoor in Chittoor district of the region presided over the meeting. He gave an extempore and stirring speech on several issues, particularly on education and influenced the participants.[56] Chairman for the Reception Committee, Kommareddi Pattabhiramaiah, spoke on different issues like protection of animals and promotion of animal husbandry, khaddar, education, social reform, and Kamma association's fund. He expressed condolences for the demise of prominent leaders, Ankineedu Bahaddar Zamindar, Parvataneni Mallikarjunudu, Sourirajula Naidu of Nagapattanam, Maganti Annapurnadevi, and Koverlamudi Gopalakrishnaiah, who had contributed enormously for the development of Kammas in all respects.[57] Other intellectuals like Bollini Muniswami Naidu and his brother, Bollini Narayanaswami Naidu of Chittoor, and Koverlamudi Gopalakrishna of Madanapalle in Chittoor district, and Avirineni Kondappa, Judgi Kottala in Anantapur in Anantapur district of the region, had participated in this conference.[58] In the same way they had participated in all the meetings of the *Kamma Mahajana Sabha* wherever they held.

In addition to these castes, other castes like Viswa-Brahmins, Agnikula Kshatriyas, Panchamas, Adi-Andhras, Niyogi-Brahmins, Edigas, Yagnyavalkyas, Malluthanulus, and Devadasis were also organized their respective caste conferences or associations to articulate caste consciousness among their respective caste people in order to uplift their communities.[59] But their associations were held more in coastal Andhra, Madras Presidency and other areas of south India than in the *Rayalaseema* region.

Even though these castes had started associations and conducted meetings, their role was confined to narrow and immediate gains. They continued to function independently of each other. Especially upper non-Brahmin castes like the Reddis and Kammas rose to dizzy heights and become chief political rivals to prove their supremacy. According to Sumit Sarkar, "The net result (of these associations) has often been the expression of socio-economic tensions through a kind of false-consciousness of caste solidarity, caste rivalry, and movements for Sanskritisation."[60] The upper non-Brahmin castes like Reddis/Kapus, Kammas and Velamas not only dominated in the formation and organization of caste associations but also appropriated or extracted the results of the associations. But the lower non-Brahmin castes were simply silent spectators and they were exploited by the upper non-Brahmins. The latter failed to develop awareness among people of the lower strata of the respective castes.

Pulivendula Conference

Another salient feature of the non-Brahmin movement of the region was the role of the Pulivendula Non-Brahman Conference. It was the first *Rayalaseema* Non-Brahmin Conference. It was held on 3 November 1917. K. Subba Reddi, a vakil of Pulivendula in Kadapa district and an active member of the Justice Party, was instrumental in organising this meeting and presided over the conference. He presented a detailed character of the Brahman oligarchy. Referring to V.S. Srinivasa Sastry's argument in the Imperial Legislative Council, that the non-Brahmin will prefer the Brahmin oligarchy to the British oligarchy, he pointed out that this statement 'serves us as an eye-opener and gives us a glimpse of the unknown regions of the south Indian Brahminic mind'. He went on to said:

> "While the British oligarchy touched us here and there and that too only superficially, the Brahman oligarchy pursues us at every turn and makes itself felt the innermost recesses of our life. While the power of the secular oligarchy is finite and can be understood that of the spiritual oligarchy is finite and inscrutable....the Brahman's claim of superiority by birth, their ill concealed sectarian bias...their powers of combination, their policy of mutual advancement and their inordinate selfishness in the past have made them dangerously formidable against the legitimate attempt at improvement made by other communities".[61]

He further stated, "that the non-Brahmin movement should only be a weapon of defense and not of offence and that while it should help to safeguard and advance the interests of non-Brahmins, never should it endanger the general interests of the country in any manner".[62] In one of its resolutions, the conference demanded that the distribution of elective seats in the Provincial Legislative Council should be in the proportion of Brahmins 5, Vysyas 4, Kshatriyas 2, Sudras 33, depressed classes 4, Muhammadans 10, Indian Christians 4, Anglo-Indians 4, Zamindars 3, Madras Corporation 1, Madras Rate Payers 2, Municipal Councils 9, University 1, Graduates 1, and Reserved 2.[63]

Print Media

Caste-Based or Sectarian Papers

The role of print media in the movement is yet another aspect in the growth of the movement in the region. Amidst the events of nationalist spirit that swayed the newspapers of the time, certain degree of caste identity could be noticed in the activities of print media. Though concrete details relating to their patronisation of castes are not available, names of some newspapers that were started in the region indicate that they could be termed as 'supporters of certain castes'. For instance, *Chraistava* (1908) of Proddatur, *Padmasali* (1924) of Periyavaram in Rajampet and *Reddi* (year not known) of Kadapa (all from Kadapa district of the region) were started as Telugu monthlies and fortnightly respectively. They were either started by their respective castes or started to patronise their castes or communities concerned. So also was the *Gethsemane* of Kadapa in Kadapa district of the region, which was started in 1923 as Telugu-English Monthly.[64]

Among these papers, *Chraistava* was started by S.B. Samos, a Christian, and *Padmasali* was founded by the Padmasali (Association) Community. *Reddi* was started by B. Subba Reddi for the interests of Reddi Caste, and *Gethsemane* was started by Chraistava Society of Kadapa.[65] So, it can be said that the promotion of caste or communities interests was coming to the fore from the beginning of the 20th Century, and the Christian interests initiated the move in that direction.[66]

Similarly R. Venkata Gowda and N. Venkata Subbaiah had started *Reddi Kula Patrika* and *Sri Padmasali* at Chittoor in Chittoor district of the region. *Sri Padmasali* was started as Telugu Monthly while *Reddi Kula Patrika* as Telugu newspaper (periodicity is not known). It was started in 1929.[67]

Coverage of the Print Media

The print culture was well versed in all respects to unfold the sensational news in those days. Erudite journalists will observe, discover, predict and publish in advance, incidents that will be sensitive, epoch making, and which creates sensation in the society. A luminary in innovative print culture, A.S. Iyengar was the first and rare one, who had not only 'political intuition' but also 'reporting ability', to publish the information on two notable incidents pertaining to the genesis of the non-Brahmin movement.[68] The print media of the region, like press of the other regions of the Presidency and Andhra, gave wide coverage on various aspects and developments of the Justice Party or non-Brahmin movement.

On Brahmin and Non-Brahmin question

The newspapers of the region had reported and covered both negative and positive aspects of the movement. For instance, the Chittoor paper *Venkatesa Patrika*, in its issue of the 2nd October1920 with the title, 'The non-Brahmin Problem', supported non-Brahmins, and criticised the government's support to Brahmins. According to the paper, "The non-Brahmin problem was created by Thyagaraya Chetti, Ramarayaningar, and Mr. Nair. The government had given them a helping hand. But the Brahmins criticised Government and demanded *swaraj*. The British Govternment promised to grant it. This would prejudicially affect the prestige and pay of European officers. It is therefore good to create a non-Brahmin party".[69] But the paper focused on the limitations of non-Brahmin movement under the heading, 'The non-Brahmin Movement an evil to the country'. The paper on the one hand exposed the defects of the British government and on the other appealed for unity between Brahmins and non-Brahmins. On this aspect it wrote, "The

British have plundered all our country's wealth and reduced it to poverty. It is due to our giving room to them by our Brahmins and non-Brahmins disunion. If our country is to develop and attain *swaraj*, we (Brahmins-non-Brahmins) must be united. When two men (a Brahmin and a non-Brahmin) fight with each other, it is third man (the English or the British) that gains".[70] Similarly, another paper, *Balabharati* of Anantapur, criticized both the British and non-Brahmins, asked for unity between Brahmins and non-Brahmins under the title, 'The Non-Brahmin Movement is the Country's misfortune'. It said, "the Non-Brahmins of the Madras Presidency can not alone obtain *Swaraj* for generations to come. We shall first free ourselves and then, if necessary, we shall take up the cudgel against the Brahmins".[71]

On Justice Ministry and Reforms

The press was unhappy with the functioning of the Justice Ministry and reforms introduced by it. Particularly, the *Venkatesa Patrika* of Anantapur was critical of the new Justice Ministry. It observed "that the Justice triumvirate, in the name of non-Brahmin advocacy, has eventually joined hands with the English, to ruin the poor people....[72] Further on 'The salary of the Deputy President' of the Madras Legislative Council, the paper opined that "Why should these Deputy Presidents not work without receiving any salary? If these people are paid, why should not the Members of the Council also be paid? If that is done so, many a selfish men will try to get into the Council, cheating the voters". [73]

Citing some of the defects of the reforms introduced by the Madras Legislative Council, Balabharati of Anantapur commented, "That the candidates of the Legislative Council are selfish. The conduct of business in the meeting of the Legislative Council since the 14th of this month, one sees that the members of the Council are denied even freedom of speech under the President who has won notoriety for wielding bureaucratic authority".[74] The *Venkatesa Patrika* of Chittoor expressed that the rule of the Justice Party Ministry under Mr. Ramarayanigar was oppressive and tyrannical. By citing 'The Chirala Municipality', it remarked that the actions of the Justice Party Ministers are foolish and arbitrary. If the Hon'ble Mr. Ramarayanigar thinks that much good will result from municipalities, why should he not constitute his own native place of Kalahasti (in Chittoor of the region) a municipality? Are the Ministers intended for enforcing an arbitrary system of Government?[75] The paper had also expressed its disappointment for the Ministry's attitude towards the Brahman employees.[76] The *Matruseva* of Tadipatri (Anantapur district) deplored the attitude of some of the Ministers in regard to the statement of Dr. U. Rama Rao in the Council that 'titles also may be sold in the same as, under the new University Reform Bill, memberships in the Senate are proposed to be conferred on those who pay Rs.10,000/-'.[77]

The paper drew the attention of the Government to the coercive punitive tax collection under the title, 'The Guntur punitive tax', and wrote, "The collection of the punitive tax at Guntur has begun, and with it the attachments also. The tax is levied according to the will and pleasure of the Collector. In fact, it has even fallen on the heads of some Moderates, *vakils* who have not renounced their profession, and also on non-Brahmins like Tripuraneni Ramaswamy Chowdari..."[78] It exposed the ambivalent attitude of the Education Minister, Mr. A.P. Patro, on the location of the Andhra University and wrote: "Our Education Minister Mr.Patro indulged in a more pompous pretension when he told his brother members in the Council that the Government preparing plans and estimates for the Andhra University and he put forward the lamest excuse when he said that members representing various districts had not yet settled the location of the University".[79] Referring to the visit of the Hon'ble Rai Bahdur K.V. Reddy Naidu to Anantapur, *Pinakini Patrika* of Anantapur observed, "...If the Ministers should only remember a little the fact that their duty lies in ascertaining the state of the people who are instrumental in bringing them to power, many difficulties can be got over. When is such a good fortune to come to us?"[80]

The Anantapur paper found fault with the Raja of Panagal for the introduction of The Madras Hindu Religious Endowments Bill in the Madras Legislative Council. It remarked, "the Raja of Panagal introduced the Bill with the help of the 'Justice Party' to contest in the elections". It further opined, "that the object of the Bill was to prevent the waste of temple property. It is true that the temple funds are wasted. But, it is also true, that the officiating priests are responsible for it to a great extent. Such wastage should be stopped; but can there be anything more horrible that to invest the people who have no faith in Hinduism"? The paper went on to say: "it is deplorable that this thought does not strike the 'just' minds of the 'Justice Party'. Although the members of the 'Justice Party' may become the officiating priests themselves, and it will in no way affect the Brahmins. But to give to men of other creeds through grudge for the Brahmins control over the gods, whom the non-Brahmins and their forefathers have worshipped for generations, is a proof of their narrow mindedness".[81] Later on, the same paper went on to criticise the Bill and said, "His Excellency the Viceroy should, by exercising his extraordinary powers, have refused to give his assent to the Act". It also commented, "Whether it is the Justice Party or any other Party, it is the Indians, that are to blame for the Act and the remedy lies in amending it in the light of experience gained in the actual working of it".[82]

The *Balabharati* of Anantapur, in its caption, 'Is it not unjust?', observed the prevalence of anomalies in the appointments made under the Government Order with reference to 'Communal Representation in Public Services'. "...If appointments are made by selection and not by seniority, there is scope for many errors to creep in. Moreover, this Government Order will apply to the gazetted officers as well. The result of it will be that the senior Brahman and the junior non-Brahmin employee are placed on the same footing".[83] Similarly, it observed 'partiality' in the appointments in favour of non-Brahmins. The paper criticized it under the title, 'Partiality', and said : "...(In Government service) seniority has been thrown into the background, and efficiency has been cast to the winds. The Government has resolved to give the posts of deputy collectors, tahsildars, and the other high appointments whenever they fall vacant to the non-Brahmins alone. What more evidence is needed to show the partiality (of the Government)?"[84]

On 'Dual Government' or 'Diarchy'

Regarding the nature of "Dual Government" or "Diarchy" granted to India, the *Balabharati* of Anantapur had expressed its disappointment to the reforms introduced under this scheme. The paper criticized its ideals and said, "The August declaration first gave hopes of the grant of self-government to India. When the Montford Scheme of Reforms were published, they thoroughly disappointed all parties. This frustrated all hopes entertained about these councils. We can well guess what may happen to the country under these circumstances".[85]

Similarly, *"Venkatesa Patrika* of Chittoor criticized the government for the introduction of 'Dual System of Government', selfishness, its negligence of the country and non-Brahmins' negative attitude towards the country."[86]

When elections were slated for Madras Legislative Council, several papers of the region gave wide publicity for new reforms in the place of 'Diarchy' which was introduced by the Justice Government. For instance, *Balabharati* of Anantapur of the 1 July 1920 under the title, 'The Legislative Council Elections', criticized the present Government's policies, and supported the Congress Party. It further said, "Complete self-government has to be secured within a limited time through the agitation in the Legislative Councils. Put an end to Diarchy soon, when it negate public opinion. Congress Party leaders, who are conversant with politics, who are active in public life, and who are thoroughly acquainted with the Reforms Act, should be returned to the Legislative Councils".[87]

Andhra Prakasika of Madras referring to the appointment of Mr. K.P. Lakshmana Rao, a Brahman, as the District Judge of Kadapa, observed that this appointment has dissatisfied all parties and added: "Such lessons only teach the moral that the non-Brahmin Party should, at least in future, leave off their affinity to the bureaucracy and turn to use their power in the public cause. We have to see how the Publicity Bureau will uphold this appointment".[88] The same paper urged, "that the Indian Ministers, who profess to be ready to sacrifice everything for the sake of non-Brahmins, should, out of patriotic motives, accept small salaries, and says that if they require large salaries, taxes can not be raised, and that if taxes be raised, it is the non-Brahmins that will suffer".[89]

On 'Empire Exhibition'

The British Government had planned to collect loans from the public to develop India by conducting Empire Exhibition. The Justice Party Ministry gave wide publicity to it. But many members of the Legislative Council suspected it, opposed this plan and they raised a resolution against it. Several newspapers of the *Rayalaseema* region were also against the bad intentions of the Government. They supported the resolution and gave wide coverage against Empire Exhibition. For instance, *Matruseva* of Tadipatri in Anantapur district observed the remarks made by K.V. Reddy Naidu on 'Empire Exhibition' and said: "Sir K.V. Reddy Naidu once said 'that the Empire Exhibition was for our good'. 'That if the people of the Empire were to see the raw products of India, there would be a great demand for them'. Perhaps Sir Reddy Naidu has thought that a like gain will accrue to us from the exhibition of dancing girls. It will be well if meetings are held at every place and the disapproval of the people expressed".[90]

Another paper, *Yuvabharatam* of Chittoor, of the region while supporting the resolution pointed out: "The resolution is timely and opportune. All countries take loans from their people but it is for useful purposes and not as in India for Railways which are intended more for the benefit of the foreign merchants and for the exploitation of the country than for the convenience of the people.[91] *Pinakini Patrika* of Anantapur criticized

Government's indifferent and negative policy on 'Empire Exhibition' and opined, "Some contend that the land-produce and minerals of India should be exhibited at the Empire Exhibition in England. They argue that, if raw materials such as cotton, fibre and silk, produced in India are exhibited at the Exhibition, they will fetch greater prices for, if the people of other countries want them, we can sell them at a dear price."[92]

On 'No-Confidence' Motion

One of the interesting developments was formation of the Ministry under Hon'ble the Raja of Panagal in Madras in 1920. But differences had cropped up between different leaders of the Ministry. Prominent leaders like Sir K.V. Reddy Naidu was removed and C.R. Reddy was not inducted. Apart from it, C.R. Reddy's 'no-confidence motion against the Ministry' and on several other issues, noted leaders of the Justice Party Ministry had thrown brick stones and mud stones on each other. Print media exposed these rifts varyingly. For instance, *Pinakini Patrika* of Anantapur wrote: "Sir K.V. Reddy Naidu has been thrown out from the new Ministry. Perhaps the Hon'ble the Raja of Panagal took Mr. Pillai into the Ministry fearing that the Tamilians might raise a hue and cry if no Tamilian was appointed. Whatever that may be, we are unfortunate in not having Mr. C.R. Reddy as the Minister of Education."[93] *Swarajya Patrika* of Vijayawada (Bezawada) criticized the mal-administration of the Raja of Panagal, and C.R. Reddy's no-confidence motion. It pointed out, "The 27th is approaching. Mr. Ramalinga Reddy has proclaimed a fight against the Ministry....The administration of the Raja of Panagal during the last three years has caused disgust to all the parties and lost the sympathy of the parties and people in all respects". The paper criticized the object of Ramalinga Reddy and said, "to remove the present Ministry, and have another in its place, his efforts are useless. It is all the same if under the present circumstances, a 'Rayaningar' or a 'Reddygar' is a Minister". It further said, "If real service is to be done to the country, Mr. Reddy must give up the ideas of forming a new Ministry, giving effect to the Reforms, and co-operating with the Government...Otherwise, the Swaraj Party whose object is to create deadlocks in the Government cannot come to his support..."[94] The *Andhra Patrika* of Madras gave more details of the C.R. Reddy's 'no-confidence' motion and attitude of the Justice Party Ministers'.[95] In the same way, the *Andhra Prakasika* of Madras expressed more details about the 'no-confidence motion'.[96] Similar views were expressed by the *Pinakini Patrika* of Anantapur. According to it, "From the fact that, in regard to the 'no confidence' motion moved in the Council, 41 elected members (excluding the Ministers) voted on behalf of the Ministers and 43 against them, it is clear that the Government by the present Ministry has not had the approval of the people."[97]

On Elections

The papers of the region unearthed yet another aspect i.e., elections-of the non-Brahmin movement and developed awakening among people. For instance, the *Pinakini Patrika* of Anantapur under the title 'An exhortation to the voters' quoted Mr. A. Kaleswara Rao as having delivered the following speech at Penukonda: "We have been suffering under the rule of the Justice Party. The Justice Party has urged that the political prisoners should be treated like other prisoners. It is that Party alone which has introduced the oath of allegiance. So you had better give your votes only to the *Swarjyist* candidates hereafter. All these proclaim the courage and greatness".[98]

Expressing its disappointment and discouragement regarding the elections to the Legislatures, the *Sri Sadhana Patrika* of Anantapur commented, "The Working Committee of the Congress has resolved that Congressmen should have nothing to do with the elections and that propaganda should be carried on to prevent voters from going to the polling booths and recording votes". It also said that "we have been sending representatives to the Legislatures for ten years past. The ryots must find out if this has any good to anybody at any place. Whether good has accrued or not, the expenses incident to the Legislatures have been unavoidable". The paper observed further, "over and above this, election jealousies have multiplied. These jealousies have degenerated from Brahman-non-Brahmin quarrel into 'Kamma' and 'Kapu' animosities and the little unity has perished by reason of the elections. Why hang on to such Legislatures? Candidates are not unaware that the Legislative Councils are useless..."[99] In the same way, the papers of the region had reported on different aspects of the Justice Party or non-Brahman movement. For instance, *Yuvabharatam* of Chittoor had written on 'Gooty Kesava Pillai'[100], and *Andhra Patrika* of Madras had reported on 'Unity between Brahmins and non-Brahmins', and 'Congress-League Reforms'[101] to articulate and awaken the people.

From these details of coverage and reports of the print media, it can be noticed that the tone of majority of the newspapers was against the non-Brahmin movement and its policies. But if one can observe the other side of the picture, the non-Brahmin movement was in full vigor so far as the election results and the power of the Justice Party were concerned. It is quite obvious, in this context, that the tone of the language that they expressed would be anti-non-Brahmin, since majority of the founders of these papers were Brahmins and all of them were nationalistic in their rhetoric. Besides, they had neglected the role played by the non-Brahmin movement or Justice Party in the articulation and awakening of the hitherto subordinate sections or castes of the society. Even, they did not and could not identify and give proper positive perspective to the introduction and implementation of some of the reforms by the Madras Government under the influence of the non-Brahmin movement or Justice Party leaders like Dr. C.R. Reddy, Gooty Kesava Pillai and others.

Other Landmark Developments or Events

Madras Mahajana Sabha

From the beginning or even before the inception of the non-Brahmin movement, several non-Brahmin intellectuals of the region were participated actively and instrumental in various organizations. For instance, Gooty Kesava Pillai of Gooty in Anantapur district of the region was nominated as the corresponding member of the Madras Mahajana Sabha (MMS). He held this position for the next three years. He affiliated his own organization, *Gooty People's Association*, with MMS. When the MMS had met, first, at Madras in December 1884, Gooty Kesava Pillai was the first intellectual, a non-Brahmin, of the region to attend the meeting. He was present at the second conference of the MMS held in December 1885, along with other leaders of Gooty, J. Srinivasa Rao and Y. Choudappa.[102] In the next conference of the MMS held between 1886 to 1887, yet another non-Brahmin, A. Sabhapathy Mudaliyar of Bellary (now in Karnataka) of erstwhile Ceded Districts participated in all its activities. He was a merchant and industrialist. He was elected as Municipal Commissioner, Bellary.[103]

Andhra Movement and Andhra Nationalist Association

A separate Andhra Movement was started by the Telugu speaking people in the Telugu areas of Coastal Andhra and *Rayalaseema* regions against the Madras State Government from 1913 onwards. Even though differences had persisted, from the beginning of this movement, continuously between Brahmins and non-Brahmins, majority non-Brahmins expressed their antagonism against the movement with the support of the colonial Government. But it is interesting to note here that more than three-fourths of the 1200 delegates assembled for the Special Andhra Conference at Bezwada (Vijayawada) in 1917 and half of the delegates participated in the next Conference held at Kadapa were non-Brahmins.[104] This shows that on the one side one section of non-Brahmins did not support the Andhra movement due to the fear of Brahmin oligarchy but on the other side another group of non-Brahmins had extended their support to it as they wanted to strengthen their position among people. Further more, when the internal differences were rampant among different groups of non-Brahmins themselves, leaders like Gooty Kesava Pillai and Dr. C.R. Reddy had opposed the non-Brahmin movement, criticized the negative policies of the Justice Party Government and supported Andhra Movement. Gooty Kesava Pillai and his followers were known as Congress non-Brahmins. This was particularly so after 1934 and 1937 elections, when they lost power and many leaders had left Justice Party and joined Congress Party.

On 13 November 1921 the General Body meeting of the Andhra Nationalist Association was held at Vijayawada Town Hall. Hundred Members from different districts had attended the meeting. On the eve of the elections for twenty-four member body, one of the participants reminded the organizers that more members should be elected from non-Brahmins. When elections were held, fourteen members were elected from non-Brahmins. From the Rayalaseema region the members elected were: Chittoor-C.V. Rangam Sreshti, Kadapa-Kethu Venkata Reddy, Kurnool-Medam Venkataiah Sreshti, Bellary-Dharmavaram Gopalacharyulu and Anantapur-Kalluru Subba Rao.[105]

Election Scenario

Till the raise of non-Brahmin movement or Justice Party, the domination of the Brahminism was at its peak in Madras as well as in Andhra areas. This angered the non-Brahmins castes and they questioned the oligarchy of the Brahmins. In addition to it, they have decided to strengthen their position in all spheres of life. This led to the bitter animosity between the Brahmins and the non-Brahmins and it can be found in the sphere of elections held to the Madras Legislative Council, which was established under 1919 Montague-Chelmsford Act.

To bridge the widening gulf between Brahmins and non-Brahmins the British official, Lord Meston, made a compromise proposal in 1920 under the Act of 1919 for separate representation in the Madras Legislative Council. He recommended reservation of two seats in the City of Madras and one seat in each of the plural constituencies for the districts of Anantapur, Bellary, Chittoor, Kadapa, and Kurnool along with other districts of Andhra to the non-Brahmins.[106] The Meston Award reflected the region so much that, as a result, many leaders or intellectuals of non-Brahmin castes were met often and interacted each other to strengthen the Justice Party position from the gross root level in order to usurp the power in the ensuing elections by capturing as many seats as possible. On 17th March 1920, the Raja of Panagal, Panganti Parthasarathi Rayaningar had written a letter from Kalahasti to one of the prominent non-Brahmin leaders of the Chittoor district, Ratakonda Venkataswami Naidu and said,

> "Now that Lord Meston has given the award, we have to see about to work to make the best out of it. You know our district has to return two representatives, one of the seats being reserved to the non-Brahmins and the other open for both Brahmins and non-Brahmins to compete for. Our sole aim should be to see that this general seat is also captured by us. It will be no easy task, unless we make a united and determined effort to achieve it. We must organize and proceed to work systematically from now. The others are already in the field. I propose for this purpose there should be a District Non-Brahmin Association at Chittoor with branches at the Taluk headquarters and if necessary at other important places working in unison with the District Association. We should prevent any competition among the non-Brahmins themselves, especially in the case of the seat open for both the Brahmins and non-Brahmins. This can be done only if we can see to it that one seat of these selected by the District Association stand for election and the other, if any redirecting back, working whole heartedly for the selected candidates. You know our District Board meeting is posted to 31st instant. I

have written to Devaraja Mudaliar, B. Muni Swami Naidu, and Arunachala Mudaliar to call a meeting of the non-Brahmins at Chittoor on that day. I request you to kindly see that you attend the meeting even it should be at the cost of some inconvenience and make our other District Board non-Brahmin members also attend. I have also written to them."[107]

The same tendency can be observed in other districts of the region. According to the Meston award, later, when elections were held in 1920, the Justice Party had won, in the absence of Congress, majority seats and formed Ministry. Similarly, in the 1923 elections also it came out victoriously as the single largest party in the tripartite contest between Justicites, Nationalists and Congress leaders and formed Ministry.[108] The region was instrumental in electing from the North Central Landholders Constituency, in which the region was a part, the Raja of Panagal, Panaganti Ramarayaningar, a Justicite, in the three successive elections of 1920, 1923, and 1926.[109] Apart from it, Justice Party had maintained its strength and domination in the District Boards, Taluk Boards, Municipalities and District Education Councils of the region during the second and third decades of twentieth century. For instance, in the Anantapur District Board among the total thirty-eight members twenty-four were non-Brahmins where as Brahmins were six only. Similarly, twenty-seven and four members were non-Brahmins and Brahmins respectively out of thirty-seven members in the Chittoor District Board. Twenty-five were non-Brahmins and six were Brahmins out of thirty-six members of the Kadapa District Board and thirty-one members were non-Brahmins and seven members were Brahmins among forty-four members of the Kurnool District Board.

Another interesting thing is elected members were more than the nominated members. For instance, in the Anantapur District Board thirty members were elected where as nominated members were eight only. Similarly, elected members were twenty-seven and nominated were ten in Chittoor District Board.

Table-II: Position of the Non-Brahmins in the Rayalaseema Region, 1923

District	*District Board*				*District Taluk*				*Municipalities*			
	Non-Brahmins	*Brah-mins*	*Other*	*Total*	*Non-Brahmins*	*Brah-mins*	*Others*	*Total*	*Non-Brahmins*	*Brah-mins*	*Others*	*Total*
Anantapur	24	6	8	38	55	20	64	139	12	3	17	32
Chittoor	27	4	6	37	52	5	3	60	16	8	8	32
Kadapa	25	6	5	35	70	19	17	106	8	5	19	32
Kunool	31	7	7	45	63	14	13	96	10	7	19	36
Total	107	23	26	156	240	58	94	101	46	23	33	132

*Data was not available on the District of Bellary in the sources consulted.

In the Kadapa District Board, twenty-seven were elected and nine were nominated and thirty-four members were elected and eleven were nominated in the Kurnool District Board.[110] All the elected members were belonged to different areas of the district concerned. This shows the influence and strength of the non-Brahmins among different sections of people in the region. But the pitiable thing is that the upper caste non-Brahmins like Reddys, Kammas and Velamas had occupied prominent place and dominant position whereas the lower caste non-Brahmins were not identified and got their due share. This phenomenon and tendency can be observed in the various Taluk Boards and Municipalities of the region from Table II:

In the District Education Councils of the region also majority members were from non-Brahmin castes. But here also the upper caste non-Brahmins had dominated at the cost of lower caste non-Brahmins as observed earlier.[112] Subsequently, the position of the non-Brahmins was weakened due to their internal bickering, especially between upper caste non-Brahmins themselves. By the end of the third decade of the twentieth century, when these differences were on the rise, the Swarajya Party on the one side and Brahmins on the other took advantage of these developments, they made scathing attack against the policies and mistakes of the Justice Party government and the attitude of the non-Brahmins. Several intellectuals and leaders of the region like Vellala Ramakrishana Sastry, Gullapalli Venkata Punnaiah, Ayyadevara Kaleswara Rao, Gadde Rangaiah Naidu, D. Venkatanagi Reddy, Kadapa Koti Reddy, and Gadicharla Harisarvothama Rao and organisations like the Andhra Provincial Congress Committee, the District and Taluk Congress Committees and press correspondents of the newspapers like *Andhra Patrika* had undertook vigorous election campaign and criticised these defects of the non-Brahmins.[113] Resultantly, several notable leaders of the Justice Party in the region were defeated in the 1926 elections. If we observe the entire Andhra scenario, before 1926 elections the strength of the Justice Party in the Madras Legislative Assembly was 43,

Table-III: Position of the Justice Party in Rayalaseema Region before and after 1926 Elections

District	Before 1926 Member Represented	Before 1926 Party	After 1926 Member Represented	After 1926 Party
Chittoor	B. Muniswami Naidu	Justice Party	B. Muniswami Naidu	Justice Party
	C. Ramalinga Reddy	Swatantra Party	C.R. Parthasarathi Aiyangar	Congress Party
Kadapa	T. M. Narasimhachar-yulu	Swatantra Party	Arcot Parasurama Rao	Congress Party
	K. Koti Reddy	Congress Party	K. Koti Reddy	Congress Party
Kurnool	K. Sarabha Reddy	Justice Party	K. Sarabha Reddy	Justice Party
	B. Sesha Reddy	Justice Party	G. Harisarvothama Rao	Congress Party
Bellary	A. Rangandha Mudaliar	Swatantra Party	A. Ranganadha Mudaliar	Swatantra Party
Anantapur	P. Kesava Pillai	Justice Party	P. Obi Reddy	Congress Party
	G. Rameswara Rao	Swatantra Party	C. Narayana Reddy	Congress Party

while Swatantra Party secured 26 seats, Congress got 23 seats and the English got 6 members among the total 98 members. But after 1926 elections Justice Party's position had decreased abnormally. For instance, out of 98 members it got only 13 seats, where as the Congress, Swatantra, and the British got 47, 32 and 6 seats respectively.[114] In the *Rayalaseema* region also the Justice Party's position had come down from four to two in the 1926 elections. Many leaders of the Justice Party in the region were defeated. Surprisingly prominent Justice Party leaders of the region, C.R. Reddy, Gooty Kesava Pillai, C.L. Narasimha Reddy, and T. Narasa Reddy had not only opposed the policies of the Justice Party but also joined Congress Party. This shows the dramatic debacle of the Justice Party in the region. This can be visualised from the Table-III:[115]

Since majority leaders of the non-Brahmin leaders left the Justice Party and joined Congress Party, Justice Party candidates were less when compared to the Congress candidates in the subsequent elections held in 1930, 1934 and 1937. Vigorous campaigning was undertaken by the Congress activists than Justicites and other party activists. In spite of it, Justice Party did not lose its identity in the region. It contested and won in other elections held for Central and Provincial Assemblies. For instance, in 1930 elections T.N. Ramakrishna Reddy of Madanapalli in Chittoor district was elected from Ceded Districts and Non-Muslim Rural Constituency to the Central Assembly where as S. Gouse Mohideen was elected from Muslim Kadapa Rural Constituency to the Provincial Legislative Assembly in 1937 as Justice Party candidates. Similarly, Munshi Abdul Wahab Saheb was elected as a Justicite from Muslim Madras North Constituency, in which the region was a part, to the Madras Legislative Council.[116] This shows the influence of Justice Party or non-Brahmin movement in the region, despite its dwindling position.

Prominent Leaders

In the *Rayalaseema* region several prominent leaders worked for the Justice Party or Non-Brahmin Movement to articulate non-Brahmin ideology and develop consciousness among non-Brahmin people. For instance, Gooty Kesava Pillai (1860-1933)[117] of Gooty in Anantapur district, C. Ramalinga Reddy (1880-1951),[118] otherwise or better known as C. R. Reddy, of Chittoor, Panaganti Raja Ramarayanigar[119] of Sri Kalahasti, and Bollini Muniswami Naidu (1885-1938),[120] Ratakonda Venkataswami Naidu (1875-1953) of Madanapalli,[121] C.R.Parthasarathy Ayyangar, Mir Hussain Saheb, Doraswami Ayyangar, and Rev. John Key of Chittoor in Chittoor district, K. Subba Reddy and Palem Doraswamy Naidu[122] of Pulivendula, C. L. Narasimha Reddy, Gangadhara Siva, and T. Narasa Reddy of Kadapa district, and K. Sarabha Reddy, D. Ranga Reddy and P. Sesha Reddy of Kurnool district played significent role in the activities of the Justice Party or non-Brahmin movement in the region.

Gooty Kesava Pillai

Gooty Kesava Pillai of Gooty was a multifaceted genius of the region. He was one of the members', who met at the residence of Mr. Ethiraj Mudaliar, High Court Vakil in 1915, to start the South Indian People's Association, from which the Justice Party was emerged in its full form. He was very much associated, from the very beginning, with the Justice Party and the Non-Brahmin Movement and he also thought that it was not so virulent in its approach towards any other group or community. Further, he played, in the beginning, a significant role in the activities of the Justice Party, because, neither the communal hatred nor aggressive attitude towards other political groups were raised. But he realized, subsequently, that the policies adopted by the Justice Party might or would lead to caste-war. He submitted a memorandum to the British Official, Evans, to make a compromise between Brahmins and non-Brahmins. He said,

> "Dear Mr. Evans, I was sorry and depressed that a compromise could not be reached between the Brahmins and the non-Brahmins. I fear that feelings may grow

more embittered, 30 out of 60 is more or less assured by the Government of India's pronouncement. I would submit shortly the views of the Madras Presidency Association of which I happen to be the President you may know that my Association is composed of what Dr. Nair's party call, pro-Brahmin or non-Brahmin. From what I was able to gather the members of my Association consider that a few more seats should be reserved, and each District or group should have half of the seats reserved. If any District is considered too small for a plural constituency, it might be grouped with another, for instance, Anantapur and Cuddapah are a group, Bellary and Kurnool with another. The non-Brahmin classes need to be emancipated from the religious and social shackles, and freed from political obstacles. The Brahmins would not have even 10 or 12 seats assigned, to them, though they are not much more than Indian Christians in population. Why? I trust and hope that His Excellency's goodwill statesmanship, and large heart, will find a solution"[123]

Apart from it, he did not like loosing his long association with the noted Brahmin intellectuals or leaders of Tamil Nadu like Vijayaraghavachariar, Sir C. P. Ramaswamy Iyer and others. His conviction made him to withdraw from the Justice Party. But he started a rival organization namely The Madras Presidency Association under his Presidentship with the leading non-Brahmin leaders such as V. Chakkari Chettiar, P.S. Guruswamy Naidu, Salla Guruswamy Chetty against the fissiparous and factious tendencies of the Justice Party. The Indian Patriot edited by Mr. Karunakara Menon was set on firm footing and functioned as mouth piece of this newly formed party. But both of them would not survive for long. Throughout his later life, he was non-committal to any political organization or party. But he had good relations with the leaders like Dr. T. M. Nair and the Raja of Panagal, Panuganti Raja Ramarayanigar of the Justice Party on the one side and other parties and leaders on the other. He was a great social reformer. He worked for the welfare of the non-Brahmin depressed classes in Tamil Nadu and Andhra as well. The Fifth Session of the Depressed Classes Conference was held under his Presidentship on 31 December 1914 at Cuddalore. He submitted a copy, of the resolutions passed in the conference, to the Chief Secretary of the Government of Madras for consideration.[124]

He had European officers as friends like Lord Pentland, Lord Carmichael, Sir Murray Hammick, Sir William Meyer, Sir John Atkinson, Sir Charles Todhunter, Sir Harold Stuart and others as Sir Mohammad Habibullah and Sir Ahmad Hussain. Similarly, Pillai was included as one among the national leaders such as Mahadev Ranade, Gopalakrishana Gokhale, Mrs. Besant, Hasan Imam, Mazhar ul Haq, Jinnah, Gandhi, Motilal Nehru, Tej Bahadur Sapru, Madan Mohan Malaviya, and Pundit Misra.[125]

Dr. Cattamanchi Ramalinga Reddy or Dr. C.R. Reddy

On the same genre came the great leader of the region, Dr. Cattamanchi Ramalinga Reddy. He was reverently known as Dr. C.R. Reddy. During his early part of his Primary Education, when he was in second form, he got a bitter experience when his caste was humiliated, sarcastically, as *'Reddy-maddi-sarayi buddi'* (Reddy-dirty-liquor vessel), by a Brahmin boy. Later, when he was doing his Under Graduate Course (B.A.) at Madras Christian College, Madras, he was astonished to note that separate hostel rooms were earmarked for Brahmin and non-Brahmin students. He stayed in one of the non-Brahmin rooms. In B.A. Course, his history teacher was Dr. Kelleth. On one occasion, Dr. Kelleth asked the students to tell their castes. Similarly, when he asked Dr. C.R. Reddy, 'What is your caste'? He replied that 'I am an Aborginee'. This surprised Kelleth, and he asked once again, 'What prompted you to name yourself as Aborginee'? Then, Dr. C.R. Reddy replied, "I don't know why people termed or named themselves as Brahmins and non-Brahmins. Since thousands of years, hundreds of communities or societies had been living in this land or country with each other. Then, is their blood surviving or living or flowing among these artificial or synthetic castes?"[126] These incidents of his early life might have had nurtured or influenced Dr. C.R. Reddy's mindset and prepared a ground work so solid that he became a staunch non-Brahmin activist or Justice Party leader in the region.

Like Kesava Pillai, he was also a multidimensional character and a rare personality of the time. As far as the Justice Party or the Non-Brahmin Movement of the region was concerned, he was a consistent politician from the beginning. Under the influence of his friend and a prominent Justice Party leader of Chittoor, Bollini Muniswamy Naidu, Dr. C.R. Reddy had left his education field, resigned for the Mysore Education Officer post, came to Madras and entered into politics in 1922. He had contested for the seat of University Constituency which was vacated by the term of Srinivasa Aiyyangar and got victorious. On 14 February 1922 he took the oath of office in the Madras Legislative Council.[127]

As he was a versatile genius and multidimensional character, he proved his credibility and identity in all respects. Even though the British Official, Montague, introduced several constitutional reforms in India, he resigned due to the pressure in the Parliament. When a resolution was passed in the Madras Legislative Council to appreciate the services he rendered to the country, Montague expressed his happiness and said, "I believe the gesture of Indian people". Later, on 22 March 1922, Dr. C.R. Reddy gave an extempore speech in which he stated that, "he (Montague) was a good friend of us, who did yeomen service to India".[128]

Subsequently, notwithstanding he belonged to Justice Party and Non-Brahmin Movement in the region, he criticized-positively, constructively and objectively - the policies of the Government. The Government was also convinced and agreed, very much, with his arguments. His speeches were not only stirring, scintillating, thought-provoking, praise-worthy and press-worthy but also lively, humorous and harmonious. Some of his notable speeches were: on the limitations of budget on 7 March 1922, his critique of over taxation on the people, on coercive economic policies of the Government, on the faulty implementation of the educational and commercial policies of the Government, on the defects of the introduction of The Madras Hindu Religious Endowments Bill in the Madras Legislative Council on 18 December 1922, on the Bill for the Reconstruction of the Madras University of 1922 on 22 November 1922, on the starting of and the location of Andhra University Bill, on the 1923-24 Budget Speech on 24 March 1923, on the Government's unnecessary and huge expenditure on Military and the Railways, on the Government's oppressive and tyrannical policies and the police atrocities in Malabar, antagonism against the inclusion of Brahmins in the musical parties during the temple festivals and on the no-confidence motion against the Justice Ministry.[129] His speech on 26 November 1928, on the 'no-confidence motion' against the Ministry was a sensation itself in the Legislative Council.[130] The print media of the Presidency had reported on this speech both in India and abroad.[131] He had parallels or symmetry with great leaders of the country like Surendra Nath Benerjee, Bipin Chandra Pal, Bal Gangadhar Tilak, Gopalakrishna Gokhale, Srinivasa Sastry, and Raghavendra Rao in this respect.[132] Like Gooty Kesava Pillai, he had several British Officials and top brass leaders' of the Government as his friends. As in Madras, he played a pivotal role in other states as well. He, along with other leaders and intellectuals, tried to unite different non-Brahmin groups and start *Praja Mitra Mandali* in Mysore.[133]

The strength of the Justice Party or non-Brahmin movement forced the government to take steps in favour of the non-Brahmins. For instance, removal of socio-religious inequality, breaking of monopoly in the public services and honorary offices, communal representation, education facilities, the uplift of the depressed classes, revival of village panchayat system, amenities in the villages, more emphasis to agriculture, rural indebtedness through co-operative societies and land mortgage banks, improvement of the condition of the tenantry in zamindary areas and economic council to co-ordinate the activities of the various nation building departments were some of the notable achievements or major changes that were brought about in favour of the non-Brahmins.[134]

Despite several efforts were made to unite different sections of non-Brahmins on the one side and Brahmins and non-Brahmins on the other, the differences persisted and this damaged the image of the Justice Party very much. In the elections, later, to the Districts Boards the Justice Party was crushed by the Congress in the region, as elsewhere. For instance, the Justice candidate was defeated in the presidential election of Kurnool District Board. D. Ranga Reddy defeated in the election said: "Had it not been for the local personal differences among the Justicites of this (Kurnool) district, there would not have been Congress success in the President's election.[135] Further more, many non-Brahmin leaders of the region were joined the Congress Party which resulted finally in the disappearance of the Justice Party. For instance, C. L. Narasimha Reddy of Kadapa district left Justice Party and joined Congress Party.[136]

Conclusion

Notwithstanding the non-Brahmin movement articulated demands of its various castes, in the initial stages. It failed miserably due to the differences between various non-Brahmin groups. Particularly, the negative attitude of the upper non-Brahmins like Reddys and Kammas on the one side and Kapus and Velamas on the other towards the lower non-Brahmin castes had weakened the non-Brahmin movement in Andhra in general and Rayalaseema in particular during the period under study. Finally, when the non-Brahmins lost in the elections in 1937, majority of the non-Brahmin leaders or Justicites had left the Justice Party and joined Congress Party. This led to the disintegration and disappearance of the non-Brahmin movement in the region. But, subsequently under the influence of the ideals of the iconic leaders like B.R. Ambedkar, Jyothiba Phule, and Narayan Guru, the consciousness had gained momentum among lower non-Brahmin castes in the socio-economic-political fields in the recent past. They have been trying their best to mobilise their respective caste people to question the hegemony of the dominant castes in the society and political fields in order to achieve their needs and aspirations and solve their burning problems. They could not put a check to the hegemony of the upper non-Brahmin castes due to their poverty and economic and societal isolation, still, from the mainstream life. The domination and hegemony of the upper non-Brahmin castes in the society as well as political system has been unquestionable and intense even now also.[137] This shows the continuation of the dominant position of the upper non-Brahmin castes in the socio-political scenario.

Notes and References

* I am thankful to **S. Mahaboob Basha**, Assistant Professor, Department of History, Dr. B. R. Ambedkar Central University, Lucknow (U.P.), **M. Bhaskarendra Rao**, Charted Accountant, Madanapalli, Chittoor District, **Dr. B.R. Prasad Reddi**, Reader in History, Silver Jubilee College, Kurnool, A.P. and **S. P. Gafar,** President, People for Social Sciences, Porumamilla, Kadapa District, A.P. for their interaction and encouragement in my academic persuit.

1. *Inscriptions of Andhra Pradesh, Kadapa District I*, Hyderabad, 1977, pp.1-4, 9-10.
2. P. Yenadi Raju, *Rayalaseema during Colonial Times, A Study in Indian Nationalism,* New Delhi, 2003, pp. 3, 10, see also Bhuman, *Charithralo Rayalaseema* (*Rayalaseema* in History) (Telugu), October 1989, Tirupati, pp. 34-5.
3. C.V. Ramachandra Rao (ed.), *Rayavachakamu*, quoted in P. Narasimha Reddi, *Pracheena Telugu Kavyallo Telugunadu*

(References to Telugu Country in the old Telugu Literary Works) (Telugu), Tirupati, pp. 65, 69.

4. Bhuman, *Charithralo Rayalaseema,* pp. 34-5.
5. *Fifth Report* from the Select Committee on the Affairs of East India Company, vol. II, Madras, 1883, p. 89. (Tamilnadu Archives (hereafter TNA)) The *mandals* of Madanapalle and Vayalpad of the present Chittoor district formed part of ceded area. The area of these *mandals* was in Kadapa district till the formation of Chittoor district in 1911. For more details see P. Yenadi Raju, *Rayalaseema during Colonial Times*, p. 10.
6. Bhuman, *Charithralo Rayalaseema,* pp. 34-5.
7. T. Kameswara Rao, *Naa Vangmaya Mitrulu*, (My Literary Friends) (Telugu), Chittoor, 1966, p. 256. See also M. Veerabhadra Rao, *Sri Sarvithama Jeevithamu* (A Biography of Gadicharla Harisarvotha Rao), (Telugu), Vijayawada, 1965, pp. 311-312, 317; P. Yenadi Raju, *Rayalaseema during Colonial Times,* p. 11; K.V.Narayana Rao, *The Emergence of Andhra Pradesh*, Bombay, 1973, p.166; and P. Azeez, *Rayalaseema Ratnalu: Sri Kadapa Koti Reddi- Smt. Ramasubbamma* (Jewels of *Rayalaseema* : Sri Kadapa Koti Reddi-Mrs.Ramasubbamma) (Telugu), Hyderabad, 1994, p. 99.
8. Adapa Satyanarayana, "Nation, Caste, and the Past: Articulation of Dalitbahujan Identity, Consciousness and Ideology", Sectional President's Address, *Proceedings of The Indian History Congress*, Bareilly, 2004, p. 416.
9. R.S. Sarma, "Importance of Regional History", Presidential Address, *Proceedings of the Andhra Pradesh History Congress*, Warangal, 1990, see also S. Gopal, "Recent Trends of History and Social Sciences", Presidential Address, *Proceedings of the Andhra Pradesh History Congress*, Vijayawada, 1978.
10. M.K. Gandhi, *Collected Works of Mahatma Gandhi,* Vol. IX, New Delhi, 1958-1984, p. 458.
11. Romila Thapar, *Cultural Pasts: Essays in Early Indian History*, New Delhi, 2000, pp. 95, 109.
12. Sumit Sarkar, *Modern India, 1885-1947*, New Delhi, reprint, 2004 (1st pbd:1983), p. 162.

13. Bipan Chandra, et.al., *India After Independence*, 1947-2000, New Dehli, 2002 (1st pbd.1999), p. 119.
14. S. Bhattacharya, "The Problems and Prospects of Regional History", (Mimeographed), Hyderabad, 1988, p.1, quoted in Adapa Satyanarayana, "Nation, Caste, and the Past: Articulation of Dalitbahujan Identity, Consciousness and Ideology", p.
15. C.J. Baker and D.A. Washbrook, *South India : Political Institutions and Political Change 1880-1940,* Delhi, 1975, Preface, p. vii. P. Yenadi Raju, "South Indian Historiography: Recent Trends", *Dravidian Studies*, (A Quarterly Research Journal), Vol. II, No. 2 &3, Special Issue, Jan-June, 2004, Dravidian University, Kuppam, A.P., p. 35.
16. The genesis of the Non-Brahmin Movement in the Madras Presidency can be traced back to 1909, when the Madras Non-Brahmin Association was formed by two non-Brahmin lawyers, P. Subramanian and M. Purushotam Naidu. Later, it was termed as Madras Dravidian Association. But it could not survive for long due to lack of organisation. Undeterred by this, a group of non-Brahmins had started, subsequently, the Madras United League under C. Natesa Mudaliar as Secretary in 1912. Then it had changed its name as Madras Dravidian Association. It conducted regular meetings and discuseed the problems of the non-Brahmins. In 1915 the non-Brahmins published a book known as *Non-Brahmin Letters*-twenty one letters-in Madras. In 1916 the Madras Dravidian Association established a hostel for non-Brahmin students in Madras City known as 'Dravidian Home'. For details see, *The Madras Mail*, 3 June 1909, O. Rangaswami Naidu, *The Origin of the Justice Party*, Madras, 1968, p. 257, R.C. Majumdar, *Struggle for Freedom,* Bombay, 1978, p. 259, K. Nambi Arooran, "The Origin of the Non-Brahman Movement, 1905-1920", in *Tamil Renaissance and Dravidian Nationalism (1905-54)*, Madurai, 1980, p. 42, and P. Chakravarthy, *Emergence of Justice Party*, Vol. iv, Trivendrum, 1977, p. 303.

17. Eugene F. Irschick, *Politics and Social Conflict in South India : The Non-Brahmin Movement and Tamil Separatism,1916-1929*, Berkeley, 1969, p. 225, see also B. Kesavanarayana, *Political and Social Factors in Andhra (1900-1956)*, Vijayawada, April 1976, p. 297.
18. Eugene F. Irschick, *Politics and Social Conflict in South India*, Introduction, see also M.N. Srinivas, *Social Change in Modern India*, Berkeley, 1966, pp.102-3.
19. The Non-Brahmin Manifesto, *The Guardian Press*, Madras, December 1916, pp.1-4, see also Eugene F.Irschick, *Politics and Social Conflict in South India*, pp. 47-48, 359-367.
20. Y. Vaikuntham, *Studies in Socio-Cultural and Political History : Modern Andhra*, Hyderabad, 2004, p. 71.
21. For more details see, M.N. Srinivas, *Caste in Modern India and Other Essays*, Bombay, 1962, p. 41.
22. This data was belonged to Andhra region which includes the Rayalaseema region. Andhra region includes the Telugu speaking districts of erstwhile or hitherto Madras Presidency: Ganjam, Vizagapatam, Godavari, Krishna, Guntur, Nellore, Kurnool, Cuddapah, Anantapur, Bellary and Chittoor. Since the data pertaining to Rayalaseema districts was not available, this can serve the necessary purpose in this context. For more details see Y. Vaikuntham, *Studies in Socio-Cultural and Political History*, p. 72.
23. Y. Vaikuntham, *Studies in Socio-Cultural and Political History*, pp. 71, 72, 73, 76, see also G.Premkumar, "Early Census Reports and the Genesis of the Dravidian Movement in the Madras Presidency", *Proceedings of the South India History Congress*, Madurai, 2005, pp. 64-67.
24. For more details see, Lakshmi Subrahmanian, *The Justice Party and the Non-Brahman Movement (1916-20)*, Madras, 1979, p. 13, Eugene F.Irschick, *Politics and Social Conflict in South India*, p. 14, and M.S. Barnett, *The Politics of Cultural Nationalism in South India,* New Jeresy (Princeton), 1976, pp. 330-331.

25. The genesis of caste society that reflected the orthodox or traditional Brahmanical view can be traced back to the Vedic or Aryan society. Romila Thapar, *The Penguin History of Early India, From the Origins to A.D.1300,* New Delhi, 2003, (1st pbd. Allen Lane, 2002), pp. 62-68. Similarly the nature of Brahman hegemony and resistance to Brahman tyranny was found in ancient India. A.L. Basham, *The Wonder that was India*, New Delhi, 1984 (reprint), (1st pbd.1954), p. 248, see also D.N. Jha, *Early India, A Concise History*, New Delhi, 2004, pp. 77-79. During medieval times the reformers questioned the pitfalls of the Brahman or Vedic dominated Hindu society and orthodox Muslim society dominated by Ulemas in the form of Bhakti and Sufi movements. D.N. Jha, "Looking For a Hindu Identity", *Proceedings of the Indian History Congress*, Visva-Bharati, Santiniketan, 2005-06, pp. 9, 14. In the *Rayalaseema* region, Pothuluri Veerabrahmam of hitherto Kandimallayapalle village and present Brahmamgari Mattam was the first non-Brahmin who opposed the Brahmanical ideology and awakened the lower sections of the society against the domination of Brahmanism in the 16th century. Chatakondu (Darsi) Subbarayudu (adapted son of Veerabrahmam), *Sri Veerabrahmamgari Jeevitha Charitramu (The Life History of Sri Veerabrahmam)* (Telugu), Kandimallayapalli, Kadapa District, 1995, sixth reprint, (1st pbd:1932), pp. 97 ff. In the modern days, the Brahman elite, who had been working in the English East India Company as tehsildars or revenue officials etc, at taluk level, supported colonial Government and showed their domination not only against the non-Brahmin subordinates like cuttubodies or village clerical staff, local non-Brahmin people but also rivaling local leaders or chieftains or Palegars. For instance, the Nossam tehsildar, Raghavachari's Brahmanic oligarchy was one of the main reasons for Vuyyalavada Narasimha Reddi of Nossam in the erstwhile Kadapa district and the present Kurnool district of the region to raise his revolt against the Company Government in the region. Tangirala Venkatasubba Rao, *Renati Suryachandrulu*

(The Sun and Moon of Renadu) (Telugu), (Appendix-I, (Bangore (Bandi Gopal Reddi)), "British Prabhutvampai Vuyyalavada Narasimhareddi Sayudha Tirugubatu" (The Armed Revolt of Vuyyalawad Narasimha Reddi against the British Government) (Telugu)), Bangalore, 2000, p. 135. The anti-Brahman tocsin was first sounded in Maharashrta in the 1870s by Mahatma Jhothiba (Jyothirao) Phule in his book, *Ghulam-giri* (1872) and his organisation, the Satyashodhak Samaj (1873). Sumit Sarkar, *Modern India, 1885-1947*, p. 57. K.V. Narayana Rao, *The Emergence of Andhra Pradesh,* Bombay, 1973, pp.26-27, and P. Damodarm Pillai, *Gooty Kesava Pillai (A Deenabandhu of South India)*, Hyderabad, 1978, pp. 9-10.

26. *Reports* of the Third, Fifth, Sixth, Seventh, Fourteenth, Twenty-third, Twenty-fourth, Twenty-fifth, Twenty-sixth, Twenty-eight, Twenty-ninth, Thirtieth, Thirty-second, Thirty-third, Thirty-fourth, Sessions of Indian National Congress, Madras, 1887, p.181, Bombay, 1889, pp. 91, 96-97, 113-140, Calcutta, 1890, pp. 117-118, Nagpur, 1891, pp. 104-105, Madras, 1898, pp. XXIII-XXIV, Madras, 1908, pp. 96, 98, 102, 106, CCCVII-XXXVIII, Lahore, 1909, Appendix C, pp. XV-XVII, Allahabad, 1910, p. 18, Calcutta, 1911, p. 2, Karachi, 1913, p. 6, Madras, 1914, pp.16-17, Bombay, 1915, pp.14-15, Calcutta, 1917, p.16, Delhi, 1918, p. 2, and Amritsar, 1919, Appendix, p. XII, XIV, XV, respectively (TNA) & (APSAH); see also *Andhra Patrika*, 12 June, 1922, p. 2; 2 April, p.14, and 12 November, p.10, 1923; 15 November, 1924, p. 10; 24 October, 1925, p. 17, 12 January, p.10 and 16 January, p. 2, 1940 (APSAH); A.M. Zaidi & S. Zaidi (eds.), *The Encyclopaedia of Indian National Congress*, Vol. I, 1885-1890, New Delhi, 1976, p. 595, and B. Rama Sastry, "Swatantrodhyamam – Kondaru Pramukhulu" in *Kadapa Zillah Samachara Darsini* (Directory of Information on Kadapa District) (Telugu), A Supplement of *Visalandhra* on Kadapa District, Kadapa, 1992, p.19.

27. Carolyn M. Elliot, 'Caste and Faction among the Dominant Caste : The Reddis and Kammas of Andhra' in Rajni Kothari, *Caste in Indian Politics*, Hyderabad, reprint, 2004 (1st pbd:1970),

pp. 121-1153. Among the Velamas, the Koka family of Audi-Velamas, a sub-sect in Velamas, migrated from Kurnool district of the region to North Arcot in Tamilnadu State. In this way, one of the great freedom fighters and one among the noted intellectuals, C.P. Ramaswamy Iyer migrated to North Arcot in Tamil Nadu. For details see C.F. Brackenbury, *Andhra Pradesh District Gazetteers, Cuddapah District Gazetteer* (reprint), (1st pbd.1915), Hyderabad, 1993, p. 81, see also David Washbrook, "The Development of Caste Organisation in South India, pp. 160-1.

28. Y. Vaikuntham, *Studies in Socio-Cultural and Political History : Modern Andhra*, p. 73. Data was not available on Bellary District in the source consulted. For instance, if we take community wise strength in the region, in 1921 the non-Brahmins were 630505, depressed classes were 113219, Brahmins were 10225, and Hindus were 753949 in Kadapa district. *The Memoranda* submitted by the Government of Madras to the Indian Statutory Commission in1928, 1928, p. 336 (Tamilnadu State Archives (TNA)).
29. Sumit Sarkar, *Modern India*, pp. 54-5.
30. Susan Bayly, *Caste, Society and Politics in India : From the Eighteenth Century to the Modern Age* (The New Cambridge History of India), Cambridge, reprint, 2005 (1st pbd.1999), p. 72. The same phenomenon can be found in the findings of Suvira Jaiswal and D.N. Jha. Suvira Jaiswal, "Inventing a Culture of Patriarchy : An Aspect of Brahmanism", Mamidipudi Venkatarangaiah Memorial Lecture, *Proceedings of the Andhra Pradesh History Congress*, Anaparti, 2002, and D.N.Jha, "Looking For a Hindu Identity", pp. 1-42.
31. Atlury Murali, "Colonialism and Caste Movements : Study of Appropriation of Past in the Madras Presidency", *Proceedings of the Indian History Congress*, Amritsar, 2002, pp. 889, 891.
32. Antonio Gramsci, the famous Italian Marxist philosopher, coined the phrase "organic intellectuals", who can think and awaken a particular and fundamental social group to achieve their basic needs and aspirations. Antonio Gramsci, *Selections*

from Prison Notebooks, London, p. 3. This perception reflected intellectuals like Mahatma Jyothiba (Jyothirao) Phule and B.R. Ambedkar of Maharashtra, E.V. Ramaswamy Naicker of Tamil Nadu and Narayan Guru of Kerala.

33. Jan Tinbergen, "Some Thoughts on Mature Socialism", in *Jawaharlal Nehru Memorial Lectures* (Bhavan's Book University), 1967-1981, Vol.I, New Delhi, 1998, pp.141-142.
34. Sumit Sarkar, *Modern India, 1885-1947*, pp.158-9, see also B. Kesavanarayana, *Political and Social Factors in Andhra (1900-1956)*, Vijayawada, April 1976, 300-302.
35. David Washbrook, "The Development of Caste Organisation in South India, 1880 to1925", in C.J. Baker and David Washbrook, *South India:Political Institutions and Political Change, 1880-1940,* New Delhi, 1975, pp.150-194, see also Uma Ramaswamy, "The Belief System of the Non-Brahmin Movement in India : The Andhra Case", *Asian Survey*, Vol.18, No. 3, March 1978 , p. 296.
36. Uma Ramaswamy, "The Belief System of the Non-Brahmin Movement in India : The Andhra Case", p. 294. Oiginally the Reddi Sangham was founded in Cuddalore, South Arcot in 1913. David Washbrook, "The Development of Caste Organisation in South India", p. 203, and *Madras Mail*, 3 June 1909 (TNA).
37. Y.Vaikuntham, *Education and Social Change in South India : Andhra, 1880-1920*, Madras, pp. 173-177.
38. Y. Vaikuntham, *Studies in Socio-Cultural and Political History,* pp.73, 79, 87.
39. *Andhra Patrika*, November 3, 1934, p.19 (Andhra Pradesh State Archives, Hyderabad (APSAH)). Majority of the *Arya Vaisya Mahasabhas* were held more in Coastal Andhra area than in the *Rayalaseema* region. But many intellectuals of the region attended these meetings.
40. *Andhra Patrika*, September 10, 1920, p. 3 (APSAH).
41. *Andhra Patrika*, June 17, 1921, p. 2 (APSAH). It is quite interesting here that Vaikuntham had mentioned that the First *Telaga Mahajana Sabha* was held in October 1923 at

Masulipatnam by referring the *Krishna Patrika* (editorial), 13-10-1923, pp. 5-6. But the *Andhra Patrika*, which I have mentioned in this reference, on the contrary, wrote that it was held in 1921. Since the *Andhra Patrika* did not mention whether it was a district level Sabha or State level one, the Sabha which Vaikuntham was referred might have a State level one where as the one that I have referred to should have a district level one. Both papers should have cleared such ambiguity.

42. Y. Vaikuntham, *Studies in Socio-Cultural and Political History*, p. 83.
43. *Andhra Patrika*, 17 June 1921, p. 2 (APSAH).
44. *Andhra Patrika*, 20 June 1921, p. 4 (APSAH).
45. *Andhra Patrika*, 10 January 1934, p. 3 (APSAH).
46. B. Sanjiva Reddy, "Caste and Social Development: The Case of Reddis in Andhra", in R. Balasubramanian (ed.), *Social and Economic Dimensions of Caste Organisations in South Indian States*, Madras, 2001, pp. 266-267.
47. It is quite contradictory here that when the *Reddi Jana Sangha* itself was formed in 1920 how can it is possible it to go back and start the First *Reddi Mahajana Sabha* in 1913. The *Reddi Jana Sangha* might have stared in 1902 instead of 1920. Another controversy, in this context is, while B. Sanjiva Reddy stated, in his article (no. 38), that the First *Reddi Mahajana Sabha* was held in Cuddalore in 1913 where as the *Andhra Patrika*, in its issue of 19 June 1916, pp. 2-3, mentioned that it was held in 1916 at Nambur.
48. *Ibid*, pp. 267-268, see also Gorrepati Venkata Subbaiah, *Dr. C.R. Reddi* (a Biography), Vijayawada, June 1963, pp. 95-98.
49. *Andhra Patrika*, 8 December 1921, p. 3, see also Ibid, 3 January 1922, p. 2 (APSAH), and B. Sanjiva Reddy, *loc.cit.*, in R. Balasubramanian (ed.), *Social and Economic Dimensions of Caste Organisations*, p. 268.
50. *Andhra Patrika*, 6 September 1926, p. 5 (APSAH).
51. B. Sanjiva Reddy, *loc.cit.*, in R. Balasubramanian (ed.), *Social and Economic Dimensions of Caste Organisations*, pp. 269-270. Later, the *Reddi Mahajana Sabha* conducted its meetings during

the pre and post-Independence periods with some minor fluctuations. Even now also one can observe its services to the Reddi community, Hyderabad as its headquarters. The entire credit for this development of the Reddi Mahajana Sabha and Reddi community goes to the intellectuals and prominent leaders like Wanaparthy Zamindar family, Kadapa Koti Reddi, and Dr. C.R. Reddi. For details see Ibid, pp. 271ff.

52. Y. Vaikuntham, *Studies in Socio-Cultural and Political History*, p. 83.
53. G. Sudharsan Reddy, "Caste Reform in Andhra, 1900-1930", *Proceedings of the Indian History Congress*, Amritsar, 2002, pp. 855, 857. It was not clarified whether this *Kshatriya* community belonged to *Arya Kshatriya or Agnikula Kshatriya* sub-sect in this regard.
54. *NPR*, (November – December), 1911, p. 1720 (TNA).
55. Seventh *Kamma Mahajana Sabha*, Presidential Speech, Nidubrolu, Guntur District, 21-22 June 1919, pp. 1-20.
56. 'Presidential Speech' of Bollini Muniswami Naidu, *Kamma Vikasam,* April 2009, pp.15-16.
57. *Speech of Kommareddi Pattabhiramaiah*, Chairman for the Reception Committee, Tenth *Kamma Mahajana Sabha*, Angaluru, 15 June 1929, pp. 1-11.
58. *M.Bhaskarendra Rao* (Charted Accountant and maternal grandson of Ratakonda Venkataswami Naidu), Madanapalle, Chittoor district.
59. For more details see, G.Sudharsan Reddy, "Caste Reform in Andhra, 1900-1930", in *loc.cit.*, pp. 855-861, Uma Ramaswamy, "The Belief System of the Non-Brahmin Movement in India : The Andhra Case", p. 294ff, and Y. Vaikuntham, *Studies in Socio-Cultural and Political History,* pp. 77ff. The people of these castes of the region might have participated in these conferences.
60. Sumit Sarkar, *Modern India,* p. 55, see also Uma Ramaswamy, "The Belief System of the Non-Brahmin Movement in India : The Andhra Case", p. 298.
61. V. Geetha and S.V. Rajadurai, *Towards a Non-Brahmin Millennium, From Iyothee Thass to Periyar*, Calcutta, reprint, 1999 (1st pbd: June 1998), pp. 43-44.

62. T. Varadarajulu Naidu, *The Justice Movement,* Madras, 1931, p. 76.
63. *Ibid.*
64. *Andhra Jyothi,* Daily, 22 and 23 March 1987, Tirupati, 1987, p. 3.
65. *Ibid.*
66. The *Chraistava* was the first newspaper to appear with the tag of a religion, that is, in 1908.
67. *G.O. No. 958-59, Public (Confidential)*, Madras, 16 August 1930 (TNA), see also K. Subramanyam, *The Press and The National Movement in South India : Andhra, 1905-1932*, Madras, 1984, Appendix-I, pp. 19, 243-244.
68. In 1916, when a heated discussion was going on, on the 'slaughter' of the candidates in the Intermediate Examination of the Madras University Results, severe criticism was raised against the under valuation. But few English professors rejected this criticism. One of them, Rev. Macphail, went to the extent and said, '...you bring *jutkawallas* (persons who pull horse carts) and *rickshawallas* (persons who pull two wheeled carts) to the examination hall, and when they fail, you complain of enormous slaughter'. The candidates, whom Macphail referred, mostly were non-Brahmins. A.S. Iyengar published Macphail's statement in the *Indian Patriot*. Similarly, he accidentally, later, observed, discovered and an eye witness of the meeting of the leaders such as Dr. T.M. Nair and P. Thyagaraya Chetty and others in Mint Street, Madras. The defeat, earlier, of Dr. T.M. Nair, by his rival Dewan Bahadur T. Rangachariar, in the Madras Corporation election, led to conduct this meeting. The leaders gave eloquent speeches against the domination of Brahmin supremacy. Further, the publication of a book entitled *Non-Brahmin Letters* by the *Indian Patriot* office also attracted them. They were planning to start a movement. Iyengar published this story also in the *Indian Patriot*. The reports on these two incidents were termed by others journalists and leaders as a 'scoop'. But, however, these developments had created an epoch making history of non-Brahmin movement in

South India and attracted the attention of leaders, scholars, historians and socialogists all over the world. For more details see, A.S. Iyengar, *Role of Press and Indian Freedom Struggle* (All Through the Gandhian Era), New Delhi, 2001, pp. 6-9.

69. *Native Newspaper Report (NPR)*, for the week ending 2 October 1920 (October to December), 1920, p.1200 (TNA).
70. *NPR*, for the week ending 28 February (January –March), 1921, p. 256 (TNA).
71. *History of Freedom Movement (HFM) Vol.78, B22, Non-Brahmin Movement 1921-1936*, for the week ending 12 February 1921, p. 249 (TNA).
72. *NPR*, 1920-1921, p. 101 (TNA).
73. *NPR*, for the week ending 12 March (January-March) 1921, p. 328 (TNA).
74. *NPR*, for the week ending 26 March (January-March) 1921, p. 391 (TNA).
75. *NPR*, for the week ending 23 April (April-June) 1921 p. 489 (TNA).
76. *NPR*, 11 June (April-June) 1921, p. 695 (TNA).
77. *NPR*, 16 December (November-December) 1922, p. 1525 (TNA).
78. *NPR*, 18 December (November-December) 1922, p. 1401 (TNA).
79. *NPR*, 19 April (April-June) 1924, p. 533 (TNA).
80. *NPR*, for the week ending 4 November (November-December) 1922, p. 1331 (TNA).
81. *NPR*, 21 April 1923, p. 498 (TNA).
82. *NPR*, for the week ending 31 January (January-February) 1925, p. 115 (TNA).
83. *NPR*, for the week ending 14 October 1922, p. 1229 (TNA).
84. *NPR*, for the week ending 14 October 1922, p. 1230 (TNA).
85. *NPR*, 17 December (November-December) 1920, 1920-1921, p. 193 (TNA).
86. *NPR*, for the week ending 23 April (April-June) 1921, p. 502 (TNA).
87. *NPR*, for the week ending 19 July (July-September) 1920, p. 303 (TNA).
88. *NPR*, for the week ending 1 January (January to March) 1921, p. 479 (TNA).

89. *NPR*, 28 January (January to March) 1921, p. 255 (TNA).
90. *NPR*, for the week ending 20 October 1923, p. 1289 (TNA).
91. *NPR*, for the week ending 3 March (March and April) 1923, p. 286 (TNA).
92. *NPR*, 29 December (November-December) 1923, p. 1616 (TNA).
93. *NPR*, for the week ending 8 December (November-December) 1923, p. 1513 (TNA).
94. *Ibid* (APSAH).
95. *Ibid*, pp. 1513-1514 (TNA).
96. *Ibid*, p. 1514 (TNA).
97. *NPR*, for the week ending 15 December (November-December) 1923, p. 1547 (TNA).
98. *NPR*, for the week ending 26 December (November-December) 1925, p. 1633 (TNA).
99. *NPR*, for the week ending 2 August 1930, p. 1206 (TNA).
100. *NPR*, for the week ending 3 March (March to April) 1923, p. 286 (TNA).
101. *Ibid* (TNA), *Andhra Patrika*, September 22 1915, p. 3, June 3, 1918, pp. 2-4, June11, 1918, p. 4.
102. P. Damodarm Pillai, *Gooty Kesava Pillai (A Deenabandhu of South India),* (a Biography), Hyderabad, 1978, p. 8.
103. *Indian Mirror,* 20 October 1886; V.L. Sastri (ed.), *Encyclopedia of the Madras Presidency and the Adjacent States*, Madras, 1921; *Administrative Report of the Madras Presidency*, 1878-1886; *University of Madras,* Calendar for 1893-94, I; and *Asylum Press Almanac & Compendium of Intelligence*, 1868, 1875, 1880 and 1886 (TNA).
104. *The Hindu*, 31 May 1918.
105. *Andhra Patrika*, 14 November 1921, p. 3 (APSAH).
106. B. Kesavanarayana, *Political and Social Factors in Andhra,* p. 302ff.
107. *Private Letter* from the Raja of Paragal, Panaganti Parthasarathi Rayaningar to Ratakonda Venkataswami Naidu, dated 17-03-1920 (procured from the maternal grandson of Ratakonda Venkataswamin Naidu namely *M. Bhaskarendra Rao,* Charted Accountant, Madanapalli, Chittoor District).

108. B. Kesavanarayana, *Political and Social Factors in Andhra*, p. 302.
109. B. Sivasankaranarayana, *Andhra Pradesh District Gazetteers, Cuddapah*, Hyderabad, 1967, p. 707.
110. *Madras Year Book, 1923, Part-II*, Madras, 1923, pp. 526-539 (TNA).
111. *Ibid*, pp. 526-539, 551-553, 565-566, 571-592, 627-628, 637-38, 641, 650-51 (TNA).
112. *Ibid*, pp.673-679 (TNA).
113. *Andhra Patrika*, 10 December 1925, p. 3, 3 March 1926, p.1, 17 May 1926, p. 17, 10 May 1926, p. 8, 17 May 1926, p. 17, 3 July 1926, p. 8, 6 July 1926, p. 5, 21 July 1926, p. 13, 31 July 1926, p. 3, 21 September 1926, p. 19, 14 October 1926, pp. 2-3, 16 October 1926, p. 6, 20 October 1926, p. 5, 21 October 1926, p. 6, 22 October 1926, p. 6, 25 October 1926, p. 4, 28 October 1926, p. 17, 2 November 1926, pp. 16-18, 16 November 1926, p. 4 (APSAH).
114. *Andhra Patrika*, 22 November 1926, p. 7 (APSAH).
115. *Andhra Patrika*, 16 November 1926, p. 4, 18 November 1926, p. 8, 22 November 1926, p. 6 (APSAH), see also B. Sivasankaranarayana, *Andhra Pradesh District Gazetteers, Anantapur*, Hyderabad, 1970, pp.810-813.
116. B. Sivasankaranarayana, *Andhra Pradesh District Gazetteers, Cuddapah*, pp.708-709.
117. Kesava Pillai hailed from Tamil Nadu. He was born on 8 October in 1860 at Pattu village in Gudiyatham taluk of North Arcot District in present Tamil Nadu State and erstwhile composite Madras State. His parents were Subbamma and Venkatachalam Pillai. He was married in the year 1879 to Salambri Ammal. He had four sons and a daughter by his first wife. When she died in the year 1898, he got married Pushpavati Ammal as his second wife. He had three issues, two daughters and a son, by her. When she was also left this world, Kesava Pillai took a third wife named Unnamalai Ammal in 1908. They got blessed with two daughters. One of his sons, Govindaraj, accompanied him to British Guiana (the present

Guyana Republic in South America) in 1921 and later served in the Military Engineering Service. Kesava Pillai completed Law and practiced as a law agent in Sankeridurg in the Salem district in 1880. Later, he worked as a clerk on a monthly salary of Rs.15/- in the Deputy Collector's Office at Gooty in 1881. He had given it up and became the Special Correspondent to the daily newspaper, *The Hindu*, at Salem. He was present when the Hindu-Muslim riots took place in Salem in 1882. He left Salem in the same year and set up practice as a lawyer at Gooty. He had completed his subsequent life of 50 years in Gooty in Anantapur district and contributed to the development of consciousness among people of the district in particular and the region in general. Hence, he was known reverently as Pattu Kesava Pillai or P. Kesava Pillai, in Tamil Nadu and Gooty Kesava Pillai in Andhra Pradesh. At last his unfortunate demise came on 28 March 1933 at Gooty in Anantpur district of the region. For more details see, *Dewan Bahadur P. Kesava Pillai, C.I.E., Birth Centenary Celebrations*, (P. Damodarm Pillai, Birthe Centenary Celebrations Committee, Podanur, Coimbatore, Tamil Nadu), 1960, p. 1-3, and P. Damodarm Pillai, *Gooty Kesava Pillai*, pp. 1-5.

118. He belonged to Cattamanchi village in Chittoor Municipality or town and district headquarters, Chittoor. He was born on 10 December 1880. His parents were Narayanamma and Subrahminyam Reddy. He completed his Primary Education at Cattamanchi and Gundlapalli villages and Higher Secondary or Matriculation in Chittoor High School in 1896. For Higher Education or Under Graduate Course (B.A.) he joined Madras Christian College in 1897, where he wrote *Musalamma Maranamu* (An Old-woman' Death) for which he got a Telugu Association Prize in1899 at the age of 19. He completed his B.A. Degree in History and Philosophy in 1901 with rare Distinctions and Awards. In the next year he was sent to Cambridge to pursue higher studies under the Government of India Student Fellowship. He got the prestigious Exhibition and Wright's Prize in 1903. In 1905, he was elected as Secretary

to the Cambridge University Liberal Club. Then, in 1906 he became the first Indian to be elected to the coveted post of Vice-President of the Cambridge Union Society. He secured First Grade in M.A. History at Cambridge. Later, admired by his intellectual excellence, the ruler of Baroda, Sayaji Rao Gaikwad, sent him to U.S.A. and Canada for study tour to observe the working of education system. Subsequently, he worked throughout the country in various capacities : Vice-Principal at Maharaja Gaikwad's College-Baroda (1908), Professor at Mysore Maharaja's College-Mysore (1909), visited Canada, Japan and Honkong to comprehend an idea as to how the Mysore University should be constructed (1914), prepared and submitted a plan for the construction of Mysore University (1915), Principal for Mysore Maharaja's College (1916-17), Inspector General of Education in the Mysore State (1919-20), President of Fourth *Reddy Mahajan Sabha* (1920), Member of Advisory Committee for All India Education Department (1921), Member of Madras Legislative Assembly (1922-26, 1935-36), Vice Chancellor of Andhra University (1926), President of Chittoor District Board (1925-36), Chairman of Inter-Universities Board (hence forth Association of Indian Universities) (1937), and Pro- Chancellor of Mysore University (1949). He breathed his last breath on 24 February 1951 in Madras. For more details see, Gorrepati Venkata Subbaiah, *Dr. C.R. Reddy,* (a Biography), Vijayawada, June 1963, pp.11, 289-290.

119. Although Panaganti Raja Ramarayaninar was originally hailed from Sri Kalahasti in Chittoor District of *Rayalaseema* region, he settled in Madras. He became the Chief Minister for Composite Madras State and played a significant role. It was because if his influence that Sri Kalahasti had became the centre of non-Brahmin activity in Chittoor district in particular and *Rayalaseema* region in general. His impact among people was so solid that as a result Andhra movement could not spread and strengthen in Chittoor district for so many years. *Andhra Patrika*, 11 June 1918, p. 4 (APSAH).

120. Bollini Muniswami Naidu was another stalwart of the region. He belonged to Chittoor in Chittoor district. He had good network and relations in Madanapalle, Chittoor and other areas of the region. From the beginning, he was a great non-Brahmin and Justicite in the region. It was he who influenced great personalities like Dr. C.R. Reddy to enter into politics and became luminaries of Justice Party and non-Brahmin movement in the region. He had two sons and four daughters. For more details see, *NPR,* for the week ending 11 June (April-June) 1921, p. 695 (TNA), and Gorrepati Venkata Subbaiah, *Dr. C.R. Reddy*, p. 100.

121. He belonged to Madanapalle in Chittoor district and one of the notable and prominent members of the non-Brahmin movement and Justice Party. He was born in an agriculture family at Madanapalle. His father was Ratakonda Gurrappa Naidu and his mother was Seethamma. He completed his education in Madanapalle and Madras. After completing Law Degree in Madras, he started his legal profession in Madanapalle Court from 1894 onwards. His forefather had worked in Police as well as Revenue Departments in Madras and Mysore Governments in various capacities besides in the Missionary Work for London Mission. Mr. Ratakonda Ramanna (spelt as Ratookonda Ramanna by the British) was the grand father of Mr. Ratakonda Venkataswamy Naidu. Mr. Ratakonda Ramanna worked in the Military Department of the Mysore State. From 6th mile from Madanapalle town was the Mysore Kingdom, where as Madanapalle was in the Madras Presidency which was under the British hegemony. Hence, it seems that the people require some testimonial from the persons of responsible position to cross the border or to go freely in the new places. It is almost like a passport. Mrs. Porter of London Mission Society visited Madanapalle also during the second half of 19th century very often as mentioned in some of the letters of Mr. Ratakonda Venkataswamy Naidu. He was honoured with different designations at Madanapalle in Chittoor district : noted Vakil at Madanapalle from 1884-1945, Chairman of Madanapalle

Union Board from 1903-1908, Member of the District Board 1918, President of Seventh *Kamma Mahajana Sabha* in 1919 at Nidubrolu in Guntur district and President of the First elected Taluk Board in 1921. He had acted as Legal Advisor to American Arcot Mission. He was invited by Garapati Anjaneya Choudari of Ellore in West Godavari to preside over the Seventh *Kamma Mahajana Sabha*. Madanapalle Union was appreciated as one of the best Unions in the entire Madras Presidency by the then District Collector during his tenure. The Governor treated him as one of the best intellectuals in Chittoor district and he used to interact with him whenever he visits Madanapalle. The *Swatantra*, a daily from Madras, had given wide coverage on the development achieved by the Madanapalle Union during his Chairman's period. He had four sons: Ramaswami, Guruswami, Rangaswami, and Ramamurthy and four daughters: Seetha Devi, Sundaramma, Padmavathi, and Sarojini. He took special efforts to educate all his children to pursue professional education in reputed institutions in different parts of India. Finally he died on 28 December, 1953 in his house at Madanapalle. *M. Bhaskarendra Rao*, his grand son, Charted Accountant, Madanapalli.

122. Palem Doraswamy Naidu was one of the prominent leaders of the Justice Party or non-Brahmin movement in Kadapa District of the region. He was a resident of Pulivendula in Kadapa district. He was elected as the President of Rayachoty Taluk Board and Member of the Senate. He started the Board High School in Pulivendula and taught there. He was a great philanthropist. He, along with other noted leaders of the district, had participated in various constructive activities in the district. But he died on 14 December 1925. In memory of his sudden demise, a grand condolence meeting was organized in Pulivendula on 27 December 1925. A Special Committee was formed, on that occasion, to take up the activities like to adorn his photo in the school, to get the permission to name the school on his name, to change and declare his death day as a holiday, and to conduct, as a great tribute, various activities. Later, on

14 May 1927, several competitions were conducted for boys and girls. Local people had felt happy and enjoyed on that auspicious occasion. In the evening, a grand procession with his photograph was held and continued throughout the night. More than 4000 people were attended and said to have had the glance of the procession. In the next day morning, a big meeting was conducted under the District Vice President, N. Ranga Reddy. Many leaders, who spoke on that occasion, appreciated his services rendered to the people and expressed their gratitude and regards. One of the leaders, N. Lakshiminarasaiah, highlighted the main events and special characteristics of Naidu's life. The meeting was concluded successfully. Two thousand people were fed on that occasion. *Andhra Patrika*, 18 January 1926, p.17, see also *Ibid*, 19 May 1927, p. 15 (APSAH).

123. *Memorandum* of Gooty Kesava Pillai to Evans, dated 14 January 1920.
124. *G.O. No.1011*, dated 24 May 1916 (Public Department) Ordinary Series, Madras, 1916 (TNA).
125. P.Damodarm Pillai, *Gooty Kesava Pillai, (A Deenabandhu of South India)*, pp. 8-12.
126. Gorrepati Venkata Subbaiah, *Dr. C.R. Reddy*, pp. 24-25, 32 and 34.
127. *Ibid*, p. 100.
128. *Ibid*, p. 101.
129. *Ibid*, p.102, see also Cattamanchi Ramalinga Reddy, "Hindumata Parinamamulo Bhajanakutamula Pramukhyata" (Importance of Musical Parties in the Evolution of Hindu Religion) (Telugu), *Samadarsini*, (Third Annual Issue), 1930-1931, Madras, p. 27. The special annual issues of *Samadarsini* were published in memory of the founders of the Justice Party and Non-Brahmin Movement in Madras, by the founder of the Paper, Pinjala Subrahminyam Chetty at Samadarsini Press in Madras.
130. Gorrepati Venkata Subbaiah, *Dr. C.R. Reddy*, p. 111.
131. See Ref. nos.66-70.
132. Gorrepati Venkata Subbaiah, *Dr. C.R. Reddy*, p. 111.

133. B. Narasinga Raja Naidu, "The Myth of the Model State Concept of Mysore-A Case Study", *Aspects of South Indian History*, Nagarcoil, 2000, p. 289.
134. B. Kesavanarayana, *Political and Social Factors in Andhra*, p. 304.
135. *Justice*, 2 January 1936 (TNA).
136. *G.O. No.710,* Public (Election) Department, dated 9 April 1937, pp. 74, 322, 336, 346. See also *Fortnightly Report, (FNR),* for the year 1945 (TNA).
137. In the recently held general elections in April-May 2009, major political parties - Congress, *Mahakutami*, and Praja Rajyam Party - had allocated more seats to the upper non-Brahmin castes than to the lower non-Brahmin castes contrary to the proportion of the population. Thus not only they denied or neglected the latter but also exploited them to the maximum extent possible to cripple the lower non-Brahmin castes' precarious position further. For more details see, Adapa Satyanarayana, "Inka Agrakuala Rajyadhikaramena? (Is Still Upper Caste Poltical Power?)", *Vaartha*, Kadapa, 10 November 2008, p. 4, "partillo kulala vareega seetlu (seats in the parties according to castes)", *Vaartha*, Telugu Daily, Kadapa, 10 April 2009, p. 3, "Caste Factor", *Deccan Chronnicle*, Anantapur, 22 March 2009, p. 2, K.V. Satyanarayana (formerly Member of APPSC, Government of Andhra Pradesh, Hyderabad), "Otlena Seetlu Leva (Only Seats but not Seats)...!", *Vaartha*, Kadapa, 13 March 2009, p. 7, B. Bhangya Nayak, "Kula Chaitanyamto Marpu Sadhyama? (Can Change Possible through Caste Consciousness?)", *Vaartha*, Kadapa, 17 March 2009, p. 4, and Kanchala Jayaraj, "Kulam Punadulapine Rajyadhikaram (Power of the Country/State on the Basis of Caste)", *Vaartha*, Kadapa, 1 April 2009, p. 4.

Index

E

Q

R

Y

Z

leaders or elites and activists of the caste associations.[illegible] As a result, each and every caste of the non-Brahmin castes formed its association. For instance, The *Arya Vaisya Mahasabha*, The *Kamma Mahajana Sangam* and The *Reddi Mahajana Sangam or Sabha* were founded in 1907, 1910, 1914 and 1920 respectively.[illegible] In the *Rayalaseema* region Vaisyas, Reddis, Kammas, Telagas, Padmasalis, were in forefront to conduct their respective caste associations.

Arya Vaisya Mahasabha

Arya Vaisyas had claimed *dwija* (twice born) like Brahmins.[illegible] The *Arya Vaisya Mahasabha* had conducted its meetings in different parts of Andhra, Madras Presidency and South India. The *Rayalaseema* region, along with other regions of South India, participated in these conferences and the region had got its identity. For instance, when the Fourth Conference was held at Bellary in 1910 and was attended by 1000 delegates from South India, Bellary was selected as headquarters for the people of the region. Apart from it, Arya-Vaisyas started a hostel at Bellary with a donation of Rs.25000 given by Mrs Subbalakshmamma.[illegible] Further, *Arya Vaisya Mahasabha* conducted some of its Sessions in the region. For instance, the Seventeenth *Arya Vaisya Mahajana Sabha* was held at Nandyala in Kurnool district. Noted Telugu poet Kalam Krishna Rao was Presided over the meeting. He pleaded for unity between the *Rayalaseema* and Coastal Andhra people. Several resolutions were passed for the upliftment of the Arya-Vaisya caste people.[illegible]

Telaga Mahajana Sabha

Telagas were termed themselves as *Kapus*. By profession they were agriculturists.[illegible] The first *Telaga Mahajana Sabha* was met at Railway Kodur in Kadapa district in September 1920. The president of the association, Nagappa, spoke on the local issues like the *Telaga* caste development, unity among *Telaga* people, national education, women education, removal of child marriages and dowry system, political awareness, and th

Even in the Indian National Congress the Brahminical influence and domination can be noticed.

In Andhra area, in which the Rayalaseema region was and is, a part, Kshatriyas, Arya-Vaisyas, Kammas, Reddis/Kapus, Balijas, Velamas (offshoot of Kapus) and Other Backward Classes including Muslims, Christians, Scheduled Castes and Tribes were, and are, the non-Brahmin castes. Among them, Reddis, Kammas, Balijas and Velamas were land-owners whereas Arya Vaisyas or Vaisyas or Komatis were traders. They were upper non-Brahmin castes while the remaining were lower non-Brahmin castes. The upper non-Brahmin castes had [illegible]

Table 1 : Distribution of Castes in Rayalaseema Districts of the Madras Presidency, 1921

Caste	Kadapa	Kurnool	Anantapur	Chittoor
Balija	13.2	10.3	10.4	19.0
Boya/Besta	4.5	4.5	6.0	4.3
Chakali	6.0	[illegible]	2.9	6.3
Golla	6.0	5.2	4.2	5.6
Kummari	4.7	6.0	6.7	5.9
Mangali	4.8	5.1	5.5	6.7
Mutrasi	1.6	0.9	1.7	4.7
Sale	3.0	1.7	1.7	2.9
Telaga	4.4	0.3	[illegible]	[illegible]
Uppara	17.6	10.5	11.2	1.9
Velama	0.5	[illegible]	[illegible]	[illegible]
Mala	8.8	[illegible]	[illegible]	[illegible]
Madiga	4.1	[illegible]	0.8	[illegible]
Muslim	[illegible]	[illegible]	[illegible]	[illegible]
Kamma	2.5	0.6	[illegible]	[illegible]
Kapu/Reddi	[illegible]	[illegible]	[illegible]	[illegible]
Komati	4.9	7.5	[illegible]	[illegible]
Kshatriya	1.5	0.8	1.2	[illegible]

The data pertaining to Bellary district was not available in the Census consulted.